The Power of Maybes

BEYOND THE MODERN

Series editors: Clive Dilnot, Eduardo Staszowski and Virginia Tassinari

To contend with the scale and intractability of the multiple and interacting crises that are threatening to engulf us is to have to change how we think of both thought and acting. The separation of critical thought and technological and economic acting-in-the-world has eviscerated the ability to bring together theory and practice for anything other than merely instrumental ends.

At the same time, neither the human sciences – which historically have feared intervention – nor models of acting that eschew depth understanding can alone suffice to redirect catastrophe. One consequence of these failures is that they cause us to lose sight of other objective possibilities for the world. Envisioning the latter must be the real subject of thought and practice today.

This is the motivation for this new series of books.

Recognizing that the key challenge of our time is to invent a modernity capable of redressing the blind march toward disaster, they focus on teasing out what is immanently possible within what-now-is. Operating at the intersections of fields previously kept distinct, they explore both the conditions of such a re-invention and the articulation of configurations of thought, material practices and politics that can potentially realize transformative possibilities in the world.

In so doing their aim is to help lay groundwork for an ontological shift; for the transformations in thought, imagination, and capability necessary for engendering peaceful egalitarian rather than catastrophic modes of bringing the future into being.

Published and Forthcoming

Relationality: An Emergent Politics of Life Beyond the Human, Arturo Escobar, Michal Osterweil and Kriti Sharma

The Power of Maybes: Machines, Uncertainty and Design Futures, Betti Marenko

(Designing) Beyond the Modern, Eduardo Staszowski and Virginia Tassinari

Contrapractice: Designing and Defuturing Now, Tony Fry and Dulmini Perera

Designing Politics: Materiality, Agency, and Embodied Deliberation, Anke Gruendel

The Possibility of the Artificial/The Urgency of the Possible, Clive Dilnot

PRAISE FOR *THE POWER OF MAYBES*

Betti Marenko has created a striking meditation on openness, indeterminacy and the call of an imminent future for theorizing, as well as making and unmaking, forms of human invention. An exciting and original project, this book provides an alternative understanding of the scope and limits of automation, industrialization and artificial intelligence by making explicit what the digital and the machine leave out or can only approximate, that is, the details and forms, the veering off from predicted courses, that self-making, art and creativity produce, the unknowable futures they make possible.

ELIZABETH GROSZ, author of *The Incorporeal. Ontology, Ethics, and the Limits of Materialism* (2017)

The Power of Maybes is a dazzling exploration of the themes of uncertainty, power, futures and designs and their relation to the epistemic, epoch-defining challenges of planetary computation and the automation of decision making. Betti Marenko makes us not only aware of the immanence of uncertainty to our computational machines but also of its potential in countering the future as a foreclosed event. Foregrounding design as a worldbuilding enterprise, *The Power of Maybes* invites us to learn how to reach out to uncertainty in its cosmic dimension, practice the art to detect the desirable futures already operating in the present and work with them to bring them into being.

TIZIANA TERRANOVA, author of *Network Culture* (2004) and *After the Internet* (2022)

Here, finally is the anti-Singularity we have been waiting for: an invitation not to merge with tech, but to verge with it. To explore, and to discover, yes, but without the illusions of command and control. Here is neither a techno-pessimism nor an optimism, but a future technics, a grimoire for a future where we have never been technologically determined unless machines, like people, have always been indeterminate. Machines overheat, get thirsty, decompose, lie dormant, go ungrieved, and above all, like their human companions, live largely interrupted lives. The history of technology and design is, as much as human history, a history of hijacked and foreclosed maybes. Only the most insipid ideology can say, 'whatever is actual is good, and the good is always actual'. For the rest of us, we cleave to the reminders offered here by Marenko, to keep hesitating, stammering, and unknowing, for there lies any and every chance for something other than the morbid illusions of necessity.

JOSHUA RAMEY, Visiting Assistant Professor of Peace, Justice and Human Rights, Haverford College

Betti Marenko's *The Power of Maybes* is a delightful, world-opening surprise. In masterful prose she documents that, counter to widespread critical wisdom, AI doesn't actually result in predictability and control and closure. To the contrary, AI increases the amount of uncertainty of lives. And Marenko encourages us readers to embrace this uncertainty as the highest good: For what is uncertainty but an invitation to imagine what could be? To help herself and her readers to navigate the always still nascent, emergent territories of uncertainty provoked by AI, Marenko introduces the concept of 'maybes'. 'Maybes' are more than just a recognition of the unknown; they are a call to action. They serve as both a practical and analytical tool, allowing us to engage with uncertainty actively and foster a more open and empowered approach to life. This book is a must-read for anyone seeking to live a life today.

TOBIAS REES, author of *Plastic Reason* (2016) and *After Ethnos* (2018), former Reid Hoffman Professor at Parsons/the New School, senior visiting fellow, Google

The Power of Maybes invites readers to revalue uncertainty and even learn to find in it an unexpected ally. Uncertainty is ubiquitous in the technological world – any design is an experiment with uncertainty – or in the living one, all life being an experiment in form, evolution dipping into the potent maybes percolating in life. Marenko takes pains so readers won't have to. The writing is consistently sharp, witty, intelligible, consequential, maybe. She describes a possible otherwise to a mechanized future those who love certainty say is unstoppable.

BARRY ALLEN, Distinguished University Professor, McMaster University

The Power of Maybes imbues the emancipatory engagement with machines and algorithms with desperately needed new life. Betti Marenko weaves together highly original thinking about the inherently unknowable aspect of machines and technology with an updated understanding of the Ancient Greek notion of technē, drawing the panorama of an updated praxis of the *metic* intelligence: a cunning, adaptive and speculative pragmatism, against which the reductive and predictive logic of planetary computation and automation, tethered as they are to the extractive frame of Integrated World Capitalism (IWC), begin to pale in comparison. Bartleby's No, as well as deliberate strategies of 'unknowing' drawn from conjecture, divination and other ancestral practices, come together in a shakedown of traditional epistemology and standard views of technology, opening the vista for a human non-human process of co-creation at cosmic scale.

CÉCILE MALASPINA, author of *An Epistemology of Noise* (2018) and Programmer for Art & Curatorial Studies at the New Centre for Research & Practice

While the future seems necessarily determined by the unpredictable unfolding of techno-capitalism, Betti Marenko invites us to design and inhabit other possible worlds. *The Power of Maybes* acknowledges the call of the untapped potentialities of life and encourages us to liberate them through an experimental approach to technology. Finally, a book that is not simply a critique of algorithmic governmentality, but a positive proposal for overcoming the limitations enforced on the creativity of being.

ANNA LONGO, editor of *Breaking the Spell: Contemporary Realism under Discussion* (2015) and *Time without Becoming* (2014)

The Power of Maybes

Machines, Uncertainty and Design Futures

Betti Marenko

BLOOMSBURY VISUAL ARTS
LONDON • NEW YORK • OXFORD • NEW DELHI • SYDNEY

BLOOMSBURY VISUAL ARTS
Bloomsbury Publishing Plc, 50 Bedford Square, London, WC1B 3DP, UK
Bloomsbury Publishing Inc, 1359 Broadway, New York, NY 10018, USA
Bloomsbury Publishing Ireland, 29 Earlsfort Terrace, Dublin 2, D02 AY28, Ireland

BLOOMSBURY, BLOOMSBURY VISUAL ARTS and the Diana logo are trademarks of Bloomsbury Publishing Plc

First published in Great Britain 2025
Paperback edition published in 2026

Cover design by Andrew LeClair

A catalogue record for this book is available from the British Library.

A catalog record for this book is available from the Library of Congress.

ISBN: HB: 978-1-3503-7727-1
PB: 978-1-3503-7731-8
ePDF: 978-1-3503-7728-8
eBook: 978-1-3503-7729-5

Series: Beyond the Modern

Typeset by Integra Software Services Pvt. Ltd.
Printed and bound in Great Britain

For product safety related questions contact productsafety@bloomsbury.com.

To find out more about our authors and books visit www.bloomsbury.com and sign up for our newsletters.

Contents

Foreword

I prefer not to, or a matter of cosmic uncertainty.
ADAM NOCEK

Long gone are the days when French philosophy could relish in the uncertainty of knowledge. In many ways, uncertainty has come to characterize our shared, if asymmetrical, planetary condition. This is so much the case that it's almost become a part of standard academic practice to list the uncertainties much of the world population faces: the uncertainty of food, healthcare, and shelter for billions; the uncertainty of democracy, peace, and geopolitical stability in a multipolar world; the uncertainty of artificial intelligence, scientific research, and verifiability; the uncertainty of climate, biodiversity, arable land, and human life on the planet. Of course, the extent to which these and other uncertainties are felt and lived is geopolitically uneven, but even the logics responsible for distributing these uncertainties are becoming less and less certain. Where for several decades the neoliberal political economic order seemed to reliably design and feed off various kinds of uncertainty, and critical theory had a fairly reliable object to critique, this political order is undergoing massive transition, and what comes next is *uncertain*.

If Design has long been in the business of mitigating uncertainties – systematically narrowing the field of uncertainties surrounding how to solve/define a problem – then we would also be remiss not to point out how Design thrives on uncertainty. Indeed, Design's own transformation into a force for 'social good' (Social Design) is born out of many of the political, social and environmental uncertainties named above. By filling in where the welfare state has backed off, Design has been able to correct for its commercial sins of the past through various forms of social innovation. But Design never lets a good crisis go to waste and in recent decades has turned uncertainty into a kind of industry. Whether the uncertainty is associated with business, healthcare and medicine, food, policy, governance, education, or the future itself, Design has done well to manage, govern and/or cultivate these uncertainties – to design for, with, and around them. Even Critical and Speculative Design (CSD), which is outwardly critical of the business of Design, is nevertheless deeply invested in the uncertainty industry: doing everything it can to make the present more malleable and thus uncertain.

Of course, there's a good deal of difference among these design practices, but whether it's alleviating or producing uncertainty this much seems clear: that risk is at the centre of what Design means by uncertainty. This is because uncertainty is understood, measured and managed in terms of the risk it poses – whether it be environmental, political, or existential risk. For Betti Marenko, risk is only a matter of perception however: it's a mode of framing uncertainty such that it poses a risk to the endurance of certain knowable and predictable patterns. Hence, uncertainty is generally perceived through the cognitive prism of risk. Sometimes a bit of uncertainty opens up a space for political imagination – for example, when it poses a risk to the persistence of oppressive political regimes; at other times, however, uncertainty risks destabilizing widely desired forms of order and stability and it must be managed.

Either way, the coincidence of Design, uncertainty, and risk is so prevalent that it almost passes for common sense. Gilles Deleuze explains that common sense is essentially 'what everyone knows' and as such largely goes unquestioned. In *Difference and Repetition*, common sense is associated with what's taken for granted, what passes for mere opinion, for *doxa*. In this context, Deleuze draws attention to literary figures like Melville's *Bartleby* or Dostyevsky's underground man who dare to question common sense, who pose questions that seem unreasonable or that don't adhere to the norms of good and acceptable thought. It's precisely in this manner that Bartleby defies common sense – through his insistence, 'I prefer not to' – and in doing so becomes what Deleuze calls an 'Idiot'. Yet the Idiot is not a pejorative term, for Deleuze, but rather names the position of the philosopher who dares to question what 'no one can deny'. The latter is another name for the 'dogmatic image of thought' or the image thought presupposes of what it means to think in a given era.

It's just this presupposed image that the Idiot protests. Here's Deleuze: 'The philosopher takes the side of the idiot as though of a man without presuppositions.' Just below, he continues:

> Such a protest [from the Idiot] does not take place in the name of aristocratic prejudices: it is not a question of saying what few think and knowing what it means to think. On the contrary, it is a question of someone – if only one – with the necessary modesty not managing to know what everybody knows, and modestly denying what everybody is supposed to recognize. Someone who neither allows himself to be represented nor wishes to represent anything ...[1]

[1] Gilles Deleuze, *Difference and Repetition*, trans. Paul Patton (New York: Columbia University Press, 1994), 130.

If idiocy is what dares to undermine what everybody knows, then this is the gift that Betti Marenko dares to give us: a text that challenges what everybody knows. When Marenko works through Deleuze and Giorgio Agamben's readings of Bartleby, this should be taken with the utmost seriousness: it provides insight into how we should approach Marenko's own thought.

To wager that uncertainty be disentangled from risk, and that this is a political proposition, is likely to sound suspicious to some, especially to Design. Even more so, her claim to root this conception of uncertainty in a cosmological vision, one that yokes Spinoza's pantheism together with Chinese philosophy, divination and a host of occult practices, has all the hallmarks of refusing to get on board with what everyone knows. In good, acceptable academic discourse, flirting with the cosmic is one thing (e.g. to the connectedness of all things, to the primacy of relations, and so on), but unapologetically affirming what tends to be the remit of theology is quite another. There is no skirting or undermining commitments to the divine, political theology, and non-Western spiritual practices in *The Power of Maybes*: The book brings these concerns squarely into contact with Design, Physics, and the empirical realities of planetary computation. When faced with keeping objective, academic work on technoscience to one side of the aisle and theological, spiritual, and cosmological work to the other, Marenko says: *I prefer not to.*

Rarely do we come across a book that treats not adhering to disciplinary legibility as a mark of success instead of an obstacle to be overcome. Still, now that transdisciplinarity has become a kind of academic common sense, there are many who are likely to champion the illegibility of their work within the confines of traditional academic knowledge production. Much more likely, however, these very same rallying cries too often find themselves propping up all the markers of an academic trans-discipline, leveraging recognizable citation practices to confirm and reproduce (trans)disciplinary knowledge.

This is not the experience we get with reading *The Power of Maybes* – thought moves in new directions and begins to feel uncomfortable with its own starting place. Why can't we speak of advanced technology and cosmic uncertainty in the same breath? Why can't the immanent force of the divine be a part of design practices? Why do secularized academics squirm when political theology mixes with their critique of capital? And why can't the style of academic thought move between fiction and social science, between empirical history and fabulation? These are the kinds of questions we are urged to wrestle with – questions that don't have easy answers and are likely not meant to be answered in any case. The questions the book raises should remind us of Isabelle Stengers' plea to 'smell the smoke in our nostrils' – to recognize that we're all still witch hunters.[2] In smelling this smoke, we're called upon to recognize how quick we are to dismiss or explain away what diverges from the agreed-upon values of secular academia – from what 'no one can deny'. Likewise, not only does this

[2] Isabelle Stengers, 'Reclaiming Animism', *e-flux* 36 (July 2012): 7, www.e-flux.com/journal/reclaiming-animism/

plea challenge us not to dismiss some claims in the book as *mere* fiction but it enjoins us to affirm this fiction as immanent to the fabric of reality.

Writing almost a century ago, Alfred North Whitehead challenged us to see fictions as real and as deserving of our attention as the material world physicists describe. In his day, Whitehead's attempt to stitch these two sides of the epistemological universe together did not always sit well with his contemporaries. And to this day, few readers of Whitehead (save theologians) acknowledge the central role God plays in bringing these bifurcating realities together. The theological Whitehead is something generations of philosophers have downplayed. And I'm no exception. Here, I'm reminded of a conversation I had several years ago with Brian Massumi. In the midst of my own efforts to do away with God in Whitehead's metaphysics, he urged me to consider how God is precisely what gives Whitehead the 'elbow room' he needs: The divine is what makes it possible to preserve all that has been without repeating it as it was. God is what allows us to entertain the *what if*, the *what may be*, without sacrificing the immanence of the past in the present and future. And while this conversation certainly helped me to grasp the importance of Whitehead's theology, perhaps more to the point: it prompted me to smell the smoke in my own nostrils – that I, too, was a witch hunter. Making Whitehead acceptable to philosophers of science meant finding a way out of his theology.

It's just this experience of hesitation and uncertainty that I felt when I brought Whitehead's theology to bear on the philosophy of science that we should experience when reading *The Power of Maybes*. We're not always meant to feel at ease when pantheism and Design are thought together or when the spiritual and the computational are brought into ever closer proximity. Is this philosophy, design, fiction, theology … ? Perhaps all of them, perhaps none of them, or perhaps not deciding and remaining uncertain is the point. It's just this pause or hesitation in judgment that both Whitehead and Deleuze critiqued Kant for not appreciating – that thinking occurs when there is no *a priori* organizational matrix for sense experience (via the categories of the understanding), and when judgment fails to secure certain knowledge. If we remain uncertain about how to categorize this book, then this is one of its greatest strengths: it opens up a space for thinking. The ontology of uncertainty Marenko puts forward is brought to life in the act of reading. Form and content coincide in *The Power of Maybes*.

Adam Nocek
November 2024
Tempe, Arizona

Acknowledgements

The Power of Maybes began to take shape in 2017 when after over a decade in academia I decided to take some time out to think. During that period of intense study and travel I have had the privilege of being invited to share ideas and work in progress in many different events and contexts, each of them providing me with wonderful opportunities for discussion, connection and reflection. I am particularly grateful for the conversations that took place at the cx Centre for Interdisciplinary Studies at the Academy of Fine Arts, Munich (thanks to Karianne Fogelberg, Maria Muhle and Susanne Witzgall for inviting me to the *Hybrid Ecologies* Lecture series); at the *Aesthetics and the Political in Contemporary India: Deleuzian Explorations* Conference at Tata Institute of Social Sciences, Mumbai (thanks to everyone at the Deleuze Studies in India Collective); at the AAAI (Association for the Advancement of Artificial Intelligence) Spring Symposium at Stanford University (thanks to Mike Kuniavsky for inviting me and helping me secure a travel grant); at the Media Design Practice programme, Art Center Pasadena (with thanks to Phil Van Allen, now at TU Delft); in Amsterdam at the *Design, Fiction and Speculative Philosophy for a Planet in Crisis* event at Spui25 and with the GeoMedia Research Network at Mediamatic (with thanks to Patricia Pisters for inviting me many times and for the warm friendship); at Goldsmiths, University of London (with thanks to Matt Ward and Duncan Fairfax for inviting me to *The Death of the Imagination. Design and the Slow Cancellation of the Future* event); with the Design Research cohort at the Faculty of Architecture, Universita' La Sapienza Roma (with thanks to Lorenzo Imbesi for inviting me to give a *Design Issues* lecture and for inviting me to be co-chair of *Design Culture(s) of Revolution* at the Cumulus conference, with Stefano Maffei, Alastair Luke and Hélène Day Fraser as brilliant collaborators); with the Animism Reading Group at the Program for the Evolution of Spirituality, Harvard Divinity School (with thanks to Natalia Schwien); with the participants to the seminar *Technē Beyond Monoculture* at The New Centre for Research & Practice (with thanks to Cécile Malaspina, for inviting me and for the enthusiasm), and with the Creative Leadership course at Musashino Art University (with thanks to Tadanori Nagasawa for inviting me to give the Interactive Innovation talk). I have been fortunate to be part of the Deleuze and Guattari Studies community for a long time and I continue to be inspired, moved and nourished by the richness of thought and the generosity of spirit I encounter, most recently at the *Intelligence, Instituting, and Archiving* conference hosted by the Architecture Department, TUDelft (with huge thanks to Stavros Kousoulas and Andrej Radman for inviting me to be camp instructor and to my co-conspirator Agnieszka Wolodzko).

Casting my mind back to the beginning of this project, I wish to express my gratitude to Terry Knight at MIT Architecture and Daniel Cardoso Llach, Computational Design, Carnegie Mellon University, who supported me with precious conversations and generous exchanges. A special thank you to David Benqué for the inspiring conversations, our Speculative Diagrams collaboration for the Research Through Design conference at TU Delft and for showing me how to weave ideas and practice in such a generous and original way.

While the book was put on hold by my involvement with the Erasmus+ project FUEL4Design, the time spent on this project proved to be remarkably generative. Thanks to the entire FUEL4Design project team, in particular my colleagues and friends at Central Saint Martins: Jerneja Rebernak, Silke Lange and Pras Gunasekera; and to Andrew Morrison, Oscar Tomico and all the other 'Fuelers' who made the project possible. I have learned a lot from all of you. I am especially grateful to Manuela Celi and Chiara Colombi at the Department of Design, Politecnico of Milano, not only for our work together on FUEL4Design but for inviting me to shape the yearly International Doctoral Summer School at Politecnico of Milano since 2020. So much of my thinking has been generated and nourished during this Summer School, a phenomenal and truly transversal laboratory of ideas, practice and research where intellectual inquiry keeps on generating possibilities (while spilling with ease into conviviality). Thank you, to you and all your formidable team, in particular Victoria Rodriguez Schon, for making me feel so at home.

An important shift in my outlook has been taking place since I became WRHI/WRH Specially Appointed Professor at the Institute of Science Tokyo (formerly Tokyo Institute of Technology) in 2018. Working alongside Japanese colleagues and students has helped me consolidate my ideas while challenging my assumptions. It has been a consistent learning (and unlearning) experience, since the moment I was gently shown the emptiness at the centre of everything. I am grateful to Kayoko Nohara for her continuous support, the long conversations, the generous collaboration and the friendship, and to Giorgio Salani and Kohei Kanomata for the fantastic teamwork.

At Central Saint Martins I am privileged to work alongside so many brilliant educators, practitioners, thinkers and makers – true *thinkerers* – whose creativity, commitment and enthusiasm never waiver. I treasure precious conversations, often snatched among the relentless rhythm of academic labour, with Heather Barnett, Jo Wheeler, Stephanie Sherman, Monika Parrinder, all my colleagues in the BA Product and Industrial Design and everyone in the Product Ceramics and Industrial Design Programme, too numerous to mention. Some very special thanks are due to John Wollaston, Sam Mitchell and Stefan Sloneczny for inviting me to curate the Hybrid Futures series of talks and symposium during the first Digital Innovation Season at Central Saint Martins, to Kaye Toland, my Hybrid Futures Lab collaborator and all-round plotter for always seeing further than me and for flawless strategizing, and to artist Maggie Roberts who in 2018 invited me to the symposium *The Shaping of a Message* at the Department of Visual Cultures, Goldsmiths, University of London, where I used 'The Power of Maybes' as the title of my talk for the first time.

Some of the research that supports this book was made possible by an Independent Social Research Foundation (ISRF) Grant and by a three-month Research Sabbatical from Central Saint Martins, University of the Arts London.

I cannot begin to say how lucky I am to be entwined with remarkable 'living experts' whose generosity, sharpness of thought and appetite for ideas (and for life) is a constant source of inspiration: Margot Leigh Butler, for cross-oceanic adventures; Leslie Atzmon, for unwavering support; Adam Nocek, for planetary conversations in Mumbai, London, Amsterdam, Milan (and the foreword); Joshua Ramey, for the unhinging and the pledge; Tiziana Terranova, for the constancy of our summer dialogues; Luciana Parisi, for the generous feedback; Roy Bendor, for the fierce mind and generous hospitality. I am especially grateful to Adam, Joshua, Tiziana, Luciana and Roy, who at various stages in the making of this book found the time to read my drafts, offer their criticism and whose advice greatly steered my thinking. Needless to say, I could never do justice to all the feedback I was fortunate to receive and any responsibility for the final version remains solely mine. I am hugely indebted to Clive Dilnot, my editor at Bloomsbury, without whom this book would simply not exist. Thank you for your editorial sagacity, but most of all thank you for believing in *The Power of Maybes* and in me.

Finally, to all my special kins, near and afar, thank you for being luminous creatures by my side, no matter what, Paulene, Stuart, Léon, Bronwyn, Miriam, Valentina, Lucrezia, Bruna, Mina, Yuri and my fearless Joy; and to Mr. Architect for the invisible scaffolding you build for me.

Deleuze once said that giving lectures is like a research laboratory, you talk about what you are investigating not what you know.[1] My biggest thanks go to everyone who has sat through my talks, lectures and workshops and shared their views afterwards. Even more, to those – like the anonymous reviewers whose bafflement sent me back to the drawing board – who asked me the questions I did not know I needed to think (and be moved) just a tiny bit more.

[1] Gilles Deleuze, *Negotiations* (New York: Columbia University Press, 1995), 139.

Introduction: Hybrid Futures

I hold out my hand to the future.
FÉLIX GUATTARI[1]

WHAT THIS BOOK IS ABOUT

This book is about uncertainty, futures, machines and design. It is also about power, intended in both senses of entrapment and coercion (*potestas*), and capacity and potential (*potentia*). I place uncertainty at the centre of a web where these lines of inquiry concerning uncertainty, power, futures, machines and design, intersect and contaminate each other. This transversality is necessary to cast uncertainty in a new light, one that illuminates the specificity of the current moment – the 'now' – while treasuring the shadows through which the 'now' tilts into the future.

I believe that the transversal inquiry into uncertainty I propose, whose aim is to reposition how uncertainty is conceptualized, discussed, handled, metaphorized and confronted, is crucial to make sense of one of the dominant issues of our time: the epistemic challenges brought by *planetary computation* – the 'most radical process of artificialization of intelligence that human history has ever seen'.[2] Planetary computation has epoch-defining effects: what counts as knowledge has been reconfigured by intelligent machines of prediction; the automation of decision-making has become a mode of governance – known as algorithmic governmentality; uncertainty is constrained into predictable grooves

1 Félix Guattari, *Chaosmosis. An Ethico-Aesthetic Paradigm* (Bloomington and Indianapolis: Indiana University Press, 1995), 134.

2 Luciana Parisi, 'Instrumental Reason, Algorithmic Capitalism, and the Incomputable', in *Alleys of Your Mind. Augmented Intelligence and its Traumas*, ed. Matteo Pasquinelli (Luneburg: Meson Press, 2015), 130.

that capture my potential, pre-empt my behaviours, foreclose my futures. As uncertainty gets seized, ambiguity is eroded, and existence is impoverished.

For me, to understand these power manoeuvres that target uncertainty, necessary in order to disengage from them and reclaim the uncertainty of futures, has directly to do with rethinking what uncertainty is and how to re-inhabit it. A transversal approach to uncertainty like the one *The Power of Maybes* proposes becomes therefore essential to the project of resisting machines' capture. My argument, which is also a wager, is that an *allyship with uncertainty is not only possible but necessary* to build an alternative to the worst excesses of algorithmic governmentality. I claim that uncertainty can be entered into, dwelled in and experienced as a way of counteracting capture and reimagining the encounter of the human with machines. This is what the *power of maybes* stands for: an endorsement to live with uncertainty by cultivating modes of knowing and being (and resisting) that hold uncertainty as an ally.

MAYBES

Uncertainty concerns *maybes*

The plural 'maybes' underpins the founding proposition of the book: that to speak of uncertainty is ultimately to speak of pure indeterminate potential prior to its capture and differentiation. Maybes stands for this unthinkable multitude of possible possibles, the ever-dynamic ungraspable *virtual ocean* of all that may be: it may be x, it may be y, it may be z, it may be *otherwise*. Maybes stands for radical contingency. It is not finite nor discrete, countable nor calculable, predicted nor predictable. It is *cosmic*. By cosmic I mean the becoming of all things, each thing existing in and of itself, unfolding in an infinite universe and ceaselessly and unforeseeably transforming.[3] Put differently, my inquiry into uncertainty leads to the metaphysical question: How do I approach the sensible totality of the world in all its incandescent and uncertain unfolding? My thought experiment is to move across and beyond the sublunary sphere – traditionally the realm of the four elements and of a changing nature – to reach out to uncertainty in its cosmic dimension: a dimension at once material and sensible, intelligent and intelligible, where undifferentiated potential swirls.

This perspective, which in Part Two I call 'cosmological orientation', is the condition I pose to my rethinking of uncertainty. By posing uncertainty as cosmic, I regain my existence in its plenitude – with all its potential, including the potential not to. By inhabiting uncertainty as oceanic experience, I access the power of the unknown, recruiting *un-knowing* and *not-knowing* not only

[3] It was the Greek pre-Socratic philosopher Heraclitus who invented the concept of cosmos (*kosmos*) to describe an ordered universe where everything is flux and change is constant, an eternal and uncreated cosmos, as the 'primordial generator of matter and energy, the constructor of all stars and planets, the agitator of each and every modification of spacetime'. Gökhan Kodalak, 'Cosmodality. Prolegomena to a New Architectural Metaphysics', *Log* 52 (2021): 133.

as modes of knowing but as ways of *feeling for* unknown futures away from the anticipatory discourses of neoliberal innovation, futureproofing, techno-determinism and instrumental reason. In short, by insisting on inhabiting uncertainty, rather than shunning it, I argue that I can learn to cultivate a vital capacity: how to be nourished by uncertainty, *whatever* it may bring.

This is why *The Power of Maybes* advocates that making friends with uncertainty is the portal to a full life, a life full, that is, of all its unforeseeable 'may bes'. It is in this *whatever* that my ultimate power resides: my *power to* as well as my *power not to*, and my power to exist and resist. With this I also seek to bring back critique to the dimension of the micro-political, the minor intervention and the tiny gesture that in themselves contain all the infinite universes I belong to already. This is the reason why I argue that this oceanic, cosmic uncertainty, in all its plenitude, is the basis for a political stance of resistance and refusal, enlisted to the project of reimagining the present and designing other ways of being against the unabated 'desertification of all modes of existence'.[4]

FUTURES

Uncertainty concerns *futures*

With futures, one of the two terms of this introduction's title, I do not simply signal a multiplicity of futures (rather than The Future); I also wish to acknowledge futures' *unknowns* as discordance. 'Futures' speaks to the challenge of moving into unknown tomorrows without imposing today's (or yesterday's) script of what the future should be.

I echo philosopher Elizabeth Grosz's pointed question: 'How is it possible to revel and delight in the indeterminacy of the future without raising the kind of panic and defensive counterreactions that surround the attempts of the old to contain the new, to predict, anticipate, and incorporate the new within its already existing frameworks?'[5] One way 'to revel and delight in the indeterminacy of the future' is by staying alert to the insidious hold of those well-rehearsed stories about the future that the Global North is so fond of: technology will save the world, progress is growth, growth is a linear upward trajectory, instrumental reason prevails, capitalism is unavoidable. Whether these stories envision the future as a territory to occupy, a resource to extract, or a disembodied realm to manage, they are all teleological stories that serve the future as a *foreclosed*

[4] Isabelle Stengers and Didier Debaise, 'The Insistence of Possibles. Towards a Speculative Pragmatism', *Parse* 7 (2017): 14.

[5] Elizabeth Grosz, 'Thinking the New. Of Futures Yet Unthoughts', in *Becomings. Explorations in Time, Memory, and Futures*, ed. Elizabeth Grosz (Ithaca: Cornell University Press, 1999), 16.

event, already given and pre-ordained.[6] As they colonize imagination, these stories mould anticipation, become naturalized, appear *inevitable*.

But nowhere is written that the future cannot be changed. The biggest story of all is the story of inevitability. Inevitability is like a bad dream from which I struggle to wake up, but wake up I must. Even if it feels unthinkable, the tracks the future seems to be on *can* be upended. These tracks lead straight to planetary exhaustion, alienation and annihilation. They *must* be upended. New futures stories ought to be spun from the unrecognizability of the truly unknown, from the 'infinite variability of the world', the 'delight of indeterminacy' and the irrevocable, oceanic, cosmic uncertainty.

Rallying against what he calls 'inevitabilism', philosopher and historian of science Andrew Pickering writes about being 'struck by an almost total absence of ontological visions that do not conjure up a regular and knowable world, that conjure up something different. We have nothing to set against what I could call the modern ontology of fixity and knowability'.[7] The only inevitability, he continues, is the infinite variability of the world, shining unexpectedly like a crystal catching the light in endless refractions, each time slightly different and new. Looking into uncertainty as if it was a crystal is how I begin to stray from a future where 'the uncontained is woven into a containing framework and the new is made recognizable and tied to the known'.[8] It is how I begin to step into the unknown.

MACHINES

Uncertainty concerns *machines*

Uncertainty goes to the core of the world of machines. That machines – the shortcut I use for computational systems, processes and their effects – rely on incomputability, thus unknowability, is not a new idea. Already in his groundbreaking 1936 paper, Alan Turing had proved the logical impossibility of predicting which machine, given a certain input, would halt and which would not.[9] This

[6] Keri Facer, *Learning Futures. Education, Technology, and Social Change* (London and New York: Routledge, 2011); Keri Facer, 'Storytelling in Troubled Times. What is the Role for Educators in the Deep Crises of the 21st Century?', *Literacy* 53, no. 1 (2019): 3–13; Keri Facer and Arathi Sriprakash, 'Provincializing Futures Literacy. A Caution Against Codification', *Futures* 133 (2021); Barbara Adam and Chris Groves, *Future Matters. Action, Knowledge, Ethics* (Leiden and Boston: Brill, 2007); Susan Harding and Daniel Rosenberg eds, *Histories of the Future* (Durham and London: Duke University Press, 2005); Riel Miller ed., *Transforming the Future. Anticipation in the 21st Century* (Abingdon: Routledge, 2018); John Urry, *What is the Future?* (Cambridge: Polity Press, 2016).

[7] Andrew Pickering, 'Science, Contingency and Ontology', in *Science As It Could Have Been. Discussing the Contingency/Inevitability Problem*, ed. Léna Soler, Emiliano Trizio and Andrew Pickering (Pittsburgh: University of Pittsburgh Press, 2015), 118.

[8] Grosz, 'Thinking the New', 16.

[9] Charles Petzold, *The Annotated Turing. A Guided Tour through Alan Turing's Historic Paper on Computability and the Turing Machine* (Indianapolis: Wiley, 2008).

showed that not everything is computable; and that the incomputable lies at the core of the computable. In fact, the history of computation is also, in part, the history of how the incomputable was colonized, randomness was tamed and any mismatch between digital and observable reality eliminated.[10] The result of this 'taming of the incomputable' is the pervasive flatness of the digital ontology that characterizes planetary computation. This flatness is not only a convenient fiction that plasters over any uncertainty inherent to computation; it is also a mystification that obfuscates the mechanisms of capture of potential.

It seems to me, then, that no rethinking of uncertainty; no reclaiming of the potential that uncertainty nourishes; no alliance with uncertainty can occur unless these mechanisms are exposed and, from that standpoint, routes for resistance strategized.

Planetary computation may appear as the condition where it is no longer possible nor meaningful to disentangle human bodies, digital devices, artificial intelligence, neural architectures, data, flesh, hardware, software, carbon, silicon.[11] It is a seductive image. However, such over-smooth, totalizing fantasies of natural-artificial communions and biological-symbolic hybrids fail to consider the genealogy of technological automation: the servo-mechanic paradigm of technology. According to this paradigm, the automation of automation is nothing but a shift from the automation of human labour in the industrial/plantation machine. The *Power of Maybes* contends that a rethinking of uncertainty is also a way of challenging this paradigm.

The cosmic dimension of uncertainty, in other words, is revealed as reaching to and across, from the microscale of chips and bits, all the way to computation's planetary hold. This is also why I take 'machine' not only as the statistical computing device designed to solve calculable problems through a discrete number of steps but as planetary computation's epoch-defining indiscernible digital hum that, operating *below* human cognition and perception, preys upon the space where undifferentiated potential swarms prior to capture.

HYBRID OPEN-ENDEDNESS

Uncertainty concerns *hybrid open-endedness*

The hybrid – the first term of this introduction's title *Hybrid Futures* – speaks to the unknowability of futures as the uneven mix of nonlinear timelines

[10] Barry Cooper, 'The Machine as Data. A Computational View of Emergence and Definability', *Synthese* 192 (2015): 1958–9; Alexander Galloway, *Uncomputable. Play and Politics in the Long Digital Age* (London and New York: Verso, 2021), 4.

[11] See for instance, the notion of 'onlife experience' describing the enmeshing of virtual and real, with the digital-online world spilling over and merging with the analogue-offline world, an almost quaint description of what planetary computation stands for. Luciano Floridi, *The 4th Revolution. How the Infosphere is Reshaping Human Reality* (Oxford: Oxford University Press, 2014).

emerging from the play of potential as it tips (or not) into actualization.[12] In my take, the hybrid highlights the transformative value of metamorphic processes stemming from my encounter with the not-yet: what happens at the boundaries where different entities meet (and I meet worlds), each with a different horizon of potential and distinct sets of available possibilities.[13] The hybrid is not about resolving differences into a homogenous whole and celebrating their anodyne merging; it is rather a figuration for future-making as a boundary place where knowns meet unknowns.[14] Philosopher of science Peter Galison's image of boundaries as 'trading zones' is useful here to illuminate this hybrid space as a zone of transit where the traffic from heterogeneity to homogeneity and vice versa yields *metastable* systems – partial, precarious and procreative.[15]

By posing 'futures' (and the making of futures) as 'hybrid' I wish to highlight their open-endedness. This notion – that futures are open-ended thus inherently uncertain – demands both attention and caution. Attention, because the 'open-endedness of futures' dives to the core of my argument: uncertainty is an ally to counteract the capture of potential and the foreclosure of futures. Caution, because the 'open-endedness of futures' is one of neoliberalism's most effective rhetorical devices, together with the 'unlocking of potential'. Both rhetorics conveniently gloss over the inherited injustices baked into neoliberal practices,

[12] The hybrid, and more precisely becoming hybrid (hybridization) is something I take seriously throughout. This notion has also informed much of my thinking and previous work. My first book, published in 1997 by Italian publisher Castelvecchi, was titled appositely *Ibridazioni* (Hybridizations).

[13] One way of describing this is through the notion of 'adjacent possible'. Peter Galison draws from, among others, theoretical biologist and complexity scholar Stuart Kauffman, to articulate the potential offered by elements outside of, yet near, contiguous, or tangential to, a system, offering opportunity for systemic expansion, connection-building and boundary-work. Stuart Kauffman, *Investigations* (Oxford: Oxford University Press, 2000). For an example of this approach in the Global South context: John Van Breda and Mark Swilling, 'The Guiding Logics and Principles for Designing Emergent Transdisciplinary Research Processes. Learning Experiences and Reflections from a Transdisciplinary Urban Case Study in Enkanini Informal Settlement, South Africa', *Sustainability Science* 13, no. 42 (2018): 1–19. I will return to adjacent possibles and contiguity in Chapter 3.

[14] The hybrid is also a figuration for epistemological contestation. See social scientist and epistemologist Boaventura De Sousa Santos, *The End of the Cognitive Empire. The Coming of Age of Epistemologies of the South* (Durham and London: Duke University Press, 2018), who uses 'hybrid' to describe non-Eurocentric renditions of Eurocentric concepts, such as *hybrid methodologies* that combine indigenous methodologies with those drawn on extractivist legacy and are redeployed 'in a counterhegemonic way' (ibid., 152), as well as 'postabyssal' concepts and theories 'in which the mixture of knowledges, cultures, subjectivities, and practices subverts the abyssal line that grounds the epistemologies of the North' (ibid., 107).

[15] Peter Galison, 'Trading with the Enemy', in *Trading Zones and Interactional Expertise. Creating New Kinds of Collaboration*, ed. Michael E. Gorman (Cambridge, Mass. and London: MIT Press, 2010), 32. See also artist and anthropologist Fiamma Montezemolo who writes about hybridization as a *circuit* rather than a location, as the possibility of a continuous fluid exchange rather than something shared. Fiamma Montezemolo, 'Tijuana, Hybridity and Beyond: A Conversation with Néstor García Canclini', *Third Text* 23, no. 6 (2009): 733–50.

systems and governance. Yes, futures may be open-ended, but not for you and I in the same way.[16] It is only by acknowledging and accepting that its conditions are not evenly distributed that open-endedness can be genuinely generative. Open-endedness makes sense only from the standpoint of how my present is accountable for its future consequences: as stewardship of uncertainty. Grosz explains lucidly what open-endedness entails (and what it does not):

> In seeking an open-ended future, one is not required to affirm that misnomer, 'free will,' but to *acknowledge* the capacity of any future eruption, any event, any reading, to rewrite, re-signify, reframe the present, to *accept* the role that the accidental, chance, or the undetermined plays in the unfolding of time.[17]

The mandate is to acknowledge and to accept: that my choice is not pitted against determination, that my position is both 'constrained and undecidable', that the uncertain is an arrow launched from the future into my present.[18] Thus, to say that futures can be open-ended is not only to say that they are uncertain. It is also to say that they can be made, remade and unmade; that they are not predetermined, but emergent; not inevitable, but contestable. That there is no script. There is no *blueprint*.

For me, to stay 'open to' open-endedness means learning how to detect futures already circulating in the present, how to perceive them in the unfolding of things – in their *propensity* – and then devise *stratagems* to work with these forces, subtly, through carefully curated *micro-interventions*. Open-endedness, then, is less about prescience, preparation and planning, and more about crafting what tunes me to *meet the unknowable*.[19]

DESIGN

Uncertainty, finally, concerns *design* – taken in its broadest possible dimension as the activity (*designing*) that produces the artificial, builds worlds and crafts futures. Design is a crucial aspect of my inquiry into uncertainty because to design is to engage in an ontological terraforming that always concerns what could have been *otherwise*. Design is both never 'done' and always in tension towards the not-yet. As many have pointed out before me, designing concerns the realm of the artificial, which is defined precisely by its otherwise-ness: the

[16] Bruno Latour, Martin Guinard and Eva Lin, Eva, 'Coping with Planetary Wars', *e-flux* 114 (2020): 1–9.

[17] Grosz, 'Thinking the New', 18 (emphasis added).

[18] Grosz, 'Thinking the New', 19.

[19] Rebecca Solnit quotes Virginia Woolf who in January 1915 writes in her diary: 'The future is dark, which is the best thing the future can be, I think'. Not only are futures harbingers of uncertainty (and darkness), here the exhortation is to dare to stay with uncertainty, to the point of being uncertain about my own thoughts (*I think*) as well. Rebecca Solnit, *Men Explain Things To Me And Other Essays* (London: Granta, 2014), 8.

artificial is 'what could have been other'.[20] If design has to do with the artificial, with contingency and with uncertainty, then, I contend, it has to do with *maybes*.

My discussion of design is embedded throughout, with considerations and reflections on design surfacing in the text whenever the chapter's theme affords it. I made this choice in order to do justice to my 'diffused' argument about design, which develops on three layers. First, if design is an ontological, future-making and worldbuilding enterprise that engages with the uncertain and the potentially other, then my repositioning of uncertainty offers a framework for (and expansion of) design into a (lost) cosmic dimension. I return to this point in the Conclusion. Second, if uncertainty demands the cultivation of specific modes, routes and techniques of engagement – what in Part Two I call stratagems – then these must be designed. It is by designing that uncertainty can become the ally I speak of and be reclaimed as a political project of resistance. *How* one enters and dwells in uncertainty becomes a design brief. Designed interventions that go on designing worlds are practices attuned not to what is, but to what *may be*, a sensibility for plenitude (pan-sensibility) that chooses to divest from the double trap of the past with its nostalgia of what has been and the safe replication of the known called The Future. But the stratagems I endorse are both 'designed' and 'designing' interventions, which brings me to the final layer – *meta-design* – which is about deploying design to reflect on design itself. What I claim for design is to experiment with rethinking uncertainty and doing so in a way that is nothing less than cosmological. What would it mean for design to be centred not on the human, the user, its outcome, or innovation, but on the truly, cosmic *uncertain*? On uncertainty's own potential?

I conclude this introduction by circling back to Pickering's quotation and his yearning for visions that dare conjure up something different out of the uncertain. My hope is that *The Power of Maybes*, with its multifaceted take on uncertainty, is like a crystal through which these visions may be glimpsed.

BOOK STRUCTURE AND CHAPTERS

This book is for thinkers, practitioners and researchers interested in thinking uncertainty anew and curious to explore ways of leaning into it. It is also for readers with an interest in transdisciplinary inquiry at the intersection of process philosophies, technology and design. This book will appeal most to those who are comfortable straddling multiple domains and feel happiest when hyphenated; those who have an affinity with an approach that treats theory and concept-making like a practice and may recognize themselves in the defini-

[20] Barry Allen, *Artifice and Design. Art and Technology in Human Experience* (New York: Cornell University Press, 2008); Clive Dilnot, 'The Science of Uncertainty. The Potential Contribution of Design to Knowledge', *Proceedings of the Ohio Doctoral Education in Design Conference* 1:41 (1998); Clive Dilnot, 'The Matter of Design', *Design Philosophy Papers* 13, no. 2 (2015): 115–23; Herbert A. Simon, *The Sciences of the Artificial* (Cambridge, Mass. and London: MIT Press, 1996).

tion of *thinkerer*.[21] My challenge however is to take the sceptical reader with me on this journey into uncertainty. I exhort them to immerse themselves in the constellations of ideas I assemble throughout and to follow the *fil rouge* unspooling *The Power of Maybes*' proposition: that uncertainty can become an ally for living differently, for living a fuller life.

I must perhaps say at this point that if you are looking for a manual of instructions on how to control uncertainty, manage risk or future-proof your business, this book is not for you. If, on the other hand, you are open to hearing why you should trust uncertainty, why you should make it into your ally and how, then read on. I should also clarify at this point that *The Power of Maybes* is not about socio-economic factors of uncertainty, nor is it about inequality. It does not mean I dismiss the deleterious impact of precarity, the asymmetry in the distribution of resources, the unjust consequences of economic instability; or that I deny that precariousness, insecurity and their tangible effects on health, life expectation, mental wellbeing and, broadly, existence, are the direct result of injustice, violence and privilege. But this is not what the book is about. *The Power of Maybes* treats uncertainty as a *cosmic condition* – irreducible, inescapable, universal, oceanic. It proposes uncertainty as a laboratory to resist the capture of potential and cultivate a richer, fuller and, yes, *a* more uncertain life. It wants you to rethink what uncertainty is, and what it can do, by reclaiming the 'power of maybes'.

The book is divided into two parts. **Part One** concerns machines and automation, and the reasons why the power they exercise in constituting subjectivities, needs resisting. **Part Two** responds to the issues raised in Part One by framing them through a cosmological orientation. This cosmological orientation informs the stratagems that turn uncertainty into an ally.

Part One opens with **Chapter 1 – Machines Work** – which looks at planetary computation, the epoch-defining artificialization of intelligence, and its implications on knowledge and cognition. It traces a genealogy of the notion of *technē* to surface the tension between the instrumental and the non-instrumental within technology, and to question assumptions around productive knowledge, instrumentality and the notion of the blueprint. It examines how predictive machines work by looking at algorithms, machine learning and automation, and considers the epistemic consequences of the automation of automation. The chapter focuses on the unknowability at the core of computation to ques-

21 *Thinkerer* is a term I am quite partial to. As the hybrid (therefore splendidly impure) of 'thinker' and 'tinkerer', it highlights how the act of thinking is the *practice* – messy, experimental, slightly chaotic – of treating ideas like material to build temporary assemblages that induce unpredictable micro-catastrophes and shocks to thought. On the relationship between theory and practice Deleuze and Foucault say: 'No theory can develop without eventually encountering a wall, and practice is necessary for piercing this wall' … 'Practice is a set of relays from one theoretical point to another, and theory is a relay from one practice to another'. Gilles Deleuze and Michel Foucault, 'A Conversation Between Michel Foucault and Gilles Deleuze. Intellectuals and Power', in *Language, Counter-Memory, Practice. Selected Essays and Interviews*, ed. Donald F. Bouchard (Ithaca: Cornell University Press, 1977), 205.

tion the discourses of enchantment and opacity, and to begin to propose an uncertainty-driven counter-epistemology. The condition for this manoeuvre is that the extractive genealogy that still informs prevailing interpretations of technology is critically reassessed. The analysis of planetary computation continues in **Chapter 2 – Algorithmic Subjects** – which focuses on the production of subjects in the regime of algorithmic governmentality. This chapter frames algorithmic governmentality through key concepts by Félix Guattari – the Integrated World Capitalism and General Collective Equipment – and contextualizes algorithmic governmentality's extractive mechanisms within capitalism's innovative techniques for the capture of potential, techniques of 'reduction' of the plenitude of existence. The chapter concludes by asking how and where the potential for resistance may be found. It uses the discussion around the production of algorithmic subjects to locate within this process the seeds (*crystals*) of a possibility of resistance. Resistance is the topic of **Chapter 3 – Resisting Reduction** – which uses Henry Melville's novel *Bartleby* as its starting point to examine the relations between potentiality and impotentiality, and to argue that resistance can be found in the 'inoperative'. The chapter draws on Agamben and Deleuze's reading of *Bartleby* to locate the possibility for resistance in the 'amphibolic' state where potential cohabits with impotential. It examines the inoperative as the condition of possibility for a richer, fuller mode of living, which it calls 'round' or 'whatever' life: a life that can be nurtured by dwelling in uncertainty as the antidote to algorithmic capture. The resistance I argue for coincides with the creation of a new art of living and calls for enablers – *stratagems* – that are conducive to (and aligned with) the conceptual frameworks of the inoperative, the non-instrumental, the amphibolic. To begin to illustrate the characteristics required by the stratagems I propose, such as adaptability, cunning and efficacy, the chapter introduces exit, opportunism and duplicity. It also highlights that they concern design. Thus, Part One concludes with a call for design to place not the human, not even the nonhuman and certainly not the user, but the plenitude of undifferentiated potential at its core – in short, a call for design to work by reaching out to the cosmic.

With Part Two *The Power of Maybes* changes tack. It moves from planetary computation to outlining the cosmological orientation that, I contend, is necessary to inhabit uncertainty as the generative space of uncaptured potential, prior to what algorithmic governmentality feeds on. **Chapter 4 – Metic Wayfinding** – swerves into the cosmic by mapping those key moments and ideas from Spinoza's philosophy – his notion of nature and his ethics – and from pantheism that, taken together with the kind of intelligence that the ancient Greeks called *mētis*, constitute the wayfinding of the title. This cosmological orientation, informed by radical non-duality and by the coincidence of intelligent matter and sensible matter, is the basis of an ethical stance vital to a project of renewal, reparation and regenesis. It is this cosmological orientation, in other words, that I deem necessary to pursue in order to enter and dwell in uncertainty. Uncertainty, finally, is the topic of **Chapter 5 – Oceanic Uncertainty**. A deep dive into what uncertainty is, how it is thought about and which (and whose) are the stories told about it, this chapter examines uncertainty as a multifaceted (and difficult to pinpoint) entity. It looks at how uncertainty is conceptualized and framed; at the relationship between uncertainty and creativity, and between uncertainty and risk. It discusses prevention, precaution and pre-emption as modes of anticipatory governance that seize uncertainty. It examines Heisenberg's principle and ideas around quantum uncertainty, drawing together the voices of the physicist (Rovelli) and the philosopher (Barad) to surface uncertainty as the entanglement of epistemological and ontological matters. What remains to be seen in detail are the stratagems that afford making friends with uncertainty by enacting a convergence of mode of knowing, acting and being that is the basis of an ethical wisdom (already outlined through my cosmological orientation). **Chapter 6 – Unknowing Stratagems** – takes up the challenge by framing its stratagems as modes of approaching the unknown also drawing on some instances of Chinese thinking. The chapter foregrounds the stratagems through the relationship between knowing and not-knowing, and by outlining the value of cultivating not-knowing, for instance through 'learned ignorance'. It then proceeds to describe the stratagems I propose to enter uncertainty and inhabit maybes: conjecture, divination, blur, vanishing into things, *wu wei*. The book closes with the **Conclusion: Whatever Designs**, which contains some reflections that connect the key ideas of the book to design and states the implications of my cosmological orientation for a potential-driven design ontology.

A Note on Method

TRANSDISCIPLINARITY

The Power of Maybes is informed by transdisciplinarity, an inquiry across disciplinary domains whose conceptual frameworks and methodological practices aim to be as malleable as what they attempt to theorize. Because of its subject matter – uncertainty – my transdisciplinary approach in *The Power of Maybes* needs to be both elastic and rigorous.[1] Something to take into account when embarking on transdisciplinary research is that disciplinary domains – be they design, philosophy, social sciences or future studies – are hardly as coherent and cohesive as they claim to be. As a consequence, their (potentially transdisciplinary) encounter will always be the encounter of *meta-stable* entities: entities in the making, traversed by competing discourses, animated by degrees of restlessness. Put differently, transdisciplinarity is the practice of building tentative bridges across already precarious disciplines and domains, and of turning the space in-between them into a trafficked, messy terrain of inquiry. When I conduct transdisciplinary research, I get to probe limits, mix things up, linger in their gaps. In these boundary zones, my inquiry is released from the constraints of purity, coherence and non-contradiction. It becomes free to experiment.[2] This process can be confusing, awkward and infuriating, until something novel emerges, and a new concept begins to shimmer.

I believe that it is the (cosmic, oceanic) uncertainty of the world, with all the world's own fractiousness, multiplicity and unpredictability, that demands a transdisciplinary approach to research; that asks for methodologies able to attune to its shifting contours. Put bluntly, if you wish to stop seeing the world

[1] I discuss historian Carlo Ginzburg's 'elastic rigour' approach in Chapter 6.

[2] John Law, *After Method. Mess in Social Science Research* (London: Routledge, 2004); Rebecca Coleman and Jessica Ringrose, 'Introduction', in *Deleuze and Research Methodologies* (Edinburgh: Edinburgh University Press, 2013), 1–22; Betti Marenko, 'Stacking Complexities. Reframing Uncertainty Through Hybrid Literacies', *Design and Culture* 13, no. 2 (2021): 165–84.

as a homogenous entity, transdisciplinarity *is* your mode of navigation. Transdisciplinarity takes the fiction of the single, unified, 'real-world'[3] and shatters it into the multiplicity of the pluriverse. It embraces practices – transversal, collaborative, transformative – of *attuning to* the multiplicity of worlds one is contributing to create.

With critical inquiry increasingly called to attend to the uncertainties, instabilities and contingencies of a restless world, new approaches, perspectives and methodologies are needed, more than ever, that can grasp instability and uncertain transformation.[4] This is why philosophies attentive to processuality and to the not-yet are transdisciplinarity's most formidable allies. Because by engaging with, and by tapping into, the forces that traverse and make up the becoming of the world, they spur new insights without immobilizing what moves.[5] Process philosophies, with post-qualitative inquiry and the notion of method as a boundary, inform the building of transdisciplinary constellations, which is *The Power of Maybes*' method of choice.

POST-QUALITATIVE INQUIRY

The literature discussing methods as emergent, caught-in-the-act, unscripted, inventive, adaptive and unafraid to experiment is rich and wide-ranging.[6] But which methods are best suited to grasp the conditions of the unknown and the not-yet? Which approaches understand best what is coming into being, rather than describe, interpret or represent what exists already?

3 In a post-Newtonian world, I can no longer assume an objective reality 'out there' waiting to be discovered, measured and described. The fiction of a single universal world, the one-world world (OWW) is a machine that generates and maintains un-justices. See Martin Savransky, *Around the Day in Eighty Worlds. Politics of the Pluriverse* (Durham and London: Duke University Press, 2021); Walter D. Mignolo, 'The Decolonial Option', in *On Decoloniality. Concepts, Analytics, Praxis*, ed. Walter D. Mignolo and Catherine E. Walsh (Durham and London: Duke University Press, 2018), 103–244.

4 While methods underline the instrumentality of specific techniques, steps or procedures when using certain tools and instruments for navigating a journey, methodology concerns the reasoning, logic or principles used for tackling a certain issue or research problem. Put differently, methods are techniques for gathering evidence not necessarily for specifying for what they are or how they should be used, which is the aim of a methodology – the broader, theory-driven framework for how a project should proceed. Elizabeth A. St. Pierre, Alecia Y. Jackson and Lisa A. Mazzei, 'New Empiricisms and New Materialisms. Conditions for New Inquiry', *Cultural Studies<>Critical Methodologies* 16, no. 2 (2016): 99–110; Phillip Vannini, *Non-Representational Methodologies. Re-Envisioning Research* (New York and London: Routledge, 2015).

5 Rosi Braidotti, *Posthuman Knowledge* (Cambridge: Polity Press, 2019); Rosi Braidotti, 'A Theoretical Framework for the Critical Posthumanities', *Theory, Culture & Society* 36, no. 6 (2019): 31–61; Rosi Braidotti and Matthew Fuller, 'The Posthumanities in an Era of Unexpected Consequences', *Theory, Culture & Society* 36, no. 6 (2019): 3–29.

6 Celia Lury and Nina Wakeford ed., *Inventive Methods. The Happening of the Social* (Abingdon and New York: Routledge, 2012); Brian Massumi, *Semblance and Event. Activist Philosophy and the Occurrent Arts* (Cambridge, Mass. and London: MIT Press, 2011); Erin Manning, 'Against Method', in *Non-Representational Methodologies. Re-Envisioning Research*, ed. Phillip Vannini (New York and London: Routledge, 2015), 52–72.

I choose to highlight what is known as 'post-qualitative inquiry' because of its uncompromising focus on the indeterminate and the uncertain.[7] Starting from a critique of quantitative and qualitative humanist methodologies, seen as instruments that reduce uncertainty, constrain the materiality of affects and seize the not-yet, post-qualitative inquiry aims to develop modes of research that are as immanent as the events it studies.[8] From the standpoint of post-qualitative inquiry, methods do not (and cannot) exist before, or distinct from, an alleged object of inquiry. Educator and scholar Elizabeth St. Pierre even argues against method when she states: 'Method proscribes and prohibits. It controls and disciplines. Further, method always comes too late, is immediately out-of-date, and so is inadequate to the task at hand. *But method not only can't keep with events; more seriously, it prevents them from coming into existence.*'[9] For St. Pierre, method itself is a trap. Like amber immobilizing an insect and freezing its movement forever, method 'often seems designed to stifle curiosity'.[10]

How would inquiry begin then? Not with a commitment to methodology but through the specificity of the researcher's encounter with the world. It is the uncertainty of the world that dictates the terms of the inquiry. Describing how this encounter with the uncertain can be embraced during research, sociologist Maggie MacLure suggests making space for affective collisions – what she calls 'micro catastrophes' – and for the 'serious play of rigorous experimentation'.[11] Practically, this means that neither 'research' nor 'researcher' will exist outside the encounter. Rather, my embodied self becomes an integral part of the process of enquiry.[12] No longer an 'external observer', I strive to attune myself to the potential of my encounter with ideas, practices, concepts. I dispose myself to pay attention to what forces thought, to what shocks my system. It is in the encounter – with its characteristics of being a threshold state, an adjacent

7 Elizabeth A. St. Pierre, 'Post Qualitative Inquiry in an Ontology of Immanence', *Qualitative Inquiry* 25, no. 1 (2019): 3–16; St. Pierre, Jackson and Mazzei, 'New Empiricisms and New Materialisms'.

8 Immanent – from the Latin *in* + *maneo* = 'to dwell in, remain in' – is that which resides in the totality of being and contains in itself its own propulsion to self-generation. Accordingly, a philosophy of immanence is concerned not with being but with becoming, not with what is, but with what is coming into being. Immanence denotes that which exists here and now, as opposed to what is perceived or construed beyond this reality (what transcends this reality = transcendence, e.g. the platonic realm of ideas, and is assumed as a world of essential, pure, universal essences). This is why, as Deleuze remarks, transcendence is an illusion. There is nothing outside of immanence: if there was something external to it, it would be transcendence. Gilles Deleuze, *Pure Immanence. Essays on a Life* (New York: Zone Books, 2005).

9 Elizabeth A. St. Pierre, 'Post Qualitative Inquiry'. Keynote Lecture, Australian Association of Research in Education, New Zealand Association of Research in Education, 2014, 16.

10 'We may well have to give up the comfort of method, which often seems designed to stifle curiosity as we move from one pre-determined step to another and another' (St. Pierre, Jackson and Mazzei, 'New Empiricisms and New Materialisms', 8). I am indebted to Roy Bendor for the image of the amber as trap.

11 Maggie MacLure, 'Inquiry as Divination', *Qualitative Inquiry* 27, no. 5 (2021): 4.

12 For MacLure, inquiry becomes 'diffractive' (the crystal, again): no longer predicated on the interrogation and analysis of data by a human agent, but by its luminous and incoherent fragmentation. This also accounts for how the 'I' enters and dissolves into an encounter.

possible, a trading zone – that something unplanned may emerge. 'We, and the data, do not pre-exist one another',[13] says MacLure. Importantly, post-qualitative inquiry stresses that expressions such as 'raw' data and 'real-world' are not only incorrect but misleading. Data is not the 'raw' material at my disposal, mute until I (the researcher) intervene with my intellectual apparatus. Far from being a meaning to represent, a symptom to interpret, an asset to code, 'data' becomes instead a swarm of intensities whose impact remains largely unpredictable.

BOUNDARIES AND HINGES

So, how do I build my methods of inquiry?

The notion of boundary returns in sociologist John Law's well-known argument that methods, and the practice of method-building, always concern boundaries. If this is true, then it will elicit the following question: Where exactly would I make 'cuts' to specify the limits of the knowledge I am producing? Indeed, methods do more than just describe the world. They contribute to creating worlds through what they afford discovering. They produce realities. Law and Urry write: 'If methods are not innocent then they are also political, they help to make realities. But the question is: which realities?'[14] Or, should I add, whose realities? As a transdisciplinary researcher, I am even more called to reflect on which, and whose, kind of realities I create with my methods. It seems to me that such questions of methods (*how* to know) go beyond epistemic matters to become ontological.[15] Put differently, if realities are continuously produced by ongoing material-semiotic interactions, including those of research methods, then my choices – as a researcher, educator, practitioner, theorist, change-maker, citizen, thinkerer, *living expert*[16] – have consequences. Acknowledging that research is implicated in these choices, especially when certain realities are 'easier' to produce than others, means attending to the ethics and the politics of my research. I will return to matters of ethics. For now, suffice to say that ethical knowledge is the convergence of my mode of knowing, my mode of being and my mode of acting: when my knowledge and what informs my conduct cannot be separated from the person I am and I am becoming through my practice.

This is significant for another reason. It also illuminates my own personal affinity for transdisciplinary inquiry as a 'way' – a line of flight – beyond academic scholarship. Reflecting on how my practice as a researcher got to be what it is, I must enlist several other trajectories alongside academia. For instance, schooled

13 Maggie MacLure, 'The Wonder of Data', *Cultural Studies<>Critical Methodologies* 13, no. 4 (2013): 229.

14 John Law and John Urry, 'Enacting the Social', *Economy and Society* 33, no. 3 (2004): 404.

15 Another way of putting this is to say that the separation between knowledge (epistemic) and being (ontological) needs rethinking, in what may be called an ethico-onto-epistemological approach.

16 I am indebted to design strategist Kaye Toland for the expression *living expert*, way more preferable to 'end user' (and the terminal devaluation it implies).

in my youth, from the late 1980s, in post-autonomist, anarcho-punk practices of resistance, subversion and production; taking part in Italian counterculture movements pushing for, practising and defending activism, occupation and alternative lifestyles as lived critique; experimenting with radical practices of embodied transformation in the body modification and BDSM subculture of early 1990s London. All this may be taken as a fitting testimony to my own idiosyncratic and un-orthodox intellectual trajectory. My reticence to be pigeonholed into a single field, a single role, a single discipline, has constantly pushed me to privilege the hyphen mode with its hinging (and disarticulating, when not disconcerting) properties. I have been a sociologist-squatter, a punk-semiotician, a raver-philosopher, an educator-dominatrix, a tattooist muse-scholar, an activist-yogini, all the while making, unmaking and remaking myself. I mention this simply to point out the extent to which transdisciplinary research is for me a movement of continuous overflowing and porosity.

To go back to the questions above – what kind of realities do I intend to create and for whom? – with *The Power of Maybes* my wish is to bring uncertainty to fruition as an ethical practice in itself, a steering principle whose vast unknowability can also become a source of delight and a vehicle to plenitude. As per the other question – how do I build my methods? – the section below explains my method of choice, what I call *constellation-building*.

CONSTELLATION-BUILDING

I propose *constellation-building* as my method, which consists of assembling different, heterogenous and even eclectic voices, positions and ideas. As a method (and as a process), constellation-building is exquisitely appropriate to transdisciplinary work for at least three reasons. To start with, it is a way of working that grasps concepts as they unfold; then, it pushes me to think anew every time the encounter with (and the collision of) different ideas produces something unexpected; finally, it enables me to experiment with how *chance* and *intuition* participate in the process of knowledge-making. Chance becomes an opportunity to make meaning otherwise unlikely to be made. By enlisting the unforeseen as part of the knowledge-making process I acknowledge forces beyond my own agency and intentionality.[17] As I craft, both intentionally and accidentally, encounters with ideas, their unplanned collisions have the power to make me think; heterogenous elements resonate with each other to create new insights. Furthermore, building constellations of eclectic and divergent

[17] The emphasis on chance, of which more in Chapter 6, is even more relevant given that my topic of research is uncertainty. As anthropologist Michael Taussig puts it commenting on the divinatory properties of a book collection: 'Because chance plays a part in how the items in a collection gravitate into one's hands, a collection can be used as an instrument of divination, since chance is the flipside of fate.' Michael Taussig, *I Swear I Saw This. Drawing in Fieldwork Notebooks, Namely My Own* (Chicago and London: University of Chicago Press, 2011), 104.

voices is a highly generative practice. Not just transdisciplinary, but *transversal* too. I borrow Guattari's notion of transversality as the practice of building connections that go on building more connections.[18]

As the reader will discover, while each chapter is based on a different constellation of voices, the *fil rouge* that weaves them all together is uncertainty in its many facets. The reader will encounter ideas on technology, algorithms and artificial intelligence; risk, prudence and precaution; Melville's *Bartleby*, Heisenberg's principle and physicist Carlo Rovelli's poetic reading of the quantum construction of reality; historian Carlo Ginzburg's conjectural method, Joshua Ramey's political take on divinatory practices, and Nicholas of Cusa's 'learned ignorance'; the Chinese notion of *wu wei*, an appraisal of pantheism and the cunning intelligence that the Greeks called *mētis*; alongside Félix Guattari's General Collective Equipments, Antoinette Rouvroy's algorithmic governmentality and Giorgio Agamben's inoperativity, among others.

I am aware that the eclectic nature of my constellations may irritate some readers; others may find it baffling and charge it (and me) with inconsistent scholarship, or superficiality. But to work across meta-stable disciplines, which is my non-negotiable standpoint, is also to accept that a degree of 'superficiality' may be inherent to the encounter. What I mean is that whatever happens in the 'trading zones' of transdisciplinary research, I do not need to agree to the full signification of whatever is being exchanged (ideas, notions, terms, concepts, epistemes, practices, experiments, and so on). There is no requirement to subscribe to universal principles of reference. It is entirely possible to share a partial, local, 'thin' understanding of an idea or set of ideas without having to take on board the full apparatus of signification, symbols and values.[19] In his praise of 'the *thinness* of interpretation rather than the thickness of consensus',[20] Galison explains this lucidly:

> Thin description is precisely what makes it possible for the experimentalist and the theorist to communicate, albeit in a register that by no means captures the full world of either, let alone both. Thinness is what makes it possible for the surface chemist to work with the atomic physicist, the virologist with electrical engineer, the computer scientist with the molecular geneticist. The theorist does not have to probe the myriad laboratory procedures that lie behind the experimentalist's confidence that liquid hydrogen has particular thermodynamic properties; and the experimentalist does not need to know the full mathematical–physical reasoning backing the theories that lie behind a calculation. What they need is consensus in a restricted zone, a zone where coordination is good enough.[21]

[18] Félix Guattari, 'Transdisciplinarity Must Become Transversality', *Theory, Culture, & Society* 32, no. 5–6 (2015): 131–7.

[19] Galison, 'Trading with the Enemy', 44.

[20] Ibid., 36.

[21] Ibid.

Rather than making grandiose claims on what transdisciplinarity is or ought to be; rather than trying to enshrine its precarity into laws, what matters to me is that I *share enough* – enough to negotiate the next step, enough to coordinate the next action, enough to craft in the *now* a tiny bit of what the *next* may be. In these trading zones where my transdisciplinary inquiry into uncertainty is produced, I seek the 'good enough', the 'sufficient to the scope', in one word, the *efficacious micro-intervention* that may take me into the not-yet.

THE SPIDER'S STRATAGEM: INTUITION AND IMAGINATION

My constellation-building also draws on Gilles Deleuze, who writes about method as something that is constituted locally, in a fragmentary manner, without having to reference a superior unity: 'I therefore see no opposition between this local constitution of fragments of method and the final revelation', he says.[22] Deleuze evokes the image of the spider, whose strategy is to wait, motionless, until a fly is caught in the web, the web moves and the vibrations precipitate a reality that brings the fly, the web and the spider into sudden co-existence. The fly exists (as a prey) only in its encounter with the web, and so does the spider (as a predator). Deleuze's method is the *spider's strategy*. The spider builds her web and disposes itself to wait; vibrations reach her; nourishment is found. Similarly, I dispose myself to waiting for the contingent to strike, I proceed to weave, my fingers braiding thoughts, my hands kneading concepts. When I open my eyes, I am met by that which nourishes me. I meet the constellations I have built.

This is how a slice of *intuition* enters constellation-building. Because intuition breaks down the intellectual barrier between observer and observed, between researcher and research object, working with intuition is another way of engaging with boundaries. Henri Bergson writes that intuition is a thinking that perceives processes in their flow. Far from being instinct or feeling, intuition is a particular kind of knowledge, a higher form of intelligence that grasps 'spirit, duration and pure change'.[23] Intuition turns my mind inward. It establishes a sympathetic communication between myself and the world; it expands my consciousness into the cosmic. Intuition is how I apprehend things on the basis of the material life-force they express. The embodied, affective apprehension of the flow of matter (something that can only be followed) is, for Deleuze and Guattari, 'intuition in action'.[24]

[22] Gilles Deleuze, *Two Regimes of Madness. Texts and Interviews 1975–1995* (New York: Semiotext(e), 2006), 46.

[23] Henri Bergson, *The Creative Mind. An Introduction to Metaphysics* (Mineola, NY: Dover Publications, 2007), 21. For Bergson, we are in constant danger of overestimating our rationality and of underestimating our intuitive traits. See also Spinoza who considers intuition the highest form of knowledge ('scientia intuitiva'), even superior to reason and imagination (Spinoza *Ethics* Part II, Proposition 40, note 2: 69); Genevieve Lloyd, *Spinoza and the Ethics* (London and New York: Routledge, 1996).

[24] Gilles Deleuze and Félix Guattari, *A Thousand Plateaus. Capitalism and Schizophrenia* (London: The Athlone Press, 1988), 409.

This does not mean to dispense with rationality, but rather, to learn to take intuitive experiences seriously, precisely because they show a glimpse of the processual character of reality. Grosz loops back intuition to the quest for a creativity that eludes instrumentality by describing intuition as:

> our nonpragmatic, noneffective, nonexpedient, noninstrumental relation to the world, the capacity we have to live in the world in excess of our needs, and in excess of the self-presentation or immanence of materiality, to collapse ourselves, as things, back into the world. Our 'artisticness', as Nietzsche puts it, our creativity, in Bergsonian terms, consists in nothing else than the continuous experimentation with the world of things to produce new things from the fluidity or flux which eludes everyday needs, or use-value.[25]

Grosz's remarks around creativity remind me that alongside intuition degrees of *imagination* are also needed in constellation-building. Specifically, enough imagination to be stirred by uncertainty without precipitating into absolute reverie. To feed imagination into my constellation-building I use abductive thinking – the speculative mode of knowing that invents explanatory and interrogative hypotheses. Abductive thinking is a generative method unconstrained by either a priori theory or a posteriori verification.[26] Rather, as Luciana Parisi puts it, it is 'primarily attuned to the unpredictable nature of fact, thought and experience' defining 'an immanent relation between the thing and its unknown potentials'.[27] Abduction ventures to the 'limits of the observable where thought becomes experimental and experiential of the future'.[28] For Parisi, abduction is like an excitable, curious probe-head that 'demands of thought to become felt, fact to become potential, imagination to supersede observation, object to affect method, method to become transformative of the object'.[29]

All the approaches, ways and modes of knowing that I have mentioned so far – transdisciplinarity, transversality, post-qualitative inquiry, intuition, chance, imagination, abductive thinking – are the building blocks of my constellations. What they have in common is that they all strive to intensify what can be thought. They are all ways to expand the pool of 'possible possibles'. As Stengers and Debaise write:

> The sense of the possible to be activated always lies in the interstices of a situation, however incapable this situation may be of validating it. It means

[25] Elizabeth Grosz, *Time Travels. Feminism, Nature, Power* (Durham and London: Duke University Press, 2005), 136.

[26] For a definition of abduction, deduction and induction see Chapter 1, note 57.

[27] Luciana Parisi, 'Speculation. A Method for the Unattainable', in *Inventive Methods. The Happening of the Social*, ed. Celia Lury and Nina Wakeford (Abingdon and New York: Routledge, 2012), 236.

[28] Ibid., 237.

[29] Ibid., 241.

> sensing the virtualities present within this situation, despite the weight of the judgements transforming its lack of guarantee into a matter of fact, tantamount to a condemnation.[30]

This intensification is, for me, the only way to resist the 'desertification of all modes of existence', the false alternatives, the spurious representations, the subjective projections, the fabricated dilemmas, while being response-able, attentive and tuned in to consequences. But another question remains: How do I keep the elements of my constellations together *enough*, enough to be efficacious but without immobilizing what moves?

SPECULATIVE PRAGMATISM

To ensure that the disparate elements I assemble in my constellations will hold, I turn to Brian Massumi's notion of 'speculative pragmatism', and I use it as the glue that keeps my constellations together while allowing the movement necessary for conceptual plasticity. In describing the coming together of the speculative and the pragmatic, Massumi explains how

> the speculative aspect relates to the character of potential native to the world's activity, as expressed eventfully in the taking place of change. The pragmatic aspect has to do with how, in the taking-definite-shape of potential in a singular becoming, the relational and speculative poles co-compose as formative forces.[31]

Speculative pragmatism allows me to stay open to invention and potential (speculative) *and* to pay attention to what is happening, the how, the method (pragmatism). I visualize the speculative and the pragmatic as *hinged*. Their connection is so generative precisely because, like a hinge, they can move both together *and* apart.[32] Importantly, pragmatic does not mean practical or non-theoretical. It is rather what mobilizes ideas and 'unstiffens' theories.[33]

Another way of putting it is to say that speculative pragmatism engages with what does not exist yet. Then, inevitably, it will be a messy, risky, subversive

[30] Stengers and Debaise, 'The Insistence of Possibles', 18.

[31] Massumi, *Semblance and Event*, 12. He explains: 'This *should* make a difference. *Could* make a difference. But *how*? *Which* difference? Could/should: speculative. How/which: *pragmatic*' (ibid., 167). For further explanation of speculative pragmatism understood as a kind of pragmatism that draws on William James's radical empiricism see ibid., 85–6.

[32] I am grateful to Margot Leigh Butler, *hingiologist* extraordinaire, for bringing hinges and their potential to my attention.

[33] I borrow this term from philosopher William James: 'Pragmatism unstiffens all our theories, limbers them up and sets each one at work'. William James, 'Pragmatism. A New Name for Some Old Ways of Thinking', Lectures delivered at the Lowell Institute in Boston (November and December, 1906), and at Columbia University, New York (January, 1907), http://pdf-objects.com/files/William-James-Pragmatism.pdf (accessed 28 October 2024), no page.

business. It could not be otherwise. Erin Manning explains it clearly when she observes that speculative pragmatism is

> interested in the anarchy at the heart of all process and is engaged with the techniques that tune the anarchical into new modes of knowledge. It is also interested in what escapes order, and especially in what this excess can do. And it implicitly recognizes that knowledge is invented in the escape, in the excess.[34]

In other words, for speculative pragmatism to work the process must be experimental. It must allow the unruliness and anarchy of experimentation. Speculative pragmatism *intimates* me to find ways to try things out; to observe, experiment and learn; to escape from what I already know; to sidestep existing grooves, and parachute myself into the discomfort of shifting terrains.

The process of using speculative pragmatism to hold my constellations together is also a curation of sort, of the concepts I assemble, both by design and by accident, to think with; some concepts will simply describe (and lock me into) what exists already, but others will move me, make space and take time; activate thought, galvanize action.[35]

What I know is that when thinking gets stuck 'in grooves', as Alfred North Whitehead puts it,[36] artifices and interventions (or *stratagems*, as Part Two shows) are needed to 'activate' thinking. Stengers and Debaise comment:

> What we need to activate today is a thinking that commits to a possible, by means of resisting the probable – fighting any interpretation subscribing to the irresistible nature of unbounded capitalism as if that were our immutable destiny, even the conduit conveying the message of progress and emancipation, whereas in fact it denotes the desertification of our worlds and our inability to think that what we care about might have a future.[37]

34 Manning, 'Against Method', 62.

35 For example, De Sousa Santos, *End of the Cognitive Empire*, shares a tremendous list of non-Eurocentric concepts to learn to build an expanded common knowledge driven by otherness. Among others: *ubuntu*, *buen vivir*, *corazonar*, *pachamama*. Each one is a portal to make me think differently. *Ubuntu*: 'I am because you are', indicating an ontology of co-existence; *buen vivir*: good living; *corazonar*: warming up reason; *pachamama*: nature as a living being and life source. I see these concepts as hinges too.

36 For Alfred N. Whitehead, 'to be mentally in a groove is to live in contemplating a given set of abstractions. The groove prevents straying across country, and the abstraction abstracts from something to which no further attention is paid. But there is no groove of abstractions which is adequate for the comprehension of human life'. Alfred N. Whitehead, *Science and the Modern World* (Cambridge: Cambridge University Press, 1926), 245.

37 Stengers and Debaise, 'The Insistence of Possibles', 18. Their distinction between the probable and the possible seems aligned with Deleuze's distinction between the possible and the virtual: 'The probable has to do with a transposition or a rearrangement of what has already taken place or what is ongoing, as shown by the calculation of probabilities. The probable belongs to a logic of conformity … The possible, however, makes important the possible eruption of other ways of feeling, thinking, acting, which can only be envisaged in the form of an insistence, undermining the authority of the present as regards the definition of the future' (ibid., 18, note 19).

I take their exhortation to commit to a possible against the probable as a call to reach out to the uncertain, the unknown, the *maybes*. This, for me, is also the meaning of Guattari's epigraph at the beginning of the Introduction 'Hybrid Futures': 'I hold out my hand to the future'.[38]

But reaching out to uncertainty is not enough. My inquiry must *resist*, too. Resist the imposition of method, the fictions of 'raw data' and 'real world', the delusion of the external observer. It must contest linear narratives and naturalized grooves. It must downplay conscious intentionality and focus instead on what can be sensed by grasping the 'propensity of things'.[39]

Ultimately, my inquiry must also be reached to, in turn, by the uncertain and become in itself a propagation node traversed by unidentified streams of potential. It is with this image that I conclude my Note on Method. By recalling that transversality is the capacity of each connection to generate more, unheard-of, connections, triggering potential across heterogenous fields. Transversality is a detonation across strata, labels and roles. It dislodges immobilism by transcending the locked orthogonal mechanics of the vertical-horizontal and plumping instead for the free-ranging beauty of the diagonal, connecting and activating each node to the next. My constellation-building is a transversal experiment in thinking otherwise. It is my own desire to create crystalline worlds, with uncertainty by my side.

[38] Guattari, *Chaosmosis*, 134.

[39] François Jullien, *The Propensity of Things. Toward a History of Efficacy in China* (New York: Zone Books, 1995).

PART ONE

1 Machines Work

Not predicting, but being attentive to the unknown knocking at the door.
GILLES DELEUZE[1]

A MYRIAD OF MACHINES

This chapter is about machines, technology and the artificial. It starts with an examination of the notion of *technē* to investigate the margin of unknowability within technology (and within technological knowledge). It goes on to show how this margin of unknowability can be deployed in my project of turning uncertainty into an ally. Next, the chapter takes this unknowability to the core of how today's predictive machines work. Finally, it uses unknowability (and the uncertainty it produces) to call for new stories and new categories for the artificial, for automation and for the human, stories and categories that question the 'inevitabilism' of mainstream narratives, and move away from instrumentality, human-centredness and anthropocentrism.

Think of how stories and cultural fictions that circulate around the artificialization of intelligence tend to conflate media hype, technological innovation, social imaginaries, ideological agendas, corporate strategies. How they spin epistemologies, regimes of truth and myth-making yarns that are hyperbolic and delusional at best, unjust and gas-lighting at worst. New stories are called for, to side-step both the hackneyed Hollywood scenario of rogue machines bent on destroying humanity, and the optimistic fervour of the singularity; stories that stay clear of both paranoid anxiety and acritical techno-solutionism, avoid the tired tropes of techno-dystopia or techno-utopia, and strive instead to express critical and creative, experimental and transversal figurations.

This chapter uses the term 'machine' to describe a particular category of machines – the computing ones – designed to solve calculable problems through

[1] Deleuze, *Two Regimes of Madness*, 346.

a discrete number of steps. These are the machines that, from Turing onwards, have ushered in the age of planetary computation. I use 'machine' also as the shortcut for the planetary condition that characterizes the present, and as a convenient (if crude) generalization to express that *digital hum* within which the human and the nonhuman swim – the immersive totalizing reality that old stories of hybridization of carbon and silicon simply can no longer express.

But to talk about machines is also to engage with the ambivalence of a notion that is both *abstract* (what machines stand for) and *concrete* (machine as a technical contraption that makes things happen). It is also about questioning assumptions concerning the (artifice of) human intervention on (assumed 'natural') environments, a relationship that is far from straightforward. Expanding on the original meaning of the word 'machine', from the Latin *machina* as 'means, contrivance, device', and by extension any technical implement or mechanism, machines designate a way of understanding the relationship between humans and the world as a relationship of mutual constitution and interdependency.[2] Machines are the connective tissue across hybrid ecosystems of the natural and the artificial.

Furthermore, as someone schooled in Deleuze and Guattari's machinic philosophy, I think through and with machines intended as arrangements of forces, assemblages of different elements coming together in variable relations of *contiguity*, discontinuous connections and provisory linkages of dynamic flows without a priori organization, nor blueprint.[3] For Deleuze a machine is 'a "proximity" grouping between independent and heterogenous terms'.[4] Made of both connections and interruptions, a machine is the temporary snapshot result of an ongoing process of densification and dilution, expansion and contraction.

On this ground, by zooming in on the peculiar machines called 'intelligent' and the stories circulating about them, the chapter reflects on how the 'artificial'

2 For art historian Andreas Broeckmann, the twentieth century was the century of the machine. Different types of machines correspond to different types of modern subjects. In his taxonomy, the *mechanical* machine affords a relation between the human body and the technical object – a tool with a specific and limited functional autonomy that assists human labour (e.g. Archimedes lever). The *cybernetic* machine (non-Archimedean) works through exchange, of atoms, electrons, electromagnetic fields (e.g. thermometer), steers procedural operations, and not only processes but also produces information. The *totalitarian* machine, shorthand for the techno-autocratic complex, is the megamachine from which nothing (or very little) can escape, fragmenting into functional pieces every instant of the life of individuals (e.g. the body-swallowing machinery of Chaplin's *Modern Times*). The *heterogenous* machine concerns Deleuze and Guattari's assemblages. Andreas Broeckmann, *Machine Art in the Twentieth Century* (Cambridge, Mass. and London: MIT Press, 2016).

3 A note concerning the translation of the term 'assemblage': Deleuze calls *agencement* what Foucault calls *dispositif* – the former rendered in English as *assemblage*, the latter as *apparatus*. As translator Martin Joughin notes, both terms *agencement and dispositif* 'suggest a reconfiguration of some of the elements in a particular situation, which "prepares" various new lines of interaction of these elements' (Deleuze, *Negotiations*, 196, note 9), *dispositif* possesses a more 'mechanical' connotation. It must be also noted that Deleuze himself translates *agencement* as *arrangement* rather than *assemblage*, to retain the sense of orientation toward an action and reconfiguration that 'assemblage' does not have.

4 Gilles Deleuze and Claire Parnet, *Dialogues* (London: The Athlone Press, 1987), 104.

in artificial intelligence (AI) is conceptualized, and what kind of (and whose) 'intelligence' is evoked by it, to foreground what the other two chapters in Part One will go on to develop: algorithmic governmentality (Chapter 2) and questions of resistance (Chapter 3).

If the challenge for critical practice is to craft stories and images of thoughts that can make sense of how the digital hum reformats reality, knowledge and what counts as human and artificial,[5] then perhaps a good place to start is by examining what the notion of technology inherited from the Greeks – *technē* – may be still able to reveal. The next section looks at this lineage to ask questions concerning the possibility of the non-instrumental and the unproductive within technology, and to argue in favour of the uncertain, the unknowable and risk as modes through which technology can be re-imagined. This leads to a discussion of the incomputable within computation. Succinctly, the chapter frames unknowability through an analysis of where technology comes from (*technē*) and where it is going (planetary computation, automation).

TECHNĒ: KNOWLEDGE AS INSTRUMENTAL BLUEPRINT

Western understanding of technology is shaped by the Greek notion of *technē*: the productive knowledge that brings forth an idea into the world. *Technē*, the root of 'technology', 'technique' and 'technicity', is usually translated as 'skill', 'art' or 'crafts'. In ancient Greece, it also evoked specific philosophical values.[6] Aristotle calls *technē* a specific type of productive knowledge with tangible manifestations in the world and whose outcomes, once completed, will have an independent life of their own, and will be measurable and replicable. *Technē* is the quintessential instrumental knowledge supporting a purposeful, pragmatic and deliberative action. It is knowledge applied, taught, learned and quantifiable.[7] This understanding of *technē* has two important implications: I call them the 'imposition of the blueprint' and the 'burden of instrumentality'.

I start with the *blueprint*. Western thought has inherited from the Greeks the view of *technē* as 'the conception of the result to be produced before its

[5] Erich Horl, Nelly Y. Pinkrah and Lotte Warnsholdt, eds, *Critique and the Digital* (Zurich: Diaphanes, 2021).

[6] Aristotle describes three types of knowledge, intended as the ability to give an account of a process: theoretical (*episteme*), productive (*technē*) and practical (*phronesis*), each possessing a specific account (*logos*) of their object. These three distinct types of knowledge still inform Western understanding of what knowledge is: *episteme* is the theoretical know-why (scientific knowledge), *technē* is the technical know-how (productive knowledge) and *phronesis* is practical wisdom (ethical knowledge).

[7] Aristotle further specifies the nature of *technē* by making a comparison between things that are crafted by deliberate intervention and things that are made through spontaneous natural or biological processes (natural growth). Such difference between *technē* and *physis* lies in the agency: while nature is self-generating, *technē* requires an outside agent (craftsperson). Thomas K. Johansen ed., *Productive Knowledge in Ancient Philosophy. The Concept of Technê* (Cambridge and New York: Cambridge University Press, 2021).

realization in the material'.[8] In other words, ideas come first, knowledge starts in my head or soul, to then guide my hand and inform what I make, which is the tangible manifestation of the executed idea. This is like saying that abstract technical information is stored in an artefact, or that an artefact is the concrete outcome of that idea, whether I refer to building a ship, manufacturing a sofa, producing a healthy person, staging a theatre drama, or writing a book. The notion of blueprint is found in the hylomorphic model of matter, in classical design theory with the authorial modernist design position (and also in Marx).[9] But to say that artefacts are the product of a mental blueprint does not really explain the genesis of form. Or, better, it explains it by assuming that an ideal form already exists, ready to be imposed from the outside.[10]

This argument, and this is the second point, leads to *instrumentality*, the notion that technology is a means to an end, and that the optimal, most efficient response to a mechanical necessity justifies any technical solution. If it works, it must be good. If only steps from plan to execution could be fully controlled, then I could have an entirely risk-free, predictable outcome. Instrumentality is also a way of thinking about causality. Thought itself becomes a technology and an instrument of authority. In this way instrumentality leads to the triumph of technical rational agency with its sense of linear progress, ushering the triad of *techno-determinism* – the progress of technology is natural, rational, positive and inevitable; *solutionism* – technology can, will and should deliver solutions to problems; and *technocracy* – instrumental reason as governance.

From here the classic technocratic argument emerges: technologies are tools, it only depends on how they are used. This rhetoric of neutrality reduces any discussion around technology to the disingenuous and toxic slogan: 'Guns don't kill people, people kill people'.[11] The same rhetoric is found in the ostensibly objective and impartial knowledge provided by technical expertise and theories about efficiency, measurement and calculability.

In short, instrumentality deals with the most effective and efficient means to reach given ends. This leads to the belief that by controlling the transition from imagined plan to execution, the most rational technical means to achieve any goal would be possible. But a world dominated by instrumentality would be acritical, extractive, dangerous and coldly violent. It would also be inher-

8 Allen, *Artifice and Design*, 52.

9 Hylomorphism (from *hyle* = matter, wood, and *morphē* = form) assumes that matter is an inert 'receiver' of an external imposed blueprint; it also implies that the process will be a distortion of the 'forming' idea. This is Plato's classical distinction between the realm of ideas (theoretically intelligible forms) and their always imperfect application to the material world. In this (Platonic) view *technē* is always a betrayal and a falsification. Technicians, craftpersons, even artists, are seen as tricksters because they deceive people into perceiving wrongly represented ideas.

10 I have written extensively on this elsewhere. Betti Marenko, 'Digital Materiality, Morphogenesis and the Intelligence of the Technodigital Object', in *Deleuze and Design*, ed. Betti Marenko and Jamie Brassett (Edinburgh: Edinburgh University Press, 2015), 107–38.

11 Andrew Feenberg, *Technology, Modernity, and Democracy* (London: Rowman and Littlefield, 2018); Andres Esmark, *The New Technocracy* (Bristol: Bristol University Press, 2020).

ently doomed to self-destruction, because it would treat all that does not fit the utilitarian schemata as unnecessary, incoherent, disposable, be it human, nonhuman, living or non-living.[12]

Most important, the histories and philosophies of technology show that 'a tool is nothing without the variable machine assemblage which gives it a certain relationship of vicinity with man, animals and things'.[13] There is no human first and tool after.[14] Deleuze explains:

> It is the machine that makes the tool and not vice versa. An evolutionary line going from man to tool, and from tool to technological machine, is purely imaginary. The machine is social in its primary sense, and is primary in relation to the structures it crosses, to the men it makes use of, to the tools it selects, and to the technologies it promotes.[15]

Put differently, technologies are never neutral. They are situated, generative, persuasive enactors of realities, including reality's unequal power distribution, injustice and social conflicts reflected in their own unequal sovereignty layout. Far from being neutral enablers, or benign reflections of what humans do, or their prosthetics, technologies mediate, orient and shape behaviours and practices, not only of humans as 'users', but as citizens, persons, human agents, living experts embedded in metastable hybrid meshworks. Technologies are not just tools. They build the social. They design it.[16]

THE ILLUSION OF INEVITABILITY

'Nothing is made as it is because only that way works', writes philosopher and sinologist Barry Allen in his work on the artificial.[17] Anything that I make could have been made, and probably has been made, in many other ways. There is no

[12] As Massumi observes, however, the point is not to demonize instrumentality but to re-imagine how it can operate. To assert that instrumental reason has no role, in this age of complexity and environmental emergency, would be self-defeating. A way forward is to stop pitching reason against affect and instead find strategies for returning reason to its affective ground, so to affirm life in all its complexity and to imagine how rationality (as it is now) can be unlearned, and then relearned as catalyst, rather than sovereign. Brian Massumi et al., 'Affect and Immediation. An Interview with Brian Massumi', *disClosure: A Journal of Social Theory* 28, no. 13 (2019).

[13] Deleuze and Parnet, *Dialogues*, 104.

[14] Beatrice Colomina and Mark Wigley, *Are We Human? Notes on an Archaeology of Design* (Baden, Switzerland: Lars Muller Publishers, 2016).

[15] Deleuze and Parnet, *Dialogues*, 105.

[16] Betti Marenko, 'Stay Alert to the Toolification of Experience. The Technocratic Shift is Here', *Social Design Institute Position Paper*. University of the Arts London, 2021.

[17] Allen, *Artifice and Design*, 59.

unique, best way.[18] Technological inevitability is an illusion, and one to which 'contemplative nonpractitioners are especially susceptible', as Allen acerbically states.[19]

Not only is form *not* following function, but form must be understood as co-generative of the forces to which it is subjected. To say that the form of an artefact manifests something immaterial and preconceived (blueprint) does not account for the continuous *reinvention* of form. Now, reinvention is not the same as reproduction. Reinvention expresses the transformative dynamism of morphogenesis, a process that inserts the uncertain and the unexpected in how form changes. It also inserts risk in the idea of *technē*.

Perhaps *technē* may be interpreted not on the basis of its task-driven productivity, measurability and functionality, but through their absence (or by a reduced focus on them). Put differently, I ask: How do I find an 'unproductive', not-instrumental *technē*, one containing ambiguity, even the useless and the unusable?[20] Reflecting on a non-productive (or less productive) kind of *technē* leads me to consider the notion of *phronesis*, a non-instrumental mode of existence that Aristotle locates in between 'making' and 'acting'.[21] Phronesis is based on the cultivation of oneself and one's own practice delinked from the effort to gain a tangible outcome.[22] It is the situational knowledge I acquire through experience, a knowledge that cannot be separated from the person I am (and am becoming) through my practice. Phronesis puts un-intentionality on the table, together with a scaling down of the authorial subject, a certain indifference to outcomes, and an emphasis on process rather than product. It also points to self-cultivation and to Spinoza's *conatus* (of which more in Chapter 4). These are all ideas I shall return to later in my quest for ways of articulating non-instrumental modes of acting, being and knowing that hinge on uncertainty.

ENCOUNTERS WITH MATERIAL NOT KNOWING

The etymology of the word *technē* reveals something else too. It originally referred to the skills of the artisan (*tektōn*) working with material, usually wood. *Technē*'s roots in woodworking and carpentry suggest that instrumental knowl-

18 Allen draws on French anthropologist Pierre Lemonnier, who puts forward the notion of 'technological arbitrariness' based on his investigation of New Guinea people, who use wildly different ways of building domestic artefacts and dwellings. Pierre Lemonnier, *Elements for an Anthropology of Technology* (Ann Arbor: University of Michigan, 1992).

19 Allen, *Artifice and Design*, 59.

20 Aristotle mentions mathematics as an example of non-productive *technē* although mathematics actually produces statements.

21 *Phronesis* is between 'making' (*poiesis*) and 'acting' (*praxis*), the former concerning outcomes that are separable from their producer and are the visible end-product of deliberate instrumental action; the latter concerning how thought, knowledge, action are embodied in an individual style of conduct.

22 Robert C. H. Chia and Robin Holt, *Strategy Without Design. The Silent Efficacy of Indirect Action* (Cambridge: Cambridge University Press, 2009), 107.

edge concerns not only ideas but also working with material forces. Beyond the constraints of the hylomorphic model, which sees matter as the passive receiver of an idea, *technē* is revealed as a mode of knowing that emerges in the tension between procedure and improvisation, a tension characterized by risk. It is this tension between *procedural knowledge* (I know which steps I need to take to accomplish a task and achieve a goal), and *improvisational knowledge* (I know how to become attuned to, and shift my attitude with, the emergent and the uncertain) that yields generative potential.

A fitting account of this tension is found in philosopher and craftperson Hugh Crawford's narration of his blacksmithing practice. Crawford uses the expression 'thinking hot' to describe working with the material as it changes shape in the heat of the forge; literally striking while the iron is hot. The cooperation between the craftperson's body and their material is more than just the coming together of mind and hand, material and tools. Instead, Crawford's account complicates and problematizes too-neat binaries (e.g. consciousness vs. instinct), acknowledging vibrations, affective resonances, topological nuances, emergent knowledge and the unknown as assets for a material wayfinding.[23] One works with, and is exposed to, the accidental and the contingent as components of a material choreography that is not, cannot be and should not be assumed (or willed) as a frictionless endeavour.

In articulating his experience Crawford draws on philosopher Etienne Souriau, who writes: 'I must insist upon the idea that as long as the work is under construction, it is in jeopardy.'[24] The work itself *is* danger, risk, vulnerability. In writing about 'the work to be done', Souriau maintains that an attitude of wonder is essential to grasp what may be emerging in the process. This

[23] Hugh T. Crawford, 'Thinking Hot. Risk, Prehension and Sympathy in Design', in *Deleuze and Design*, ed. Betti Marenko and Jamie Brassett (Edinburgh: Edinburgh University Press), 84–106. Crawford deepens the distinction between a craftmanship of *certainty* and a craftmanship of *risk* first articulated by designer and woodworker David Pye. See David Pye, *The Nature and Art of Workmanship* (Cambridge: Cambridge University Press, 1968). While the former operates with highly uniform materials and significantly regulated tools (and workers), a craftmanship of risk grapples with the divergent possibilities enabled and demanded by material intelligence, tools, constraints, skillsets, while contending with unpredictable outcomes. Far from being the glorification of a free-form, no-rule approach to making, a craftmanship of risk calls attention to how the engagement with materiality can be at the same time procedural and improvisational, ambiguously shaped by normative formalizations *and* glitchy sensations alike. See also Manuel DeLanda's distinction between well-disciplined materials and untamed materials. The former, stripped of impurities and transformed into reliable resources, are both homogenous (uniform in composition) and isotropic (with identical properties in all directions); their behaviour is entirely predictable, and their performance rigorously standardized. The latter possess a richer material complexity, richer material information and higher morphogenetic capacities. An example is wood, which is heterogeneous, anisotropic and subject to irregularities. See designer Achim Menges for examples of architectural work that uses these properties of wood. Manuel DeLanda, 'Material Complexity', in *Digital Tectonics*, ed. Neil Leach, David Turnbull and Chris Williams (Chichester: Wiley, 2004), 14–21.

[24] Etienne Souriau, *The Different Modes of Existence* (Minneapolis: University of Minnesota Press, 2015), 229.

attitude demands not a script but an openness to what may happen; not a blueprint but the effort of letting go of prescriptions, steering the work away from the (modernist, extractivist, imperialist, colonialist) notion of the craftperson/designer as The Maker. Souriau also writes poetically about the halo of hope and the iridescence that pervades the situation when one is immersed in their work. Tellingly, this is also about the *love* one has for their work as something that simply must be done – be it wood-carving, black-smithing, word-crafting – regardless of the unknowns ahead.

But how do I work with the unknown? How do I cultivate openness to what may happen? Certainly, this is not about giving in to chance and hoping for the best. Rather, it is about figuring out how I cooperate with material forces and attune myself to their intensity. The work to be done demands the cultivation of the art of entering encounters – encounters with material not knowing[25] – and this is a risky business, one that can only be experimented with.

I will return to this point in Chapter 4 in my discussion of Spinoza. For now, I must change direction and begin to investigate a specific kind of technological machines: the calculating machines of prediction that are called 'intelligent'.

CALCULATING MACHINES AND THE EROSION OF AMBIGUITY

Computers are not only machines that calculate and compute things.[26] They have become a model for how knowledge is made. As computation produces its own mode of knowing, it serves as a metaphor for knowledge and cognition, like the seventeenth century saw the universe as a powerful, practical and elegant machine, with God as the divine *mechanikos*.[27] That computation is the go-to metaphor for how human intelligence works is plausible, but increasingly unsatisfactory. Computers are no longer universal transference machines – a metaphor for metaphor – with the capacity to transform 'anything into anything else via the medium of information'.[28] No longer can they be seen as the window to the world as the early 1990s trope had it.[29] Computation happens everywhere, far from human eyes (it is *invisible*); its complexity means that it is not fully understood (it is *unknowable*); its reach is planetary (it is *pervasive*). It is

[25] Crawford offers a list drawn on his practice as a woodworker: encounters with the grain of the wood, the sharpness of the axe, the aching of muscles, sweat-blurred vision, the sweet smell of sap.

[26] Originally (early seventeenth century) the term 'computer' described 'someone who computes', that is, a person performing mathematical calculations. From the late nineteenth century onwards, it was mostly teams of female workers who performed calculations.

[27] Horst Bredekamp, *The Lure of Antiquity and the Cult of the Machine. The Kunstkammer and the Evolution of Nature, Art and Technology* (Princeton: Markus Wiener Publishers, 1995).

[28] Wendy Chun, *Programmed Visions. Software and Memory* (Cambridge, Mass. and London: MIT Press, 2011), 57.

[29] Anna Friedberg, *The Virtual Window. From Alberti to Microsoft* (Cambridge, Mass. and London: MIT Press, 2009).

now the fundamental architecture of social, affective, corporate, institutional, administrative governance. But what kind of knowledge is computation? What are the implications of taking computation as a model for how I know? Why is human intelligence still the blueprint for artificial intelligence?

To explore these questions and to look at the tropes of invisibility, unknowability and pervasiveness, I draw on some of the ideas circulating at a time when the digital revolution was on the brink of taking place, between the end of the 1970s and the early 1990s. It seems to me that the most lucid thinkers of that time can offer rich insights on how to do critical inquiry today. One of the first to reflect on the impact of computation on knowledge was French philosopher Jean-François Lyotard. In his *The Postmodern Condition. A Report on Knowledge*, published in 1979, Lyotard writes: 'the miniaturization and commercialization of machines is already changing the way in which learning is acquired, classified, made available, and exploited'.[30] And he continues:

> The nature of knowledge cannot survive unchanged within the context of general transformation. It can fit into the new channels, and become operational, only if learning is translated into quantities of information. We can predict that anything in the constituted body of knowledge that is not translatable in this way will be abandoned and that the direction of new research will be dictated by the possibility of its eventual results being translatable into computer language ... along with the hegemony of computers comes a certain logic, and therefore a certain set of prescriptions determining which statements are accepted as 'knowledge' Statements.[31]

Lyotard's predictions have become reality. How knowledge is produced and acquired has changed. The point is not simply that knowledge has become a tradeable asset, or that it is instrumentalized, commodified, monetized. This is nothing new. What is new, however, is the extent to which knowledge has become subsumed in algorithmic governmentality.

The next chapter discusses algorithmic governmentality at length. For now, suffice to say that algorithmic governmentality is the regime of automated reason that relies on calculating machines of prediction to foreclosure futures, and whose anticipatory mode of interfacing with the world tends to replace causality. Lyotard had already identified in the new unit of information (*bit*) and in the translation of information into code a fundamental issue whose full-blown impact is experienced now: the erosion of ambiguity.[32] To understand how the erosion of ambiguity has become the defining character of planetary computation, the next section examines some key moments in the artificialization of intelligence.

[30] Jean-François Lyotard, *The Postmodern Condition. A Report on Knowledge* (Minneapolis: University of Minnesota Press, 1984), 4.

[31] Ibid., 4.

[32] Ibid., 86, note 14.

INTELLIGENCE AND THE ARTIFICIAL

Artificial intelligence (AI) is 'the study and development of intelligent agents, which includes any device that perceives the environment and takes actions to maximize its chance of achieving its goals'.[33] By extension it is any machine mimicking or simulating human cognitive functions such as problem-solving and decision-making. In the words of computer scientist Stuart Russell: 'a machine is intelligent to the extent that what it does is likely to achieve what it wants, given what it has perceived'.[34] Put differently, the goal of AI is the automation of rational behaviour to be achieved by building 'intelligent' machines that do the right thing.

For some, it is misleading to suggest a similarity between computation and the way the human brain works simply because computation cannot account for the creative embodied, intuitive, affective, empathic nature of cognition.[35] In this view, computation is unlike human cognition. Human abstract reasoning and computation cannot be equivalent. Turing himself wrote in 1947: 'If a machine is expected to be infallible, it cannot also be intelligent.' With AI performing in ways that are beyond 'mimicking or simulating human cognitive functions' this is also a compelling argument for the 'non-commensurability' between human and artificial.[36]

For others, the analogy and in-breeding between machine and human cognition should go even further. For instance, French philosopher Catherine Malabou, known for her work on plasticity, describes intelligence as impersonal, artificial and collective. In her genealogy, intelligence shifts from being a measurable entity (IQ) to the product of 'epigenesis'[37] to its current metamorphosis leading

[33] Manuel Del Campo and Neil Leach, 'Can Machines Hallucinate Architecture? AI as Design Method', *Architecture Design* 92 (2022): 7.

[34] Stuart Russell, *Human Compatible. AI and the Problem of Control* (London: Allen Lane, 2019), 41. While 'AI' covers a wide range of systems (learning, robotic, game-playing and natural-language systems) it is mostly used as a shortcut for machine learning (when the machine programs itself) and for deep learning (a category of machine learning based on multi-layered neural networks).

[35] As Cooper puts it: 'the mind does not feel, or appear to compute, like a Turing machine – given the role of creativity, consciousness, intuition'. Barry Cooper, 'Incomputability, Emergence and the Turing Universe', in *Causality, Meaningful Complexity and Embodied Cognition*, ed. Arturo Carsetti (Dordrecht: Springer, 2010), 145. See also Russell, *Human Compatible*; Cooper, 'The Machine as Data'; David Golumbia, *The Cultural Logic of Computation* (Cambridge, Mass.: Harvard University Press, 2009).

[36] Beatrice Fazi, 'Beyond Human. Deep Learning, Explainability and Representation', *Theory, Culture & Society* 38, no. 7–8 (2021): 55–77. Fazi poses a radical incommensurability between human and machine and between their distinct ways of producing knowledge. An example is High Frequency Trading (HFT) algorithms, which are distributed across technical devices and humans, and process data too fast for human consciousness to follow. What HFT algorithms generate, not bound to the speed and slowness of human cognition, goes beyond rational thinking.

[37] Epigenetic describes a process where changes are due to environmental influences.

to a removal of the 'rigid frontiers between nature and artifice'.[38] Her argument is that plasticity is the basis for biological-symbolic hybrids and that the future of AI will be biological as a result of its plastic autonomy. Commenting on (and enthused by) Ray Kurzweil's singularity (and not wanting to be accused of reactionary technophobia), Malabou reads the recursivity of machines as their programmable plasticity. The image of the homeostatic interaction of brains and machines mutually affecting and changing each other through plastic interaction is alluring; but what appears to be missing in this otherwise compelling argument is the asymmetry within the automation of reason.

As this chapter will explain, not only does this gap leave unanswered questions around the genealogy of technological automation. It is also paradigmatic of much of the critical inquiry into the transformation of cognition in the age of machines and the fixation on human-machine hybrids. For instance, when Malabou writes that the question is to accept 'the simultaneity of the epigenetic becoming of natural intelligence and artificial intelligence',[39] and that the machines of today are designed to appear natural, one cannot help but wonder which (and whose) notion of nature is evoked here.[40]

Whichever camp one wishes to endorse on how computation and cognition should (or should not) relate, one thing seems certain. What counts as intelligence, as cognition, as thinking, as knowledge; what counts as human in the era of intelligent machines is being rewritten by automation and by the ways machines 'think'. This rewriting is far from straightforward. Indeed, 'rewriting' may not even be the right word, but nor is overlapping, overwriting, aligning or mimicking. Matters of terminology – which words I use to express the concepts I think with – are not insubstantial. For instance, that artificial networks are called 'neural' and that artificial systems are called 'intelligence' cannot but emphasize how narrow the repertoire of stories and images in use actually is. This also draws attention to the extent to which human intelligence remains an inadequate litmus test for an intelligence that is artificial. Ultimately, to insist on human-centredness is hubristic not only because of the anthropocentric bias that poses human intelligence as the benchmark for the artificial one, but also because it severely restricts the terms of the debate on automated reason that is urgently and seriously called for.

THE UNKNOWABILITY OF ALGORITHMS

The algorithm has been catapulted into the public consciousness as the signifier of the overreaching power (good and bad) of machines. Beyond its status as an automated set of instructions that tells a computer what to do, the algorithm has become a cultural object lodged in our daily lives, an invisible and little-

[38] Catherine Malabou, *Morphing Intelligence. From IQ Measurement to Artificial Brains* (New York: Columbia University Press, 2019), 15.

[39] Ibid., 118.

[40] Ibid., 50.

understood entity whose inscrutable workings generate visible and tangible outcomes.

While their unknowability exists (in part) because most algorithms are proprietary and covered by corporate trade-secret protection, there are other reasons that make the automation of decision-making and the 'reasoning' that algorithms enable so inscrutable. Algorithms are the building blocks of artificial systems that quickly become impenetrable black boxes. As algorithms make decisions by calculating millions of interdependent variables, layers and parameters, even computer scientists do not fully understand how, nor are able to gauge the exact decision-making criteria behind the choices of a system. For example, in the case of driverless vehicles that teach themselves how to drive by observing and analysing human behaviour, even the engineers designing them struggle to isolate the reason behind each single action. There is no existing mathematical model that can be analysed to pinpoint causation.[41] What gets classified, from which training data, how data are selected, how models are built and what actions are taken based on their output, is all algorithm-generated – and quickly becomes human-un-accountable too.[42]

There is a genre of media and scholarly discourse that, to draw attention to the problems inherent to unknowability, ends up evoking a mysterious presence ruling human existence beyond human comprehension and control. Researcher Tarleton Gillespie expresses this when he writes that 'there may be something, in the end, impenetrable about algorithms. They are designed to work without human intervention, they are deliberately obfuscated, and they work with information on a scale that is hard to comprehend (at least without other algorithmic tools).'[43] But the unknowability of algorithms is also a design function. It is perpetuated in how algorithms are designed, as discriminating agents that operate by identifying patterns and separating the exception from the norm. Their value systems normalize the reproduction of the prescriptive categories at the heart of technologies of statistical classification, e.g. the category of average-white-able-body that underpins racial categorizations and informs profiling, predictive policing and surveillance. Because of the bias baked into them, algorithms blindly reproduce categories of race, class, sex, gender, income, etc. thus propagating patterns of social injustice, exclusion and inequality.[44]

[41] Will Knight, 'The Dark Secret at the Heart of AI', *MIT Technology Review* 120, no. 3 (2017): 7.

[42] Cathy O'Neil, *Weapons of Math Destruction* (London: Penguin, 2016); Kate Crawford, *Atlas of AI. Power, Politics, and the Planetary Costs of Artificial Intelligence* (New Haven and London: Yale University Press, 2021); Ed Finn, *What Algorithms Want. Imagination in the Age of Computing* (Cambridge, Mass. and London: MIT Press, 2017).

[43] Tarleton Gillespie, 'The Relevance of Algorithms', in *Media Technologies. Essays on Communication, Materiality, and Society*, ed. Tarleton Gillespie, Pablo J. Boczkowski and Kirsten A. Foot (Cambridge, Mass. and London: MIT Press, 2014), 192.

[44] Paul Dourish, 'Algorithms and their Others. Algorithmic Culture in Context', *Big Data & Society* 3, no. 2 (2016): 1–11; Gillespie, 'The Relevance of Algorithms', 167–93; Tarleton Gillespie, '#Trendingistrending. When Algorithms Become Culture', in *Algorithmic Cultures. Essays on Meaning, Performance and New Technologies*, ed. Robert Seyfert and Jonathan Roberge (London: Routledge, 2016), 52–74; Tarleton Gillespie, 'Algorithm',

What deserves most attention, however, is how unknowability gets interpreted and 'translated', cascading in and shaping public perception. I refer to the twinned discourses of *enchantment* and magic on one side, and of *opacity*, accountability and explainability on the other. Broadly speaking, the first interpretation poses the human as powerless in front of machines, while the second poses the human as a too-powerful agent.

UNKNOWABILITY AS ENCHANTMENT

The first way in which unknowability is interpreted in public discourse is through narratives where algorithms are magic spells, AI is a threat beyond human control and technology is *enchantment.*[45] Because the automation of decision-making and what appears to be machine reasoning seem to defy human understanding, discourses of enchantment, magic, even esoteric occultism, tend to gain traction in this space of unknowability. After all, it is easy to impart animacy to things that move and transform other things.[46] It is easy to call them 'smart'. Equally easy is to fetishize the machine as an entity where rationality and mysticism, knowability and unknowability go mysteriously hand in hand. No matter how irrational, these explanations remain attractive not because of credulity but because of convenience, in the same way in which the audience of a magic show is perfectly aware that they are complicit in an (unfathomable, performative) sleight of hand.

The problem is that once machine reasoning is framed through enchantment it becomes shielded from accountability, its opacity takes on an otherworldly quality, conveniently obfuscating the intensification of processes of classification that produce very real and very deterministic discrimination. As Kate Crawford and Alexander Campolo show, the mystification of the unknown as esoteric depth is a powerful rhetorical device in the narratives around AI, what they eloquently call 'enchanted determinism': 'a discourse that presents deep learning techniques as magical outside the scope of present scientific knowledge,

in *Digital Keywords. A Vocabulary of Information Society and Culture*, ed. Benjamin Peters (Princeton: Princeton University Press, 2016), 18–30; Nick Seaver, 'Algorithms as Culture. Some Tactics for the Ethnography of Algorithmic Systems', *Big Data & Society* 4, no. 2 (2017).

45 From Arthur C. Clarke's dictum 'Any sufficiently advanced technology is indistinguishable from magic' (1961) onward. For recent examples, see the 2022 *New Worlds* season at Somerset House, London: 'an experimental series, merging magic and technology to explore the interconnected topics of sound and ritual, myth-making, non-linear storytelling, ecological futures, and more-than-human narratives', https://www.somersethouse.org.uk/whats-on/new-worlds#:~:text=New%20Worlds%20is%20an%20experimental,more%2Dthan%2Dhuman%20narratives.... My work has contributed to this discourse: Betti Marenko, 'Algorithm Magic. Gilbert Simondon and Techno-Animism', in *Believing in Bits. Digital Media and the Supernatural*, ed. Simone Natale and Diana Pasulka (New York: Oxford University Press, 2019), 213–28.

46 For an animistic reading of smart objects see Betti Marenko, 'Neo-Animism and Design. A New Paradigm in Object Theory', special issue: *Design, Thing Theory and the Lives of Objects*, ed. Leslie Atzmon, *Design and Culture* 6, no. 2 (2014): 219–42.

yet also deterministic, in that deep learning systems can nonetheless detect patterns that give unprecedented access to people's identities, emotions and social character'.[47]

The challenge therefore is how to understand (and re-purpose) the unknowability at the core of machines without reverting to the tropes of wonder and mystery. Kate Crawford and Vladan Joler's *Anatomy of an AI System* points to a way in which this can be done.[48] This project breaks down the *Echo* AI as a socio-technical assemblage, constitutive of (and constituted by) uneven ecosystems made of computational networks and physical infrastructures; computer scientists, coders, interface designers and the population of users impacted by them; data flows, property laws, cyber security policies, political agendas supporting the harvesting of material and immaterial resources; corporations, institutions and agencies providing all these services and, last but not least, the social scientists studying them, the journalists writing about them and the artists responding to them.

This relational mapping suggests a way to shift from the *what* to the *how* of machines. In other words, *how* machines participate in mechanisms of knowledge production (and not only to decision-making), and *how* the legitimacy and authority that come from their claims of statistical objectivity must be scrutinized and made accountable, can be apprehended only through a *machinic* approach (in the Deleuze-Guattari sense of assemblage).[49]

UNKNOWABILITY AS OPACITY

The other way in which unknowability gets framed is as *opacity*, a key concern in the field of critical algorithms studies.

> If one is a recipient of the output of the algorithm (the classification decision), rarely does one have any concrete sense of how or why a particular classification has been arrived at from inputs. Additionally, the inputs themselves may be entirely unknown or known only partially. The question naturally arises, what are the reasons for this state of not knowing? Is it

[47] Kate Crawford and Alexander Campolo, 'Enchanted Determinism. Power Without Responsibility in Artificial Intelligence', *Engaging Science, Technology, and Society* 6 (2020): 3.

[48] See Kate Crawford and Vladan Joler, 'Anatomy of an AI System. The Amazon Echo as an Anatomical Map of Human Labor, Data and Planetary Resources', AI Now Institute and Share Lab (2018).

[49] Golumbia, *The Cultural Logic of Computation*; Madeleine C. Elish and danah boyd, 'Situating Methods in the Magic of Big Data and AI', *Communication Monographs* 85, no. 1 (2018): 57–80; Adrian Mackenzie, *Machine Learners. Archaeology of a Data Practice* (Cambridge, Mass. and London: MIT Press, 2017). Mackenzie's expression 'machine learners' (describing human-machine ensembles) is useful to see algorithms through a logic of assemblage (and consequently through public scrutiny, open debate and intelligent legislation), rather than insisting on their invisibility which tends to reinforce their inscrutability.

because the algorithm is proprietary? Because it is complex or highly technical? Or are there, perhaps, other reasons?[50]

Inquiries into opacity lead to debates on (the lack of) accountability which, in turn, raises the issue of explainability. The removal of human agents from the decisional loop and the impenetrability of the black box create what is known as a 'responsibility gap'.[51] Why did a certain model reach a certain decision? How can this be explained, especially to non-expert users?

These are some of the questions posed by the field of Explainable Artificial Intelligence (xAI) – 'machine learning techniques that enable human users to understand, appropriately trust, and effectively manage the emerging generation of artificially intelligent partners'.[52] In the context of xAI, 'interpretability' refers to the degree of human comprehension of a given black box model or decision, and 'explanation' refers to how information about the functionality of a model and its decision-making process is circulated to different stakeholders. Both are driven by attempts to interpret and explain AI by cracking open the black box.[53]

But unknowability cannot be reduced to a problem to solve by 'more' explanation and 'more' interpretation. Explanation and interpretation raise matters that concern the epistemological and ontological nature of uncertainty, of the unknown and of unknowing, all matters that remain flatly unaddressed by the instrumental approach of xAI.[54] To counteract this I would argue that unknowability requires not less but more *complication*, not less but more *problematization*.[55]

[50] Jenna Burrell, 'How the Machine "Thinks". Understanding Opacity in Machine Learning Algorithms', *Big Data and Society* 3, no. 1 (2016): 1.

[51] Andreas Matthias, 'The Responsibility Gap. Ascribing Responsibility for the Actions of Learning Automata', *Ethics and Information Technology* 6 (2004): 175–83.

[52] David Gunning et al., 'XAI – Explainable Artificial Intelligence', *Science Robotics* 4, no. 37 (2019): 6.

[53] Tim Miller, Piers Howe and Liz Sonenberg, 'Explainable AI: Beware of Inmates Running the Asylum. Or: How I Learnt to Stop Worrying and Love the Social and Behavioural Sciences', *ArXiv* abs/1712.00547 (2017).

[54] This is not to say that explainability is not relevant. Explanations are increasingly required to comply with legislation, improve system functionality and build trust between any given system and those who are affected by its decisions, especially in sectors such as precision medicine, autonomous vehicles, security, finance. See Arrieta Barredo et al., 'Explainable Artificial Intelligence (XAI). Concepts, Taxonomies, Opportunities and Challenges Toward Responsible AI', *Information Fusion* (2019); Brent Mittelstadt, Chris Russell and Sandra Wachter, 'Explaining Explanations in AI', FAT* '19: Conference on Fairness, Accountability, and Transparency (FAT* ACM, New York, 2019).

[55] The term 'complication' contains the root of the Greek word *plekein* [pli, fold]. Deleuze describes 'complication' as the characteristic chaotic state of the virtual, and also as the movement from the virtual to the actual and vice versa. It is a state characterized by intense multiplicity and the power of metamorphosis. Deleuze, *Difference and Repetition*, 280. Problematization concerns the understanding of how and why certain things (behaviour, phenomena, processes) *become a problem*. See Michael Foucault, 'Is It Really Important To Think? An Interview with Michel Foucault', *Liberation* 30–31, (May 1981); Isabelle Stengers, 'Putting Problematization to the Test of Our Present', *Theory, Culture & Society* 38, no. 2 (2021): 71–92; Celia Lury, *Problem Spaces. How and Why Methodology Matters* (London: Polity Press, 2020).

In fact, posing the matter as one of explainability diverts from the true issues at stake: the systemic injustice baked in algorithms on one side, and unknowability as a potential epistemic resource on the other. Both demand a radical rethinking, one that, I argue, should be rooted in uncertainty taken seriously as the hinge of a critical and creative mode of engaging with the artificial, including artificial thinking.

THE MACHINE PRODUCES UNKNOWNS

The thing is: machines – intended as automated decision-makers – produce unknowns. Their procedures orbit around a core of unknowability. Locating this view historically, computer scientist Paul Dourish observes:

> During my years of computer science training, to have an algorithm was to know something. Algorithms were definitive procedures that lead to predictable results. The outcome of the algorithmic operation was known and certain. Much of the debate about 'algorithms' at the moment focuses on a particular class of algorithm – statistical machine learning techniques – that produce, instead, *unknowns*. More accurately, they produce analyses of data that are known and understood on some terms (in terms of the formal properties of the data set – its patterns and regularities) but *unknowable* in others (in the terms of the domain that the data represents). When my credit card company deems a particular purchase or stream of purchases 'suspicious' – they know that there's something odd but they don't know what it is.[56]

This lack of understanding concerns specifically machine learning AI. Unlike 'good old-fashioned' AI (GOFAI) based on procedural logic and human programming, machine learning is recursive. The machine learns by itself to produce probabilistic results using algorithms that crunch huge quantities of data, correlate variables and self-refine their models in real time. In this way, machine learning generates algorithms based on example data and desired output, with no need for programming.

Let me briefly recall how these two ways of doing AI differ. The first (GOFAI) is based on rule-programming and deduction.[57] The second (machine learning)

[56] Dourish, 'Algorithms and their Others', 7 (emphasis added).

[57] *Deduction* is to make an inference based on widely accepted facts. It explains things through the causal relation between A and B. It moves from the general rule to the specific application. In deductive reasoning, if the original assertions are true, then the conclusion must also be true (e.g. math). *Induction* is to make an inference based on an observation, e.g. by using a sample and then moving to a generalized conclusion from that sample. It relies on empirical facts and evidence to draw predictive hypotheses and is built on probabilities drawn from past occurrences. *Abduction* is to make a probable conclusion from what you know. The process of inventing explanatory hypotheses, abduction is fine-tuned to the unknown, the potential, the not-actualized yet, therefore it is highly speculative and imaginative.

is a learning-by-doing. Instead of algorithms deducing a desired result (output) from a given set of data (input), machine learning works in the opposite way: 'in goes the data and the desired result and out comes the algorithm that turns one into the other'.[58]

Simply put, machine learning algorithms are algorithms that make other algorithms and enable computers to write their own programs. Crucially, this process enlists unknown information (the incomputable) in automated pattern-formation exceeding any programmed rule. As the chapter will examine, this unknowability of algorithmic systems that learn as they go along, trawling constantly refreshed, potentially infinite quantities of data is what Parisi describes as the alienness at the centre of automation.[59] Before looking at Parisi's argument, however, I must turn first to a deep implication of machine learning systems: that they produce realities.

A FULLY FORMED REALITY EMERGES

Machine learning is an historically specific form of calculation that shapes the space of future predictions. Starting from observable behaviours captured and expressed in the form of data, machine learning builds verifiable models of the behaviour it is analysing. By ploughing through continuously refreshed environmental variables, it performs a non-stop automatic revision and refinement of its models to predict the occurrence of similar behaviours in the future. Thus, machine learning can be described as a form of inductive reasoning that draws rules and models from a vast training data set by using statistical operations (e.g. clustering, classifying, categorizing, patterning, matching). The larger the data sets on which the models train, the more accurate their prediction.[60] Models are built recursively, which means that data is used to generate more data, which produces more and more patterning.

Think of the very common, very banal experience of online browsing. My user behaviour is compared to others with similar online profiles and decision-making points. Patterns are detected and refined. Proprietary algorithms, in particular the FANG ones (Facebook, Amazon, Netflix, Google), but others too, decide which search results, newsfeeds, recommendations, suggestions and pages I will be shown and in which order. Sidebar adverts, personalized to my profile by sorting algorithms that analyse my demographic, past clicking patterns and purchasing behaviours, are sold to the highest bidder in nanoseconds. With each click and each lingering browse, I contribute to the algorithm's optimiza-

[58] Pedro Domingos, *The Master Algorithm* (London: Penguin, 2015), 6.

[59] Luciana Parisi, 'The Alien Subject of AI', *Subjectivity* 12, no. 1 (2019): 27–48.

[60] Mackenzie, *Machine Learners*; Adrian Mackenzie, 'The Production of Prediction. What Does Machine Learning Want?' *European Journal of Cultural Studies* 18, no. 4–5 (2015): 429–45. For an explanation and demystification of machine learning see Meredith Broussard, *Artificial Unintelligence. How Computers Misunderstand the World* (Cambridge, Mass. and London: MIT Press, 2018).

tion, making it more accurate in how it evaluates and tailors the relevance of content to me and people exactly like me, guessing (almost inevitably correctly on the basis of the data it is fed) that I will like those recommendations because people like me did so. Based on what I (and people like me) chose in the past, the algorithm predicts my possible future choices, which are then served to me as the result of my search for information.

What matters is that these predictive analyses are served to me as a fully formed reality. Matteo Pasquinelli and Vladan Joler vividly describe this data-driven objectivity as a new hallucinatory regime of truth.[61] Because recursive systems appear to respond in real time to real data, the norms according to which they calculate and predict behaviours seem to emerge from reality itself, even though past behaviour should not be taken as a reliable indicator that something will occur again in the future. I will return to this point at the end of the chapter.

There are two significant implications of this data-driven immanence, one for the production of knowledge, one for the production of subjectivity.

To start with, there is the impact of predictive machines on the production of knowledge. There is a difference between a machine programmed by humans to search data for patterns that make sense to us (human-compatible), and a machine that trawls data 'to identify the patterns first and then see if they can be made sense of for human needs'.[62] These are two different modes of knowing, two distinct epistemes: the former driven by causation and the latter by correlation.[63]

As seen earlier, machine learning algorithms are not only powerful generalizers and predictors; the non-linear regression analysis they use computes by deciding on the most plausible correlations among available data.[64] This process indicates the probabilities and possibilities of relations, but not causalities as such. It therefore produces a mode of knowledge (probabilistic, extractive and deterministic) that preys on data and is predicated on a distorted understanding of what data represents. Data is not the cloud, nor the digital traces I scatter online. 'Data' (from the Latin *datum* = what is given), originally describes what exists, objectively and factually, beyond any argument. However, in computation, data is not 'given' but 'captured', literally. A more apposite definition of data is *in-formation*, data that has been given a binary form.

As Pasquinelli and Joler explain, this distortion of meaning of 'data' gives rise to 'data essentialism': the idea that data is the essence of knowledge-making, rather than some trail we leave behind. It becomes 'data orthodoxy': the idea that

[61] Matteo Pasquinelli and Vladan Joler, 'The Nooscope Manifested. Artificial Intelligence as Instrument of Knowledge Extractivism', *AI and Society* 36 (2021): 1263–80.

[62] Dourish, 'Algorithms and their Others', 7.

[63] Given two variables, causation means that changes in one variable bring about changes in the other; correlation is an association between variables.

[64] Plausible does not necessarily mean possible. This is why the patterns built by machine learning have been described as 'statistical hallucination' (Pasquinelli and Joler, 'The Nooscope Manifested', 1264).

everything is made of data flows, data are the building block of both computers and humans, and computers should be modelled on the brain. Ultimately, it is a small step from thinking that everything is data, to the idea that data offers an objective picture of the world, to say that by controlling data I can predict the future. Enter 'dataism' or even 'data mysticism': the idea that knowledge about the future can be produced by relying exclusively on data.

As per the second point, concerning the impact of predictive machines on the production of subjectivity, when predictive algorithms classify and order information in the most advantageous ways for the advertisers, they classify and order people too. Technology and ethics scholar Lucas D. Introna describes this experience as the constitution of 'a market of one':

> The higher the quality and quantity of data they [the models] have to work from the better they perform. That is why Google wants us to interact with its applications 'for free', because these interactions generate data, and data allows for a finer-grained individuation of the subject. The more individuated the subject the more valuable it is, in terms of impressionability. Through machine learning algorithms such individuation can happen automatically in order to produce the unique, highly impressionable subject, a market of one.[65]

In this market of one, I am no longer a conscious agent, nor a 'living expert'. I am turned into a sequence of 'user profiles' distributed across a plethora of platforms and networks, each requiring my affective labour in the form of consumption, participation, contribution and sharing. With my multiple digital selves dis-aggregated and re-aggregated into indexes and databases in real time, I am not even an individual 'subject' to speak of, but only observable instantiations captured and rendered through profiling, each one marked by void (of causality, agency, memorization) and by depletion (as default). My digital traces are instantly dispersed once they have been stripped bare of value, only to be re-compacted at the next ping or search. Through this continuous assembling, disaggregation and reassembling of data (already predicted by Deleuze's dividual),[66] my digital identities – dis-integrated but highly disciplined – are formatted for monetization. As Parisi puts it, 'enveloped in precarious, casual and fast decisions and enclosed in a bubble of self-satisfaction, this

[65] Lucas D. Introna, 'The Algorithmic Choreography of the Impressionable Subject', in *Algorithmic Cultures*, ed. Robert Seyfert and Jonathan Roberge (London: Routledge, 2016), 39.

[66] Deleuze's dividual is an entity continuously being made and re-made in real time, construed of discrete components, numerical fragments, digital bits, detached lines of codes and spread over interconnected multifaceted platforms. Commenting on this he writes 'Felix Guattari has imagined a town where anyone can leave their flat, their street, their neighbourhood, using their (dividual) electronic card that opens this or that barrier; but the card may also be rejected on a particular day, or between certain times of day; it doesn't depend on the barrier but on the computer that is making sure everyone is in a permissible place, and effecting a universal modulation' (Deleuze, *Negotiations*, 181).

subject has no consciousness'.[67] An illusion of cohesion remains, however, in my temporary identity as user and content creator. This transient 'me' feeds on the awe induced by the machine, is kept feverishly alert by its compulsive mechanisms of social sign-up, and autistically numb by the relentless capture of affects and potential.

If the landscape I have described seems bleak, it is because it probably is. In this landscape, computation occurs within temporal frames incommensurable to my perception and to the scale of my experience. I am always already engaged in a pre-personal mode of contact with the technomedia environment that modulates my affective sphere below my direct perception.[68]

I heed sociologist of technology Adrian Mackenzie's warning when he asks: 'What if the production of prediction changes the world that prediction inhabits?'[69] And I add: How can I resist the production of prediction? If machines produce realities, where can I find seeds of invention and emergence, divergence and dissensus, resistance and defiance? How do I resist the capture of potential? But I am getting ahead. Before examining how potential is captured and how it can be reclaimed, I must continue exploring the production of unknowns within machines. I turn therefore to the incomputable at the core of computation.

THE COMPUTABLE AND THE INCOMPUTABLE

As I have shown, unknowability tends to be framed either as enchantment or as opacity; but as I have also shown, both these interpretations are less than satisfactory. Neither addresses the problem of the systemic injustice baked into machines, nor can acknowledge uncertainty as the counter-engine of new modes of knowing. Faced with an epistemic blind spot between two decision-making processes (the human and the machine), the challenge remains how to do critique in the digital age in ways that afford working critically *and* creatively with this unknown at the core of computation – the 'opaque' (Burrell), the 'incommensurable' (Fazi), the 'hallucinatory' (Pasquinelli), the 'alien' (Parisi) – mindful of, and keeping away from, both enchantment and determinism.

Can the unknown be reclaimed, neither as a sign of a hidden, occult, magic, unfathomable, incomprehensible power, nor as the obscurity that must be cleared and explained, but rather as the condition of a mode of knowing in itself? Can the unknown become potential for retooling and resistance?

As already mentioned in the Introduction, that the incomputable lies within the computable is not a new idea. Computer scientist Barry Cooper points out that the model of computation inherited from Turing arrived with 'a

67 Parisi, 'The Alien Subject of AI', 35.

68 Anna Munster, *An Aesthesia of Networks. Conjunctive Experience in Art and Technology* (Cambridge, Mass. and London: MIT Press, 2013); Katherine N. Hayles, *Unthought. The Power of the Cognitive Nonconscious* (Chicago and London: University of Chicago Press, 2017).

69 Mackenzie, 'The Production of Prediction', 441.

mathematically simple avatar of incomputability on its back'.[70] In his comments to Turing, who had already proved the logical impossibility of predicting which machine, given a certain input, would halt and which would not, Cooper notes that blind faith in algorithmic procedures demands the elimination of the 'mismatch between the digital and the observable wider reality'.[71] In other words, although not everything is computable, the 'pervasive flatness of this implicit digital ontology'[72] leaves no space for incomputability.

Of course, something may be not computable for other reasons, for example limitations of analogue, rational or pragmatic nature. Indeed, as Alexander Galloway suggests, 'part of the history of computation is the history of the incomputable being colonised by the computable'[73] through the industrialization of randomness. But the dream of an omni-comprehensive intelligence sufficiently vast to afford no uncertainty is a fiction (and a potent delusion too).[74] The incomputable of machines is the springboard to understand how uncertainty can be reclaimed, to resist the capture of machines of prediction and push back against their systematic injustice.

DEEPER INTO UNKNOWABILITY

Scholars studying the incomputability at the core of machines tend to draw on mathematician Gregory Chaitin's idea that computation is made of unknowable probabilities. Chaitin calls algorithmic randomness, or the incomputable, the discrepancy between input and output where a transformation occurs. In Parisi's definition, the incomputable is 'increasing yet unknown quantities of data that characterize rule-based processing'.[75]

For Parisi, one of the most original thinkers working in the field of philosophy of computation, algorithmic automation signals the irruption of an entirely alien mode of reasoning. This machine reasoning is no longer based on deduction, causality, instruction-giving and the recognition of existing patterns, but is driven by adaptive learning that produces patterns of non-observable events. This is how it tends to coincide with the emergence of non-conscious intelligence in automated cognition. Epistemically, this concerns the shift to the open-endedness of hypothesis-driven knowledge production (abduction), which

70 Cooper, 'Incomputability, Emergence and the Turing Universe', 138.

71 Cooper, 'The Machine as Data', 2015.

72 Ibid., 1959.

73 Galloway, *Uncomputable*, 4.

74 As Lyotard writes: 'The ideal fulfilment of this condition is clearly expressed in Laplace's fiction of the "demon": he knows all of the variables determining the state of the universe at a moment *t*, and can thus predict its state at a moment *t'*>*t*. This fiction is sustained by the principle that physical systems, including the system of systems called the universe, follow regular patterns, with the result that their evolution traces a regular path and gives rise to "normal" continuous functions (and to futurology…)' (Lyotard, *The Postmodern Condition*, 55).

75 Parisi, 'Instrumental Reason, Algorithmic Capitalism, and the Incomputable', 133.

supersedes models of deductive rationality of the past (rooted in cause-effect) and inductive rationality of the present (rooted in observable phenomena and behaviours).

Thus, for Parisi, the growing autonomy of algorithmic thinking – the automation of automation – is rooted in the incomputable, where the output is always greater than the input, and which has become the 'absolute condition' of computation. Post-cybernetic intelligent machines have the capacity 'to observe, evaluate, and predict the behaviour of data, testing the range of effects that certain strings can have on others, while counting on the unpredictability of the results'.[76] This process creates a 'new kind of empiricism in which data is "liberated" from the static condition of the given. Data is now stretched to embrace potentiality, indeterminacy, and contingency'.[77] As machines behave as evolutive and adaptive cognitive systems, cognition seems to expand into the nonhuman territories of the machine. 'While it seems still premature to conclude that machines are subjects able to know and change their own rules', Parisi cautiously writes, 'it would be myopic to deny that computational automation has exposed the transcendental schema of reason to the experimental becoming of thought'.[78]

In other words, algorithmic patterning creates opportunities for new modes of thinking that radically question existing structures of thought. This is where Parisi's ideas become especially provoking.

THE SERVO-MECHANIC PARADIGM

Machines have been evolving. They are developing their own logic, a mode of abductive thinking that uses indeterminacy to generate speculated, non-observable realities. By positioning the abductive logic of machine reasoning as an alien system of cognition, Parisi suggests that a new mode of thinking, which is both reason and imagination, can develop. This form of speculative agency not only escapes the capture of data normativity but can push back against the dominant paradigm of technicity.

It is on this basis that the important argument of the genealogy of technicity mentioned earlier fully emerges. The Critical Computation Bureau explains: 'Within the history of machine epistemology, industrial capital took on the prototype of automation, replacing the archetype of enslaved labour. With the invention of the robot, the enslaved became enfleshed in machines as much as machines became the host of already brutally wounded flesh'.[79] This model – the 'servo-mechanic paradigm' of technology – frames the automation of automa-

[76] Luciana Parisi and Antonia Majaca, 'The Incomputable and Instrumental Possibility', *e-flux* 77 (2016): 4.

[77] Parisi and Majaca, 'The Incomputable and Instrumental Possibility', 4.

[78] Parisi, 'The Alien Subject of AI', 43.

[79] Critical Computation Bureau, 'Editorial. Dialogues on Recursive Colonialisms, Speculative Computation, and the Techno-Social', *e-flux* 123 (2021): 2.

tion as a shift from the automation of human labour whose prototype is the enslavement of bodies by the industrial/plantation machine.

However, this model is still a rather blunt (and obtuse) instrument for understanding technology because it remains based on the 'default image of technology as either an instrument in the hands of man or as entrapping man's freedom into its mindless procedures'.[80] In other words, it concerns on one side the Promethean mastery of tools with its anthropocentric prominence informed by an historically specific notion of the human; on the other, it is predicated on the extraction of value from labour – from the plantation first, then from the assembly-line, finally from cognition, affect, attention, eyeballs.

The legacy of this servo-mechanic model of technology, with its assumptions around what counts as human, and its inherent predatory and violent exploitation, cannot be undone nor ignored. No critique of automation, no critique of technology, no critique of planetary computation can take place unless the question of colonialism as the founding project of the servo-mechanical model of technology is concomitantly addressed.

This is also why images, albeit alluring, of hybrid mergings of human and machine remain unsatisfactory and inadequate: because they cannot account for, and unhinge, the nexus of technology, capital, colonialism, enslavement expressed by the servo-mechanic paradigm.[81]

For Parisi and the Critical Computation Bureau, it is precisely this model that is being challenged by the new, alien mode of automated reasoning emerging in the unknowability of machine thinking. What is at stake, therefore, is that the transformation of reason occurring in machine thinking offers the opportunity to move beyond the realm of the universal rational human and its Enlightenment legacy, and away from a recursive and extractive system that continues to be imbued with the violence of colonial episteme.[82]

IT IS REALITY THAT MAKES ITSELF POSSIBLE

As it should be clear by now, the automation of automation produces fundamental changes in episteme and ontology. Phenomena are no longer understood by causality but predicted through correlation. Data patterning – the search for patterns in data – gives a distorted indication of what may happen. This new data-driven immanence generates an onto-epistemic shift in what counts as knowledge and as existence. Once prediction is funnelled into a single objective truth a coincidence is given between machine reality (*what there is*) and

80 Parisi, 'The Alien Subject of AI', 30.

81 Luciana Parisi and William Morgan, 'What is (Machine) Philosophy?', *Qui Parle* 30, no. 1 (2021): 188.

82 Recursivity is defined as 'the self-regulation, self-adaptation, and self-regeneration of systems – including the recursive regeneration of the colonial episteme' (Critical Computation Bureau, 'Editorial', 1).

potential (*what may be*). In short, predictive machines appropriate potential and turn it into the only version of the real. They erode ambiguity.

As the next chapters will examine, predictive machines predate on, and monetize, this erosion of ambiguity with the result that what *a* life could be, in all its potentialities and plenitude, is terminally flattened.

For now, and to conclude this chapter, I wish to return briefly to the point I made earlier concerning 'prediction' and predictive machines, in order to reframe it philosophically. Cosmic uncertainty tells me that past behaviour should not be taken as a reliable indicator that something will occur again in the future. Let me explain. Deleuze writes that when the future is predicated on past occurrences, it is nothing but a doubling up of the real, a pre-planned version of what exists already. It is a mode based on anticipatory resemblance, where the 'possible' looks like what has gone on before and is therefore contained within a narrow and predictable range. This mode is derivative. Its mechanical grasp strips the unknown of its potential or, more precisely, strips potential from the unknown. Nothing new and unexpected has the space for surfacing. It is, to use Deleuze's words, a mystifying 'sleight of hand'.[83]

Deleuze reprises Bergson's formidable insight that to see the possible as what precedes the real is the 'mirage' of the present into the past. To explain: When I assume that tomorrow is already contained in today and call this illusion 'the possible', I am naively mistaken. My error is to postulate a 'retroactivity' (or future anteriority, or front-to-back remodelling) carried out by the present *into* the past. The mirage is to believe that something will have been possible once it has occurred. But this is not only an error of perception or an illusion. It is a delusion; one that, says Bergson, everybody is prey to. This is the mirage that Bergson shatters when he affirms that 'it is reality that makes itself possible, and not possibility that becomes real'.[84]

I take heed of Bergson's challenging insight and let it percolate in my reflections. If it is always reality that makes itself possible (and not, vice versa, the possible and the probable that become real), then it means that it is the full plenitude of the real that becomes possible. In other words, the making itself possible of reality cannot but contain the uncertain, the unknown and risk. It is the oceanic, cosmic uncertainty of the world that relentlessly makes itself possible. I will return to these themes in Chapter 4.

[83] Gilles Deleuze, *Bergsonism* (New York: Zone Books, 1991), 98.

[84] Henri Bergson, 'The Possible and the Real', in *Key Writings* (London: Bloomsbury, 2002), 271–83. Originally published in the Swedish journal *Nordisk Tidskrift*, based on a lecture delivered at the University of Oxford in 1920.

For now, there are questions that still need addressing: 'How to emancipate ourselves from a data-centric view of the world'?[85] How do I ensure that my 'maybes' are not captured and flattened before I make time for hesitation? How do I resist the modulation of my pre-personal, pre-cognitive sensibility? The theme of resistance will be addressed in Chapter 3. First, the next chapter dives in on algorithmic governmentality and how the micro-engineering of sensibility and potential produces 'algorithmic subjects'.

[85] Pasquinelli and Joler, 'The Nooscope Manifested', 1277.

2 Algorithmic Subjects

> Strolling 'freely' down a street, or in the country, breathing fresh air, or singing a bit loudly have become quantifiable activities from a capitalistic point of view.
>
> FÉLIX GUATTARI[1]

WHERE AND HOW ARE NEW SUBJECTIVITIES BEING PRODUCED?

'Where and how are new subjectivities being produced?' is the question posed by Deleuze during a 1986 conversation with journalist Claire Parnet.[2] With its insistence on the mechanisms and logics that practically shape individuals, Deleuze's question has lost none of its actuality. I take it as the entry point for this chapter's inquiry into algorithmic governmentality – the regime that feeds on 'the inactual, potential dimensions of human existence, its dimensions of virtuality, the conditional mode of what people "could" do, their potency or agency'.[3]

What types of subjectivities are those produced today in the context of algorithmic governmentality? What are the mechanisms and the dispositives of production? The chapter argues that in order to understand the production of 'algorithmic subjects' this must be located within the refinement of capitalist and post-capitalist techniques of extraction and commodification of potential. The chapter draws on selected ideas from Félix Guattari, in particular the

1 Félix Guattari, *Soft Subversions. Texts and Interviews 1977–1985* (New York: Semiotext(e), 2009), 257.

2 Deleuze, *Negotiations*, 115.

3 Antoinette Rouvroy, 'The End(s) of Critique. Data Behaviourism versus Due Process', in *Privacy, Due Process and the Computational Turn. The Philosophy of Law Meets the Philosophy of Technology*, ed. Mireille Hildebrandt and Katja de Vries (Abingdon and New York: Routledge, 2013), 155.

notions of Integrated World Capitalism and the General Collective Equipment, to illuminate algorithmic governmentality's extractive mechanisms in the context of capitalism.

INTEGRATED WORLD CAPITALISM: THE GIANT CALCULATOR

In his work, Guattari was greatly concerned with the analysis and the 'disassembling' of the mechanisms that capitalism uses to extract value from human and nonhuman potential. Besides, he was one of the first thinkers to understand these extractive manoeuvres as *planetary*. In a text from the early 1980s, he introduces the expression 'Integrated World Capitalism' (IWC) to describe the shift in the capitalist strategies of control and exploitation of basic human and nonhuman potential. With the IWC, Guattari anticipates the tendencies of future neoliberal globalization with its integration of technologies, infrastructures, economic control and fantasies of limitless planetary flows.[4] Moreover, Guattari is also one of the first to compare the IWC, with its planetary over-reach, to a giant 'prediction machine',[5] a global calculator, a proto-computer,[6] thus envisioning the seeds of what is now known as algorithmic, platform, Big Data or surveillance capitalism.[7]

Encroaching perceptions, senses, affects, cognition, language, behaviours, the IWC targets and extracts value from life itself in all its material, cognitive, biological and affective dimensions. What characterizes the IWC is that it 'no longer rests on the sole mode of semiotization of financial and monetary Capital, but more fundamentally, on a whole set of technico-scientific, macrosocial and microsocial, and mass media procedures of subjection'.[8] These 'procedures of subjection' require continuous refinement, upgrading and innovation. That is why the IWC contrives to be the 'homing head of innovative techniques'[9] for the extraction of surplus-value and potential from the living and non-living. Carefully designed macro and microsocial procedures turn this potential into tradeable assets. Leisure is commodified. Rest is monetized. Desire weaponized. Experience of the present, anticipation of the future, past memories. They all become targets of the IWC.

[4] Félix Guattari, *Il Capitale Mondiale Integrato. Piano Sul Pianeta* (Bologna: Cappelli, 1982).

[5] Guattari, *Soft Subversions. Texts and Interviews 1977–1985*, 267.

[6] A 1965 essay by Polish economist Oskar Lange where the market is compared to a computing device seems to pre-date this connection. See Oskar Lange, 'The Computer and the Market', in *Socialism and the Market. The Socialist Calculation Debate Revisited*, ed. Peter Boettke (London: Routledge, 2000), 158–6.

[7] Betti Marenko and Pim Haselager, 'Marx in the Smart Living Room. What Would a Marx Oriented Approach to Smart Objects Be Like?', in *Designing Smart Objects in Everyday Life. Intelligences, Agencies, Ecologies*, ed. Marco Rozendaal, Betti Marenko and Will Odom (London: Bloomsbury, 2021), 169–84.

[8] Guattari, *Soft Subversions. Texts and Interviews 1977–1985*, 250.

[9] Ibid., 267.

Guattari sees these extractive manoeuvres as coinciding with the process that produces subjectivities. In short, the IWC's two-pronged manoeuvre – extracting potential and producing subjects – works like this: potential is captured, subjectivity is de-potentialized, its acquired value is turned into the raw material that the IWC feeds on to sustain itself, so that the IWC keeps on growing by capturing more potential, sucking the lifeforce from more subjects, and so on and on – in an integrated vampiric cycle. Guattari discusses these themes in a talk given in 1985 at the University of Vincennes when he explains how subjectivity has become a commodity among commodities, tantamount to a mass-produced object. Subjectivity, he says, is the raw material the IWC needs in order to manufacture everything else – goods, forms of sociality, modes of living, conditions of existence.[10] Rejecting any nostalgia for the allegedly sovereign individual subject, Guattari goes on to say that there is no such thing as a 'natural' subjectivity, and that subjectivity has always had a fully *artificial* character. Exactly like a designed product.

It is important to note that both Guattari and Deleuze see subjectivity as an ongoing process of social production whose outcomes are never given once and for all. There is no finished 'subject', but only subjectivities constantly being produced. While this process of production of subjectivity is not too dissimilar from how it was in past precapitalistic societies, what has changed today are the techniques used to enact it, which are based on capitalist integration and, at present, on the automation of automation. Consequently, it is impossible to understand how subjectivities are produced today without understanding first the key mechanism through which the IWC's power is exercised, what Guattari calls the 'General Collective Equipment': the systematically distributed, material-semiotic, embedded, invisible and normative architecture that constitutes the lived fabric and connective tissue of all social experience.[11]

THE GENERAL COLLECTIVE EQUIPMENT

The General Collective Equipment is one of the most distinctive ideas to emerge from the lively cultural and political milieu of post-1968 French thought, yet one that has received surprisingly little attention.[12] Introduced to examine the role of 'equipments of power' in the development of capitalism from the sixteenth century onwards, it first appeared in the issue titled *Les Équipements du Pouvoir*

[10] Félix Guattari, 'Singolarità e Complessità', *Millepiani. Pensiero Globale, Cervello Sociale* (Milano: Mimesis, 2001), no. 20, 7–26. Talk given by Guattari on 22 January 1985, translated in Italian by Ilaria Dal Canton.

[11] Félix Guattari, *Lines of Flight. For Another World of Possibilities* (London: Bloomsbury, 2016).

[12] Notable exceptions: Susana Caló and Godofredo Pereira eds., *CERFI: Militant Analysis, Institutional Programming and Collective Equipment* (Rotterdam: Het Nieuwe Instituut, 2022). See also Anne Querrien's interview (2022): https://www.versobooks.com/blogs/news/5492-the-critique-of-the-school-in-post-68-french-thought-2-interview-with-anne-querrienuntitled

of the journal *Recherches*, published by CERFI (*Centre d'Études de Recherche et de Formation Institutionnelle*), a French collective of researchers, urbanists, philosophers and activists operating across the late 1960s and early 1970s.[13] CERFI studied social change with the (loose) aim of informing government policy. Initial projects focused on urban planning and the city, which a seminal text describes as a computer as early as 1973.[14]

The General Collective Equipment can be described as the assemblage of structures, apparatuses and systems, from the microscale of domestic routines to the global reach of finance, mass-media and the entertainment-techno-scientific-military complex that together fabricate the environments where subjectivities are produced, narrativized and spatialized. While the General Collective Equipment includes all the infrastructures that organize and shape major functions in the life of citizens, such as transportation (roads), education (schools), health (hospitals), utilities (water and sewage systems) and so on, it is more than just the material and architectural (infra)structure.

As Guattari puts it, the General Collective Equipment is not only 'walls, offices, circulations, transmissions of orders and information, but also and above all, a modelling of attitudes, of rituals of submission that are imposed across multiple semiotic components'.[15] Thus, following Guattari's (deliberately vague) formulation, the General Collective Equipment can be said to stand for *structures of relations* that are *material*, *semiotic* and *affective*. As such, it articulates how the production, consumption, circulation and traffic of symbolic signification takes place across all these dimensions. Fundamentally, the General Collective Equipment is what produces 'the conditions of possibility for all capitalist economic infrastructure'.[16]

In this sense, the General Collective Equipment is also the convergence of apparata of every kind and size in an integrated productive function whose

[13] This issue (no. 13, December 1973) inaugurated the series *Généalogie Du Capital*. See http://www.editions-recherches.com/revue_detail.php?id=13. For extensive analysis of CERFI see François Dosse, *Gilles Deleuze and Félix Guattari. Intersecting Lives* (New York: Columbia University Press, 2010).

[14] The text titled *La Ville-Ordinateur* (The Computer-City) by François Fourquet and Lion Murard (*Recherches* 13, 1973) was CERFI's response to a government call for tenders. It describes the city as a 'tool that occurs and breeds himself, like a living cell, a machine that is self-generating and can reproduce itself, a social machine who is its own operator, a meaningful machine that does not mean nothing but that gathers, connects and intersects all the chains productive, institutional, scientists, etc. The city is not outside the production of chains; it is not reduced to space inert and external to the trial of production (we must reject a purely spatial representation of the city): the city is a computer who makes his own program, an information machine' (1973). An important conversation took place with Deleuze, Guattari, Foucault and Fourquet responding to this essay. Michel Foucault, Félix Guattari, Gilles Deleuze and François Fourquet, 'Equipments of Power. Towns, Territories and Collective Equipments', in *Foucault Live. Michel Foucault Collected Interviews, 1961–1984*, ed. Sylvère Lotringer (New York: Semiotext(e), 1996), 105–12.

[15] Guattari, *Lines of Flight*, 50.

[16] Ibid., 12.

'machinic tentacles'[17] reach everyone, everything, everywhere. It is totalizing: 'everyone participates in this tremendous network of collective equipments. Through them, integrated global capitalism carries out vast cross-fertilizations of territories, representations, images, and systems of control.'[18] Guattari continues: 'This network, both ramified on the microsocial and the planetary scale, has become an essential element of Capital.'[19]

Historically, the General Collective Equipment emerges at the intersection of power, territory and systems of production, crystallized in recognizable social institutions. On this basis, the specific historic reality of the IWC – different from previous societies whose cohesion depended on precapitalistic structures such as cities, castes and classes – functions precisely through the General Collective Equipment's multi-scalar, tentacular domains. From the microsocial to the planetary, it produces modes of existence by way of power interventions and activations that are the result of both design and accident.

This is why understanding how the IWC and the General Collective Equipment converge in producing subjects is of paramount importance. It is through the General Collective Equipment that the IWC achieves its full integration, and that 'semiotic subjugation' – the regulation and modulation of epistemic dispositives – takes place across all domains. In Guattari's words: 'We should tackle this problem [the General Collective Equipment] and all of its aspects in depth, in order to explore the production of contemporary subjectivity.'[20]

EQUIPMENT AS A DESIGN BRIEF

The notion of the General Collective Equipment I have outlined is relevant to my inquiry for a number of reasons. First, it poses a continuum across domains (State and state apparatuses; media complex; public sector and private life) claiming that they can no longer be taken as separate entities. Second, its integrated approach spans and incorporates all the resources predisposed to the manufacture of the social (health, education, leisure and so on); the media, whose function is not only communication but 'modelization'; the spatialization and traffic of bodies, through the systems of transportation that dispose and arrange bodies in space. Third, it gives equal weight to the 'institutions and infra-individual mechanisms, systems of perception, of behaviour, of imaginary representation, of submission to hierarchies and dominant values'.[21] Most importantly, it materializes how power gets distributed over a territory and renders

[17] Guattari, *Soft Subversions. Texts and Interviews 1977–1985*, 259.
[18] Ibid., 48.
[19] Ibid., 255.
[20] Ibid., 48.
[21] Ibid., 47.

visible its most hidden mechanisms; it illuminates how material installations of power are manufactured and experienced as *designed* interventions.[22]

The discussion on the production of subjectivity seen earlier acquires renewed relevance, because, from the standpoint of the production of subjectivity, the General Collective Equipment is the material-semiotic-affective 'condensator'[23] that charges and recharges the *design and manufacture* of desirable lifestyles and modes of living. Individual subjects are at once its basic constituent and its terminal product. They are fabricated, manufactured, designed by the General Collective Equipment. Thus, in reverse of the notion of human mastery, it is not the human designing objects, systems, environment, infrastructures, but the opposite. It is objects, systems, environments, infrastructures, in short, the General Collective Equipment that *designs* the human.

By using Guattari's concepts as analytical tools there is an opportunity to read (and reverse-engineer) the General Collective Equipment as a *design brief* through which the designed world is revealed as a nexus of power formations whose mechanisms – entrenched and largely invisible because hidden in plain sight – all participate in the production of subjectivity. Then the question will be: How could this brief be unpacked, and responded to?

FROM SUPER EQUIPMENT TO CRYSTALS OF THE POSSIBLE

The integration and tentacular reach of the General Collective Equipment is expressed once more by what Guattari calls (terrifyingly) a '*Super Equipment* that is at one and the same time everywhere and nowhere, which crosses national borders, linguistic barriers, antagonisms of class, race and sex, the constellations of families, bodies, organs and even mental "faculties"'.[24] In what can be read as a prescient description of the regime of algorithmic governmentality, he continues: 'In order to be everywhere at once it multiplies its one face, with its *central-black-hole-eye*, which dispenses universal guilt, or delegates to different personae the concern with chanting refrains which, although apparently antagonistic, in reality play on the same range of faciality traits.'[25]

Precisely when the bleakness of the Super Equipment seems to become all-encompassing, all-pervasive and inescapable, Guattari introduces, with another enigmatic expression, what he calls 'optional matter' (*matière à option*) – transformational matter 'composed of the *crystals of the possible* which catalyze

[22] Although Guattari (on his own and with Deleuze) made only cursory references to design, those few instances remain startling. For instance, when he mentions the social need for 'design techniques' in order to 'calm people down' [see epigraph Chapter 3] what he refers to is design as a powerful normative intervention. See also Betti Marenko and Jamie Brassett, 'Introduction', in *Deleuze and Design*, ed. Betti Marenko and Jamie Brassett (Edinburgh: Edinburgh University Press, 2015), 1–30.

[23] Guattari, *Soft Subversions. Texts and Interviews 1977–1985*, 258.

[24] Guattari, *Lines of Flight*, 48.

[25] Ibid. (emphasis added).

connections, destratifications, and reterritorializations both in the living and inanimate world'.[26]

The key to comprehending the meaning of optional matter is in the image of the 'crystals of the possible', which evokes the capacity of a system to go through a continuous energetic amplification.[27] Like a crystal, where every stratum can indefinitely grow on the previous one, optional matter is what affords my capacity to grow, bit by bit, into making a stance; to resist, and push back against the mechanisms of the General Collective Equipment and its glassy black eye.

I will return to the optional matter later on in this chapter. For now, I continue to investigate the General Collective Equipment as the mechanism through which *algorithmic subjects* are being produced in the regime of algorithmic governmentality.

Before proceeding with this, it is useful to locate the genesis of the term 'governmentality', coined by Michel Foucault in the late 1970s by combining 'government' and 'rationality' to describe a type of government enacted through a rational and systematic approach to the management of people and things.[28] In his inventory of modes of government, an inquiry into 'how to be ruled, how strictly, by whom, to what end, by what methods, and so on',[29] Foucault defines government as 'the right disposition of things, arranged so as to lead to a convenient end'.[30] As a way to unpack his definition: 'things' refer to the complex of humans *and* things (networks, assemblages, ecosystems of the human and the nonhuman). Their disposition is a matter of 'multiform tactics' oriented to shape via guidance, incentive and control (rather than prescription), the decision-making environment within which behaviours occur.[31] 'Government' is less about laws and more about how to *dispose things* so that specific outcomes are reached.

On this ground, governmentality concerns the complex of tactics, plannings, laws, administration, bureaucracy, security and so on, deployed to produce subjectivities through rational techniques and means, for instance via systems of classification that order populations, groups and individuals. Governmentality

[26] Félix Guattari, *The Machinic Unconscious. Essays in Schizoanalysis* (New York: Semiotext(e), 2011), 16 (emphasis added).

[27] On the figure of the crystal as an emblematic materialization of the virtual, see Giulio Piatti, 'The Life and the Crystal. Paths into the Virtual in Bergson, Simondon and Deleuze', *La Deleuziana* 3 (2016), 51–8.

[28] Used by Foucault in his talk 'Governmentality', originally part of the course 'Security, Territory, and Population', given at the Collège de France in the academic year 1977–8. See Michel Foucault, 'Governmentality', in *The Foucault Effect. Studies in Governmentality*, ed. Graham Burchell, Colin Gordon and Peter Miller (Chicago: University of Chicago Press, 1991), 87–104.

[29] Michel Foucault, *The Essential Works of Michel Foucault, 1954–1984. Vol.* 3, ed. James D. Faubion and Robert Hurley (London: Penguin Books, 2002), 202.

[30] Foucault, *The Essential Works of Michel Foucault*, 208.

[31] Strategy defines long-term goals and the plan to achieve them. Tactics are more concrete, often concerning smaller steps and a shorter time frame along the way.

is therefore 'intimately bound up'[32] with statistics, whose advent as an actuarial science paved the way for today's regime of algorithmic governmentality. What makes this regime so unique is not only that calculation is at its very core, but that, for the first time in history, calculation has become fully *automated*.

ALGORITHMIC SUBJECTS

As it should be clear by now, algorithmic governmentality is the statistical governance of the 'real' made possible by predictive machines – machines that 'think'. It deploys the anticipatory mode of the automation of automation to produce today's existences via refined strategies that hijack my orientations, propensities and tendencies before they become manifest. Such strategies are underpinned by a new-normal kind of rationality that turns contingency (*what may be*) into discrete chunks of controlled experiences (*what will be*).

This is how algorithmic governmentality produces algorithmic subjects: by feeding on 'the capacity we have to suspend any definition of ourselves, our capacity "to think of ourselves beyond ourselves" in a cultivation of ecstasies or self-transcendence, self-overcoming or self-deconstruction'.[33]

The reserve of potential where pre-personal vitality simmers, in all its oceanic plenitude and mystery, is what algorithmic governmentality preys upon, moulding the yet-to-be. At the same time, my subjectivity gets moulded too by interventions that mobilize me at a preconscious stage, such as the unremitting distraction of alert-mode. Each new notification I receive shoves my body into an automatic response. Each ping is an algorithmically generated, designed artefact that demands an instant reply by conditioning me to invest attention accordingly. It is important to note that my behaviour is not entirely intentional but gets activated at a preconscious level. The micro-computational expansion and re-distribution of my pre-cognitive sensibility happen not simply *before* I register these mechanisms at a conscious level but *below* the threshold of my human sentience.

And so it is that my forthcoming behaviours are predicted, not simply before they happen, but before I might even *think* of making them happen. The flow of potential I am traversed by is captured and siphoned a micro-instant *before* I have made a decision as to how to channel it.[34] I no longer am the sum of all the potential that makes me into a not-fully-predictable horizon of possibilities,

[32] Michel Foucault, *Politics, Philosophy, Culture. Interviews and Other Writings, 1977–1984* (London: Routledge, 1988), 77.

[33] Antoinette Rouvroy, 'Technology, Virtuality and Utopia. Governmentality in an Age of Autonomic Computing', in *Law, Human Agency and Autonomic Computing. The Philosophy of Law Meets the Philosophy of Technology*, ed. Antoinette Rouvroy and Mireille Hildebrandt (Abingdon and New York: Routledge, 2011), 131.

[34] See the harvesting of neural patterning data through FMRI, a technique that measures brain activity by detecting changes associated with blood flow. Based on the evidence that cerebral blood flow and neuronal activation are coupled, researchers can detect spikes of interest registered by the brain before the individual can consciously be aware of what they are seeing.

both taken and non-taken. Instead, I have become a selected quantification of that potential, available for capture, my vital ambiguity eroded to the bone. As causality dissipates in numbers and objects of knowledge are continuously reassembled in real-time by the fine-tuning of machine learning models, my lived experience is captured with little to no mediation. The time dedicated to decision-making, reflection, pause, hesitancy, ambiguity – *maybes* – evaporates, gets eliminated as useless, non-functional, non-instrumental. The 'calculative ontology of prediction' reigns.[35]

Algorithmic governmentality's totalizing equipment effectively designs my tendencies for living, being and existing.[36] With its pre-emptive character, which, as the next chapter explains, separates actualization from the potential to actualize, algorithmic governmentality evaluates and anticipates automatically, paraphrasing Rouvroy, what my body could do (its potentialities) rather than what I am actually doing.[37]

To reiterate this point: What I could or *may* do (or not) – my potential – becomes instead what I *will* do, now given as the only possible mode of actualization. Algorithmic governmentality captures the possibility I have of making *a* choice (*whatever* choice, including no choice), rather than *the* choice (given, predicted, specific). It captures the possibility that, in making *a* choice, I might bring into existence something unplanned, un-anticipated, off-grid (or nothing at all).

This is why my attention is the target. Every time I am alerted, attracted, distracted, side-tracked, seduced and pinged, it is my attention that gets captured, and through it my potential: potential that by definition could go in manifold directions (or none), but that once taken, is siphoned into one specific direction. Crucially, potential could also *not* go in any direction. I will address what happens in this case – the 'potential not to' – in the next chapter through Giorgio Agamben's notion of 'impotentiality'. For now, suffice to say that once captured, the potential becomes the only given 'possible possible'. It becomes the only present homing in and clamping down on the open-endedness of futures.

By constraining potential, what algorithmic governmentality does (very well) is to compress uncertainty in the forms that can be co-opted by predictive machines. In this regime, 'prediction and avoidance of danger have replaced the identification and remediation to its causes'.[38] Prevention of risk, pre-emptying of insecurity and

[35] Mark B.N. Hansen, 'Feed-Forward', in *Simulation, Exercise, Operations*, ed. Robin Mackay (Manchester: Urbanomic, 2015), 59.

[36] Mark B.N. Hansen, 'The Operational Present of Sensibility', *The Nordic Journal of Aesthetics* 24, no. 47 (2014): 38–53.

[37] 'Algorithmic governmentality thus exhibits a new strategy of uncertainty management consisting in minimizing the uncertainty associated to human agency: the capacity humans have to do or not to do all they are physically capable of.' Rouvroy, 'The End(s) of Critique', 152. This is the same radical uncertainty contained in Spinoza's famous statement: 'No one has yet been taught by experience what the body can do', (*Ethics* Part III, Proposition 2, note: 86). One can only find out by experiment and by observing that body's interaction with the environment, that is, with the totality of other bodies. Gilles Deleuze, *Spinoza. Practical Philosophy* (San Francisco: City Lights Books, 1988), especially 17–18.

[38] Rouvroy, 'Technology, Virtuality and Utopia', 126.

erasure of uncertainty are proffered as the pursuit of the most efficient, convenient and bespoke mode of existence that an individual could possibly desire.

ALGORITHMIC EQUIPMENT

On the ground of what I have discussed so far, I frame algorithmic governmentality as the form taken by the Integrated World Capitalism and the General Collective Equipment in the context of planetary computation. I see this convergence – which I call 'algorithmic equipment' – as a system that appears to function as seamlessly as the digital media platforms performing their fantasy of frictionless usability, uniformly designed to be addictive and to conveniently pre-empt my decisions.[39] These digital architectures are today's 'equipments'. The modes of living they foster are designed to equate convenience with desirability via user journeys crafted to nudge behaviour (one-click payment), elicit keen participation (content sharing) and anticipate what the user will ('choose' to) do next (tailored recommendations). It is through these modes of living fostered by the algorithmic equipment that the production of algorithmic subjects comes to fruition in a fully integrated system (the Super Equipment).

Again, the landscape appears bleak. In another instance of lucid prescience from over thirty years ago, Guattari discusses 'the society of integration, of subjective integration, in and by which the subject is modelled so as to function as a *social robot*'.[40] And if to be called a 'social robot' is indigestible to some, Guattari is quick to point out that there is no need for control nor surveillance for this integration to take place. A social robot is a willing, albeit unaware, one. After all, 'capitalism seizes individuals from the inside',[41] asserts Guattari. Capitalism harvests my pre-personal flows and my most vital internal organs: desire, unactualized potential, affect, hesitation, ambiguity. Every time I log in, upgrade, check, post, tweet, upload, download and interface with digital platforms, I am enveloped and trained, my affects modulated; my body tensions adjusted. I fit the machine. But to say that I am becoming a digital self is only one part of the story.[42] Control is exercised throughout every aspect of my life. It affects 'the inner springs of life and human action'.[43] 'I' turn myself into a social robot.

[39] Natasha D. Schüll, *Addiction by Design. Machine Gambling in Las Vegas* (Princeton: Princeton University Press, 2012).

[40] Félix Guattari, 'The Vertigo of Immanence', in *The Guattari Effect*, ed. Eric Alliez and Andrew Goffey (London and New York: Continuum, 2011), 27 (interview with John Johnston) (emphasis added).

[41] Guattari, *Soft Subversion. Texts and Interviews 1977–1985*, 262.

[42] John Cheney-Lippold, *We Are Data. Algorithms and the Making of Our Digital Selves* (New York: New York University Press, 2017).

[43] Ibid., 261. There are echoes here of Deleuze's seminal essay 'Postscript on the Societies of Control' about the shift from discipline to control, which first appeared in *L'Autre Journal*, in May 1990. Reprinted in Deleuze, *Negotiations*, 177–82.

Importantly, these very same mechanisms of control impact profoundly on what I consider 'real'. When reality is being reduced to what can be predicted, what counts as real is transformed. Data-given reality becomes the only version. What happens in real-time becomes the totality of the real. The immediate, continuously updated, just-on-time manifestation of things becomes a sign of their inherent authenticity and value. This construction of reality is both mystifying, because it claims a data-driven objectivity that it does not possess, but also comforting, because it offers the illusory reassurance of futureproofing.

To clarify: by data-driven objectivity, I mean a statistical mode of knowledge-production according to which something is either written in data or it does not exist. Either it is countable, or it does not count. Put differently, when whichever hypothesis modelled by algorithms coincides with *the* known, *the unknown of knowledge* is eroded, as Lyotard wrote decades ago. I will return to this in Chapter 6. For now, I shall reiterate that what I know about the world shrinks to what is made available by data. My modes of knowing cease to be made by unknown quantities. The excess of potential and the chaotic simmering of uncertainty are flattened into the viable version of the real, which lands in my search box as an all-encompassing truth. This is more than using algorithms to calculate probabilities. The real aim of algorithmic governmentality is to grab what cannot be calculated, what escapes probability: the 'excess of the possible on the probable'.[44] The incalculable. Again, I echo what Stengers and Debaise mean when they denounce the 'desertification of all modes of existence', that is, power's drive to flatten what cannot be explained, contained, counted.[45]

POTENTIAL NEEDS CAPTURING BECAUSE IT ESCAPES

Up to this point, the chapter has looked at the production of subjectivity from the perspective of the mechanisms of algorithmic governmentality. In the section that follows, I change my vantage point to examine subjectivity from the perspective of potential. To do that I must go back to, and further problematize, the production of subjectivity.

I start from an observation that Deleuze makes in his book on Foucault where he points out that the process that creates subjectivities is a struggle against different kinds of capture and competing power claims. Thus, it always involves resistance. He writes:

> The struggle for a modern subjectivity passes through a resistance to the two present forms of subjection, the one consisting of individualizing ourselves on the basis of constraints of power, the other of attracting each individual to a known and recognised identity, fixed once and for all. The struggle for

[44] Antoinette Rouvroy, 'The Digital Regime of Truth. From the Algorithmic Governmentality to a New Rule of Law', *La Deleuziana* 3 (2016): 8. Conversation with Bernard Stiegler.

[45] Stengers and Debaise, 'The Insistence of Possibles', 14.

> subjectivity presents itself, therefore, as the *right to difference, variation and metamorphosis*.[46]

But how do I affirm my 'right to difference, variation and metamorphosis'? Massumi explains that individuals are continuously exposed to 'varying degrees of choice at successive threshold states'[47] and their willingness either to mutate or to stay the same is less the act of a unified, intentional agency, and more the expression of 'a state of self-organized indeterminacy'.[48] In other words, indeterminacy is revealed as constitutive of the process of subjectivation.

Therefore, any intentionality I still associate with myself as a sovereign subject will need to be downplayed. Rather than fixating on identity, I shall seek to cultivate my capacity to detect margins of indeterminacy and to modulate the intensities traversing me accordingly. The image of the membrane visualizes this process effectively. A membrane is a surface whose faces are (ontologically so) both inside and outside.[49] A membrane is always a double-edged surface, tilted both ways, which illustrates well that space of 'self-organized indeterminacy' when I am shot through by intensities that I scarcely recognize or identify because they traverse me at a pre-cognitive, pre-personal level before any denomination. Massumi further explains:

> Preemptive operations dip into the field of emergence, taking the commotional potential stirring there as their object. This is potential that has not yet taken determinate form. It is flush with the field of emergence. There is a margin of indeterminacy as to which existing modes of existence it might feed, or what forms of life it may emerge into. It is proto-formal: still a formative force whose conclusion is not foregone. It remains highly charged with the force of futurity. Because of this ontological indecision, the form-takings that will eventuate are struck with a high level of contingency.[50]

What Massumi describes here is not simply how pre-emption works. He also draws attention to the important point that the field where pre-emption

[46] Gilles Deleuze, *Foucault* (Minneapolis and London: University of Minnesota Press, 1988), 105 (emphasis added).

[47] Brian Massumi, *A User's Guide to Capitalism and Schizophrenia. Deviations from Deleuze and Guattari* (Cambridge, Mass. and London: MIT Press, 1992), 81.

[48] Ibid.

[49] Gilles Deleuze, *The Logic of Sense* (New York: Columbia University Press, 1990). See also Humberto R. Maturana and Francisco J. Varela, *The Tree of Knowledge. The Biological Roots of Human Understanding* (Boston and London: Shambhala, 1992). In biochemistry, the membrane is a chemically active agent capable of selecting between the substances that are useful to the molecule and those that are not. Through its filtering operations, the membrane is instrumental to the production of an 'inside' and an 'outside'. Only when these conditions of stability and flexibility were satisfied, life, as a continually self-reproducing and autopoietic system, effectively began. In other words, membranes are essential to life.

[50] Brian Massumi, *99 Theses of the Revaluation of Value. A Postcapitalist Manifesto* (Minneapolis and London: University of Minnesota Press, 2018), 63.

happens is a threshold space of 'ontological indecision', a space of ambiguity and liminality – a space of maybes. Elsewhere, he also observes that the field of emergence where potential simmers 'is rife with germinal potentials of all kinds which are not capitalistic per se – capitalism wouldn't have to "capture" tendencies if they weren't liable to escape'.[51] In other words, the space of 'ontological indecision' is also the space of resistance.

If my subjectivity is also made by an uncertain, potential, virtual dimension (will I always do what am I capable of doing? Nobody knows what my body can do), then what algorithmic governmentality strives for, through its modes of incessant alerts that target my preconscious reflexes, is the capture of this space of virtuality. But *capture is needed precisely because the prey is slippery* and can get away like an octopus in a blur of dark ink.

As the next chapter examines, the totalizing aspect of algorithmic governmentality, which feeds on ambiguity and enthusiasm, hesitation and desire, but also refusal and recalcitrance, is also paradoxically what may be nurturing forms of resistance. Margins of choice persist where the potential exists of doing or not doing, of being or not being – an outcome that is not given or known in advance. Even micro interventions, tiny movements, minimal glitches and micro-sabotages expressing refusal and recalcitrance can become agents of friction and may be cultivated, so that re-liquified potential can flow freely bearing its strange, lively, incongruous, unexpected, *whatever* consequences.

CRYSTALS OF THE POSSIBLE AGAINST THE GRID

It is time to return to Guattari's optional matter: the transformational matter made of the crystals of the possible, a space that contains all possible routes, routes to swerve capture, undo extraction and carve escape pathways. This zone of indeterminacy before a decision is taken is the space of ontological ambiguity prior to capture. It is where the *power of maybes* is to be found.

Guattari asks: How is the optional matter 'produced and mobilised, behind the supposedly neutral architectural and institutional facades of this equipment'?[52] He goes on to say he wants to show:

> By what procedures situations that are apparently open are played out in advance; and that the real margin of choice can nonetheless subsist for people who want to escape from the system. Given a gridding of equipment, what politics of a collective assemblage is it possible to envisage? Where to begin?[53]

[51] Brian Massumi, *The Principle of Unrest. Activist Philosophy in the Expanded Field* (London: Open Humanities Press, 2017), 100.

[52] Guattari, *Lines of Flight*, 36.

[53] Ibid.

The General Collective Equipment has an architectural and institutional façade that appears to be neutral. Equipments 'grid the slightest nook and cranny of the social field'.[54] I visualize it as a grid criss-crossed by either/or binary coordinates. The appearance of neutrality, the grid-like pervasive and invisible architecture, the foreclosure of futures, the binary mode; taken all together describe accurately how algorithmic governmentality produces algorithmic subjects: the algorithmic equipment.

But I read Guattari's questions above also as a prompt to think about design as a Janus-like equipment: one through which power is enacted and reproduced in tangible spatial interventions *and* also one that is able to strategize and implement micro acts of resistance. When Guattari writes that 'all the power formations have been miniaturised and are concentrated in the general collective equipment, which enable them to delimit, control, neutralize, recuperate and redefine any embryos of collective assemblages or revolutionary power',[55] I read his words not only as foreseeing planetary computation and its 'invisible' digital infrastructures, but also design's power to naturalize and neutralize, to contain and constrain, as well as to enable, to afford and to ignite. Design always goes both ways. It has two faces: one that highlights design's own implicated-ness with the most insidious and invisible power manoeuvres that govern (as in, *dispose*) systems, structures, spaces and subjects; and the other that concerns how to design, re-design and un-design the strategies, mechanisms and modes of the General Collective Equipment. In short, can the General Collective Equipment be disassembled through, and as, a design brief? Can it become the site of micro interventions, tiny movements, minimal glitches and micro-sabotages?

DIVERGENT SUBJECTIVITIES

Given the IWC's 'monstrous systems of stimulation'[56] that reduce heterogeneity, flatten difference, promote mono-thought and thrive on standardization; given that processes of subjectivation freeze into coded (therefore calculable) grooves; given that captured subjectivity becomes the one-dimensional, deaf-to-alterity subjectivity of generalized equivalence, where production, consumption and the obsession with growth take the precedence over existence, difference and creation, the questions Guattari asks (and I with him) are: How can one live when potential is extracted, desire seized and singularity appropriated? How can divergent subjectivities be created away from what keeps on devastating the social field? Reading the world as furiously running towards self-destruction (but also self-renewal), Guattari calls for an urgent rethinking of modes of existence. He calls for nothing less than a new art of living.

[54] Ibid., 29.
[55] Ibid., 47.
[56] Félix Guattari, *The Three Ecologies* (London and New Brunswick: The Athlone Press, 2000), 31.

How this 'new art of living' may be achieved is framed through his ethico-aesthetic paradigm where the emphasis is on the ethical implications of a creation committed to expanding the 'richness of the possible'[57] far from 'dominant equilibria'.[58] He argues that resistance 'against the steam-roller of capitalistic subjectivity' can be enacted through the pursuit of heterogeneity, dissonance and dissent.[59] In Guattari's 'ecosophical' perspective encompassing the three ecological registers of environment, social relations and human subjectivity, my whole existence is seen as a precondition for the production of a subjectivity whose most vital mandate is to continue enriching its own relation to the world. It is by way of subjectivities permanently off-centre that a new ethics of living can be seeded.

Guattari offers a passionate argument in favour of manoeuvres that enable a tilting toward resistance, divergence, creation and subversion – manoeuvres that *The Power of Maybes* calls *stratagems*. As Part Two proposes, these are stratagems that unlock mutant affects and carry one beyond the familiar; that afford the breaking of habits and the unhinging of grooves; that prioritize getting unstuck as a project of liberation. This is why the role of minoritarian practices, marginal knowledges and micro gestures is so important: because they foster novel, possibly non-homologated trajectories and afford entering the blurry zone of potential. It is through the intensities produced by questions and practices that confront the existent that a new art of living can be tried out, one invested in expanding the richness of the possible.

But creation brings accountability. To speak of creation is also to speak of responsibility in regard to what I create. This concerns the ethical positioning I take. I will return to these matters in Chapter 4. For now, suffice it to say that to make ethical choices in favour of the process of creation concerns, in a very Spinozian sense, that I learn to select good encounters to enter into. Put differently, to make ethical choices is a pragmatic alliance with the forces of change and the simmering of potential. It is nothing less than an alliance with uncertainty.

To conclude, Guattari, who was writing at a time of profound social transformation, helps me to make sense of the present. Through his actual and astute thought, I am reminded that subjectivity means to be simultaneously subject and subjected; that society's aim is to keep on producing subjectivities and to refine techniques for handling, controlling and manipulating life-surplus (potential); that pliable subjects are created by siphoning their potential into convenient categories and normative identities. I am also reminded that these procedures are nothing but ways of governing, that is, of *disposing things*, which ultimately concerns designing.

But I am reminded of something else too: that the production of subjectivity is a process that cuts across discrete social formations, individual or collective, that is, is trans-individual and transversal. Again, not subjects as discrete

[57] Guattari, *Chaosmosis*, 29.

[58] Ibid., 77.

[59] Ibid., 90.

entities, but processes whose continuous doing, re-doing and un-doing means that there will always be margins of potential, crystals of the possible, edges that remain open, un-finished, indeterminate, something whose tendencies, capacities, propensities – whose unknowns – are not, cannot be, given a priori. These margins, these unknowns, are where seeds of resistance can germinate.

And it is to resistance that I turn next. How do I make a stand against 'a depoliticised, statistical governmental rationality indifferent to the causes of phenomena and chiefly oriented towards the annihilation of contingency'?[60] How do I reclaim the inactual that dwells in potential? How do I *resist reduction*?

[60] Rouvroy, 'Technology, Virtuality and Utopia', 135.

3 Resisting Reduction

People are so lost, so maddened by the deterritorialisation of the gears of the social, of space and time, like frightened animals, power feels the need to calm them down, to put [soft] music in lifts, to make them parade and to channel them in a continuum space modelled by design techniques.

FÉLIX GUATTARI[1]

AGAINST THE STEAMROLLER

This chapter, which borrows the title from Joichi Ito's volume, is about resistance.[2] It contends that the 'steamroller' discussed in the previous chapter – capture of potential, erosion of lifeworld, desertification of existence, siphoning of possible possibles, in short 'reduction' – must be resisted. Reflecting on some of the recurring themes in Guattari's work – the analysis of the forces that traverse and mould society; what connects production of subjectivity and spatialization; the uneasy alliance between regimes of power and design techniques – and the deeper significance these themes have acquired today, this chapter offers my take on both 'reduction' and 'resistance' to illuminate how the capture of potential (reduction) can be counteracted (resistance).

I frame both resistance and reduction through selected aspects of Guattari and Agamben's thought, alongside a reading of Herman Melville's short story *Bartleby, the Scrivener: A Story of Wall Street* (1853), chosen to reflect on the meaning not only of the potential but of the *impotential* too. Following Deleuze and Agamben's reading of *Bartleby*, I argue that grasping impotentiality

1 Guattari, *Lines of Flight*, 46.

2 Joichi Ito, ed., *Resisting Reduction. Designing Our Complex Future with Machines* (Cambridge, Mass. and London: MIT Press, 2019).

is essential in building resistance as an ontological practice. The implications of this gesture for design will become clear in Part Two.

For now, suffice it to say that it is through Agamben's take on the potential and the impotential that my argument begins to consolidate. Specifically, I propose to take the 'power not to' – the surplus of potential in relation to the act – as the space where a richer mode of living can flourish. As the chapter illustrates, this can only happen on the condition that I tune in to the 'quantum of potential': the *maybes*. From this standpoint, resistance will also mean figuring out how to *design modes of existence* that embrace uncertainty in its cosmic, oceanic plenitude.

WE MUST TALK (MORE) ABOUT BARTLEBY

In Melville's short story *Bartleby, the Scrivener*, Bartleby is the office clerk who, one day, starts uttering the sentence *I would prefer not to*, promptly dis-engaging from all his tasks and duties.[3] Repeated demands from his increasingly exasperated supervisor lead to nothing. Bartleby does not obey orders. He appears to be idle, and yet he does not leave the office premises, nor does he formally reject or negate his role. He does not work, but he does not seem possessed by the antagonism of the refusal. He simply prefers *otherwise*, as he keeps on repeating: *I would prefer not to*.

Published over 170 years ago, this short story with its unforgettable protagonist and his enigmatic words has been the object of intense and varied critical analysis ever since. A plethora of interpretations has projected onto Bartleby a range of modes (apathy, nihilism, rebellion, mutiny, intransigence) and roles: the politicized Bartleby, the originary Bartleby, the whatever Bartleby.[4] Among these, the interpretation I favour is by Deleuze, for whom Bartleby resists all interpretation and is resolutely *not* a symbol.[5] In his commentary Deleuze describes Bartleby's utterance, *I would prefer not to*, as the 'formula of creation',[6] a formula that is nothing less than:

> devastating because it eliminates the preferable just as mercilessly as any nonpreferred. It not only abolishes the term it refers to, and that it rejects, but also abolishes the other term it seemed to preserve, and that becomes impossible. In fact, it renders them indistinct: it hollows out an ever-expand-

3 Herman Melville, 'Bartleby, the Scrivener: A Story of Wall Street', *The Piazza Tales* (New York: Dix & Edwards; London: Sampson Low, 1856).

4 Armin Beverungen and Stephen Dunne, '"I'd Prefer Not To". Bartleby and the Excesses of Interpretation', *Culture and Organization* 13, no. 2 (2007): 171–83.

5 Gilles Deleuze, *Essays Critical and Clinical* (London and New York: Verso, 1998).

6 Giorgio Agamben and Gilles Deleuze, *Bartleby. La Formula della Creazione* (Macerata: Quodlibet, 1993).

> ing zone of *indiscernibility* or indetermination between some nonpreferred activities and a preferable activity.[7]

Neither an affirmation, nor a negation; neither a refusal, nor an acceptance, this formula signals rather a state of suspension, an in-between which is neither inaction nor passivity, neither rebellion nor dissent, neither indifference nor negligence. *I would prefer not to* is the formula that maps that 'ever-expanding zone of indiscernibility' where the potential to do (potentiality) and the potential to *not* do (impotentiality) co-exist. This coexistence, where a multiplicity of different contingencies are contained, and none is chosen, is the condition of all possibility.

With poetic expression Agamben calls this space 'the luminous spiral of the possible'[8] that 'shows itself on the threshold between Being and non-being, between sensible and intelligible, between word and thing'.[9] Potentiality (which is not an act of will) and impotentiality (which is never a necessity) continuously recharge each other, like two 'phases' of an alchemical loop. It is precisely because it plunges into this loop where it affirms the power *to* as well as the power *not to* that Bartleby's utterance is the true 'formula of creation'. Precisely because something might, indifferently, be or not be, the formula underpins a philosophy of radical contingency. Contingency here coincides with the space of human freedom.[10]

Perhaps a word of caution is needed at this point. It would be easy to misread Bartleby as a cipher for the refusal of labour, the rebellion against petty authority, or for disaffected apathy. But, following Deleuze and Agamben, it seems to me that the most generative and transversal interpretation – in the sense of affording the propagation of new thoughts and unexplored connections – is Bartleby as impervious to being attributed a role. With his refusal to engage, he unhinges social structures, breaking the link between power and willingness. Conversely, any interpretation that attempts to turn Bartleby into a hero or a martyr fails to grasp Bartleby's devastating stance. For instance, to interpret Bartleby as 'lazy' or 'unproductive' remains subsumed in the neoliberal discourse on entrepreneurial innovation that reframes idleness and boredom as routes to galvanize productivity through the kind of spontaneous creativity that 'taps into' and 'unleashes' potential.[11]

7 Deleuze, *Essays Critical and Clinical*, 71 (emphasis added).

8 Giorgio Agamben, *Potentialities. Collected Essays in Philosophy* (Stanford: Stanford University Press, 1999), 257.

9 Ibid.

10 Giorgio Agamben, *La Comunita' Che Viene* (Torino: Bollati Boringhieri, 2001); Giorgio Agamben, *Nudita'* (Rome: Nottetempo, 2009); Giorgio Agamben, *L'Uso dei Corpi* (Vicenza: Neri Pozza, 2014); Giorgio Agamben, 'The Power of Thought', trans. Kalpana Seshadri, *Critical Inquiry* 40, no. 2 (2014): 480–91.

11 Tim Christiaens, 'Neoliberalism and the Right to be Lazy. Inactivity as Resistance in Lazzarato and Agamben', *Rethinking Marxism* 30, no. 2 (2018): 265. I will return to the neoliberal rhetoric around uncertainty in Chapter 5.

In this sense, Bartleby embodies the 'haunting phantom' presence of the non-productive within production. As American literature scholar Andrew Knighton puts it:

> The ambiguous productivity of the unproductive has proven the haunting phantom unascertainable by economic theory. Despite modern capitalism's tireless efforts to understand the relationship between productive and unproductive activity (and, whether through the scientific management of labor or the development of the consumerist 'leisure economy', to turn it into profit), the basic indeterminacy of these categories has presented a chronic problem for economic and cultural thought.[12]

Marx had already noted how this latency constitutes the contradiction inherent to capitalism. Capital tends to absorb as productive even those activities that are not related to work, thus muddying the distinction between the productive and the unproductive, the useful and the useless. Think at how every iota of 'free', that is, potentially undifferentiated time, is harvested and turned into commodity. Whether it is about experiencing leisure, building memories, savouring moments, investing in wellness, exercising mindfulness, unleashing potential, every facet of my 'unproductive' existence can and will be colonized. However, something else Marx already noted is the paradox at the core of capitalism, namely, that this undifferentiated remains immeasurable, its value ultimately not fully known, nor fully graspable. It is this space of 'undifferentiated activity that, outside of measure and remuneration, nevertheless generates the lives of subjects and their ontological horizon'.[13] This ontological horizon is the oceanic space where the power of maybes can be found and acted upon (or, indeed, not).

THE IMPOTENTIAL

One theme Agamben repeatedly returns to in his work is the relation between potential and act. He asks: What happens to potential when I act? Where does it go? Does it get exhausted? And what happens to it when I do not act? Agamben draws on the classical argument put forward by Aristotle to answer these questions: An architect retains the capacity to build even when they are not building; a pianist retains the capacity to play even when they are not playing; a writer, of writing. Potentiality is also impotentiality. In other words, at the core of my power lies a fundamental ambivalence. My capacity to be, to do, to know, is intrinsically woven to my capacity to not be, to not do, to not know. Their relationship however is far from symmetrical because the transition from

[12] Andrew Knighton, 'The Bartleby Industry and Bartleby's Idleness', *ESQ: A Journal of the American Renaissance* 1, no. 2 (2007): 196.
[13] Ibid., 207.

potentiality to actuality – 'passing to the act' – does not really exhaust potential. On the contrary, for Agamben potential is, first, the power *to not* pass to the act. While my potential (to be, to do, to know, etc.) operates within a specific horizon of possibility, my potential to not (be, do, know, etc.) has its own potential as the object.[14]

When a wedge is inserted in the space of impotentiality, that is when capture happens. Once I am separated from my capacity to exercise my power to not do – the architect who does not build; the pianist who does not play; the writer who does not write (because her attention is shattered into a million rabbit holes) – that is when I have lost any agency over my existence. There is nothing worse than to be estranged from impotentiality, because to have *lost the capacity to not* do means to have *lost the capacity to resist.*

To reiterate this point: When I am separated from my power to act (my potential) I can still resist through my power to not act. But when I am separated from my impotentiality, then I no longer have the capacity to resist, the energy to push back. While this is the zone routinely usurped by authoritarian regimes, it is also the zone preyed upon insidiously by the extractive manoeuvres of the Integrated World Capitalism, of the General Collective Equipment, of algorithmic governmentality. As they impinge on my impotentiality, I get disconnected from my *power to not* exercise my potential. Conversely, it is only when impotentiality is not detached from the totality of my experience, not exploited and not put to 'use' that, for Agamben, life can be said to be 'full', when impotentiality remains not-appropriated and not-appropriable.[15]

It is by dwelling in the suspension of potential, in Bartleby's alchemical loop, that a full, rich mode of living can be reclaimed, one that coincides with the totality of its potential prior to actualization and capture. A full life. The sum of unrealized potential before any qualifier is assigned. The impersonal, oceanic flow of intensities before their individuation, what Agamben calls *form-of-life* and Deleuze *a life.*[16] What I call *the power of maybes.*

THE INOPERATIVE

As I have shown, my active capacity to experience both potentiality and impotentiality can yield a life that can fully inhabit its richness. I imagine such a life as a 'round' one, and it is the experience of this 'round' existence, in all its

[14] For Deleuze, this is the counter-actualization inherent to actualization. If actualization imprisons an event into its realization, counter-actualization is what liberates it; what 'give us the chance to go farther than we would have believed possible. To the extent that the pure event is each time imprisoned forever in its actualization, counter-actualization liberates it, always for other times.' Deleuze, *The Logic of Sense*, 182.

[15] Agamben describes this as a life that fully coincides with its forms. The examples he offers are forms of life characterized by ascesis, poverty, contemplation, such as monasticism. However, I argue for less extreme, more accessible and embedded modes where life and its forms coincide.

[16] Agamben, *L'Uso dei Corpi*, 2014; Deleuze, *Pure Immanence*, 2005.

cosmic reach, that generates self-contentment.[17] In this proposition, a life is full, round and self-content when it is no longer predicated exclusively on operativity and instrumentality. Recall the notion of non-instrumentality in Chapter 1, re-emerging here through the coexistence of potentiality and impotentiality. This coexistence is the great *amphibolic* status of power.[18] The undifferentiated cohabits with the realized, without ever being exhausted in it. The beauty of unrealized potential is that it remains open to multiple possibles. It remains, to use another term in Agamben's lexicon, *inoperative.*[19]

The inoperative is not only the 'political substance of the Occident, the glorious nutrient of all power',[20] writes Agamben, but also irreducible resistance. In his outline for a poetic and politics of inoperativity, Agamben goes as far as to suggest that to be human is nothing but to be an inoperative living entity.[21] Again, this is not about being inert, nor passive; it is not about refusal. Inoperativity is a special kind of action where potential is in continuous looping relation with its own impotentiality: an *active not-doing.*[22] When I dwell in inoperativity, I delink my possible endeavours from instrumental performativity, remaining open to what *may be.* By reclaiming the inoperative before any social and economic de-marcation, I release it from the necessity of usability. By reclaiming the inoperative before any habitual behaviour, I gain an understanding of what my body can really do. By reclaiming the inoperative and its multiple uncertainties, I learn to cultivate a life whose vertiginous, oceanic roundness becomes the mode of existence to strive for.

To reiterate this point: Inoperativity is not idleness, inertia, passivity or cessation of activity. When I cast inoperativity as the opposite or the negative of work, or as lack (of labour, efficiency, hustle), then I cannot release it in its full power to yield a life.[23] On the contrary, inoperativity as a positive endeavour is the condition for a mode of existence dwelling in maybes.

[17] Spinoza's notion of 'self-contentment' is 'pleasure arisen from the fact that man regards himself and his power of acting' (Spinoza *Ethics* Part IV, Proposition 52, proof: 173, 52) and is given as the highest thing to aspire to.

[18] From the Greek *amphibolos*, 'ambiguous, struck on both sides'.

[19] For a comprehensive critique of Agamben's thought, in particular his notion of inoperativity, see Sergei Prozorov, *Agamben and Politics. A Critical Introduction* (Edinburgh: Edinburgh University Press, 2014).

[20] Giorgio Agamben, *The Kingdom and the Glory. For a Theological Genealogy of Economy and Government* (Stanford: Stanford University Press, 2011), 246.

[21] Giorgio Agamben, *Creazione e Anarchia. L'Opera nell'Eta' della Religione Capitalista* (Vicenza: Neri Pozza, 2017).

[22] Chapter 6 will expand on the significance of 'active non-doing' by looking at the Chinese notion of *wu-wei*, which means exactly that. To my knowledge, however, Agamben makes no reference to Chinese thought in his work. My constellation brings them together in what I believe to be a fruitful gesture.

[23] This is where otherwise brilliant eulogies of inoperativity: Kazimir Malevic, *L'Inazione Come Verità Effettiva dell'Umanita* (Napoli: Cronopio, 2022) and of laziness: Paul Lafargue, *The Right To Be Lazy and Other Writings* (New York: New York Review of Books, 2023) fall short. This is also the limit of proposing the conceptual personas of the exhausted, the loser, the dispossessed, the depressed as paradigmatic of inoperativity

WHATEVER-NESS

The striking relevance of Bartleby – and the reason why I use his tale to further my inquiry – is that his active non-doing reveals the undifferentiated beneath, which I see as the zone of maybes. In his obstinate dwelling 'in the abyss of potentiality',[24] in his not-engaging (with work, with instrumental production, with actualization) Bartleby burrows in that zone of indeterminacy where things are possible precisely because the imperative to actualize them is eluded. His inoperative stance is a spanner in the machine, a *sabot* in the mechanisms that parse and harvest the undifferentiated.

But the inoperative is challenging too. It is elusive. It is 'a suspension that cannot be reabsorbed by the figures of negation and identity'.[25] Thus, it must find other routes for expression, away from conventional forms of identity politics and agential power. Before any qualifying determinations, before the potential acquires an individuated form of expression, inoperativity coincides with 'whatever': when something may go in many different directions, or none.[26] This *'whatever-ness'* is the genuine value of the inoperative. Following Agamben, I take inoperativity as the condition to build a full, rich, round life. But how?

To start with, instrumentality will need to be de-emphasized to accentuate the useless, the uncertain, the amphibolic; protocols and performances of usability will need to be disactivated to make space for modes that disengage from a logic of instrumentality.[27] These gestures lead into ethical territories as they very much concern the *how*: What matters is not *what* I am – the identities I cling to, the fictions I use to in-groove my futures, what I am stuck in and give a name to – but *how* I am, *how* I know, *how* I act. In short, my modes of being, knowing, acting: ethical wisdom (phronesis, again). *How* has to do with my position, my stance, and the *contiguity* my stance affords. I will return to contiguity shortly. Before, I introduce some ways in which a resistance founded in the inoperative may be practiced through some of the stratagems (*hows*) that afford the roundness of whatever without flattening its unknowability.

(Christiaens,'Neoliberalism and the Right to be Lazy', 269). I would argue that these roles are still performing within the same extractive and performative dynamic demanded by capture, thus they do not reach the genuinely undifferentiated. It is not a coincidence that for the ancient Romans, it was work [*neg-otium*] to be taken as the negative and opposite of the contemplative life [*otium*].

24 Agamben, *Potentialities*, 254.

25 Giovanni Marmont and German E. Primera, 'Propositions for Inoperative Life', in *The Politics, Ethics, and Aesthetics of Inoperativity*. Special Issue. *Journal of Italian Philosophy* 3 (2020): 16.

26 Whatever, 'in any way', is the sense of the Latin term *quodlibet*: indicating the many modes that express a single substance.

27 Agamben calls this 'destituent power', suggesting dis-activation not as destruction but as liberation from, or suspension of, instrumentality.

EXIT, OPPORTUNISM AND DUPLICITY

Since the mid-1990s, Italian philosopher Paolo Virno has been proposing *exodus*, *exit* and *defection* as strategies of liberation and resistance.[28] I borrow these modes of action based on engaged withdrawal and foundational leave-taking to illuminate my reflections on reduction and resistance, and to begin anchoring them to 'active not-doing'. Virno writes that exodus is 'neither exiting on tiptoe through the back door nor a search for sheltering hideaways. Quite the contrary: what I mean by Exodus is a full-fledged model of action, capable of confronting the challenges of modern politics'.[29] Exodus is 'not a negative gesture, exempt from action and responsibility. On the contrary, because defection modifies the conditions within which conflict takes place, rather than submit to them, it demands a particularly high level of initiative – it demands an affirmative "doing"'.[30]

For Virno exodus is a strategy that changes the existing conditions, context and horizon of a problem and its given solutions. Similarly, exit is 'free-thinking inventiveness that changes the rules of the game and disorients the enemy'.[31] Because of the abundance of possibilities it manifests; because of the wealth of creative collective imagination it expresses, 'nothing is less passive than flight', he writes.[32]

I read Virno alongside the complementary position of Italian philosopher Massimo De Carolis, who proposes a 'phenomenology of *opportunism*' and the cultivation of a kind of wisdom 'directed not at establishing universal laws, but at discovering the sense of what is accidental, material, and unrepeatable'.[33] This 'phenomenology of *opportunism*' foregrounds the *metic* intelligence and the 'ruses of the intellect' (together with its animal guides: the octopus and the fox) which will be discussed in Chapter 4. Divested from its negative connotations, opportunism concerns being able to perceive the directions of things *before* they start moving. It is the refinement of my capacity to perceive how the current might flow, so that I can follow it. It is about grasping *propensities*.

Opportunism is also about what Massumi calls 'creative *duplicity*'[34] to suggest an efficacious strategy (or better, a *stratagem*) for dealing with neolib-

[28] Paolo Virno, 'The Ambivalence of Disenchantment', in *Radical Thought in Italy. A Potential Politics*, ed. Paolo Virno and Michael Hardt (Minneapolis and London: University of Minnesota Press, 1996), 13–34; Paolo Virno, 'Virtuosity and Revolution. The Political Theory of Exodus', in *Radical Thought in Italy*, ed. Paolo Virno and Michael Hardt (Minneapolis and London: University of Minnesota Press, 1996), 189–210.

[29] Virno, 'Virtuosity and Revolution', 197.

[30] Virno, 'The Ambivalence of Disenchantment', 33.

[31] Virno, 'Virtuosity and Revolution', 199.

[32] Ibid.

[33] Massimo De Carolis, 'Toward a Phenomenology of Opportunism', in *Radical Thought in Italy*, ed. Paolo Virno and Michael Hardt (Minneapolis and London: University of Minnesota Press, 1996), 44.

[34] Massumi, *99 Theses of the Revaluation of Value*, 69 (emphasis added).

eral capture. Creative duplicity is the cultivation of 'the fuzzy-set capacity of the dividual to truly belong to two sets at the same time, but not in like manner, rather with simultaneous divergent tendencies in co-operation'.[35] These words re-evoke the images, encountered earlier, of the *hinge*, which both articulates and dis-articulates, and the *membrane*, which both unites and divides. These images render well the kind of complicity that 'should be *practiced* strategically, in ways aimed at always upping the ration of escape over capture'.[36]

The notions briefly introduced here – exit, escape, exodus, defection, opportunism, cunning, duplicity – all participate in the active practice of 'not-doing' (*wu-wei*) and taken together, make me alive and attuned to sensing the propensity of things. This is how the inoperative can turn into action without losing its hook into the undifferentiated. But there is more. As Chapter 6 will examine, these practices of active not-doing are affirmative stances that do not just simply happen. On the contrary, they are stratagems that require dedication, astuteness and plotting. They require cultivation, unlearning and *designing.*

THE SPATIAL INTIMACY OF CONTIGUITY

I mentioned *contiguity* earlier to draw attention to how my stance in the world concerns my ethical position. Contiguity denotes proximity and the orientation that emerges when surfaces, and their interstices, are adjacent. From the Latin *contingere* (*cum* = with + *tangere* = to touch, be connected with),[37] contiguity with all that exists – human, nonhuman, whatever – is exquisitely suited to express connections 'to come', connections (not given nor expected) that are on the verge of happening. I find contiguity to be a formidably generative image for modes of living that hinge on pure potential, more than the insistence on and invocation of 'relationality'. To be clear, I do not question relationality; but as a concept, it quickly sinks into the indifferent generalist universality of 'everything is connected', losing the generative power that I crave in concept-building.

I choose instead to endorse contiguity, adjacency, proximity, propinquity as modes of *spatial intimacy* inclusive of all the divergences, asymmetries and uneven distributions that make up *adjacent possibles*. I read adjacence, and being at *ease* in this space of 'nearby-ness'[38] as a mode of spatial intimacy where movement happens before any determination, where proximity coincides with favourable timing, and where contiguity is woven into the practice of crafting propitious encounters. This space of nearby-ness, contiguity, adjacence, of

[35] Massumi, *The Principle of Unrest*, 31.
[36] Massumi, *99 Theses of the Revaluation of Value*, 68.
[37] The same root is also found in *contingency* and *contagion*.
[38] From the Latin *ad-jacens*.

being on the verge of touching, is like 'a house that magically expands with each door you open'.[39]

Contiguity affords the opportunity to act through tiny, even imperceptible movements. The smallest gesture can precipitate the greatest shifts. 'It suffices to move just a little bit' says Agamben,[40] in an echo of Deleuze's 'inconspicuous events' that have the power of eluding control 'however small their surface or volume'.[41]

Eluding control and resisting are reframed as a matter of small gestures. In the tiny movement, in the humble, ordinary, seemingly negligible act, *worlds* are contained. The tiny act, the tiny gesture, the tiny movement, the 'little bit', are neither insignificant nor negligible steps, but rather the expression of an intoxicating attention to potential as it flows into and across adjacent possibles. They are a *micropolitics* of practices too.

Micropolitics refers to the immediate, day-to-day, sphere of concerns, preoccupations and modes of inhabitation rooted in affect, perception, desire (from the personal, domestic and familial, to the collegiality of networks, collectives and shared practices), and to the way in which such concerns, preoccupations and modes express, and are connected to, wider social and cosmic dimensions. Importantly, micropolitics is defined 'not by the smallest of its elements but by the nature of its "mass" – the quantum flow as opposed to the molar segmented line'.[42] I borrow Deleuze and Guattari's expression 'microinjections'[43] to characterize the leaky, capillary, infiltration-al, de-centred dimensions of the micropolitical, and how it may inform a renewed mode of design. Put differently, I envision a *micropolitics of design interventions* operating in contiguous spaces and interstices, to activate (and agitate) adjacent possibles and to experiment with stratagems of the micro (the 'little bit', the 'microinjection'). These are the ways through which I enter into the zone of indiscernibility, and I make a home inside Bartleby's alchemical loop.

INCUBATING DESIGN

I conclude this chapter by connecting its salient points to some reflection on design and by proposing a shift to inoperativity as a way out of design's instrumental fixation.

[39] Steven Johnson, *Where Good Ideas Come From. The Natural History of Innovation* (London and New York: Allen Lane, 2010), 31. See also Lennart Björneborn, 'Adjacent Possible', in *The Palgrave Encyclopaedia of the Possible*, ed. Vlad P. Glaveanu (Cham, Switzerland: Springer, 2023), 16–28; Stuart Kauffman, 'Beyond Physics: The Emergence and Evolution of Life'. Keynote speech. *Kreyon* Conference, The Complexity of the Future (Rome, 2017).

[40] Agamben, *La Comunita' Che Viene*, 24.

[41] Deleuze, *Negotiations*, 176. In this conversation with Toni Negri (first appeared in the journal *Futur Antérieur* 1, 1990) Deleuze frames this micropolitics of gestures through *pietas* – a community-building affect of justice, honesty and fairness (not religion or morality), drawing on Spinoza for whom *pietas* is the desire 'of doing good, which is engendered in us by reason of the fact that we live according to the precepts of reason' (*Ethics* Part IV, Proposition 37, note 1: 163).

[42] Deleuze and Guattari, *A Thousand Plateaus*, 240.

[43] Ibid., 225.

In practice, this would mean to add 'inoperativity' and 'whatever-ness' to the design brief seen earlier as a proposal to critique, disassemble and counteract the General Collective Equipment. The thought experiment scaffolding the brief I propose is this: Imagine design stemming from, and going toward, not the functional and the instrumental, but the indeterminacy of whatever-ness. Imagine a design practice that alights from this premise, that takes the roundness of life as its propeller, a design practice designing a (*and for a*) full life, designing a (*and for a*) undivided existence. A design centred on potential, therefore on the impotential. A design centred on maybes.

This trajectory speaks not only to design's engagement with the making and unmaking of worlds as an ontological force; to design's effort for materializing the unthinkable and bringing into existence realities; to design as the construction of the artificial. More to the point, it concerns the challenge of design as an agent of (and for) a micropolitics of interventions. Seen in this way, with potential/impotential at its centre, design would be the practice of acting in the present by enabling the present's multiple declensions, while resisting the manoeuvres that insist on divesting the present from its totality of potential. The present must be inhabited fully by refuting dependency on past structures, the constriction of anticipatory governance, and the delusional postponement of utopias.[44] Put differently, to work with potential/impotential, through contiguity and micro-infiltrations, means to treat the space of maybes, with all its unknowns, as an *incubation* space.[45] And this is a practice that must be crafted.

It is in this sense that this chapter's argument around potentiality and impotentiality, inoperativity and whatever-ness – and my initial outline of stratagems for the inoperative – feeds into the larger project of design as an *ontological* force, and the hiatus it poses with both its extractivist lineage and its instrumental projection into the future, as well as with its founding notion of the human as the terminal user. As current design critique lucidly points out, design is called to resist the extractivist procedures that empty life of its potential, whether by algorithmic governmentality, by optimization, by colonization or by the normalization of fear.[46]

For design to repattern itself around potential and inoperativity, as I suggest, means first of all to take them both seriously as the condition for the creation of new modes of knowing, living and being. If the key question that design is facing, as philosopher and design theorist Adam Nocek puts it, concerns under which conditions the radical futural difference, or what he calls the 'coming

44 Carlo Salzani, 'Quodlibet. Giorgio Agamben's Anti-Utopia', *Utopian Studies* 23, no. 1 (2012): 212–37.

45 The etymology of *incubation* refers to the practice of sleeping in a sacred space, like a temple or a sanctuary to receive divine revelations, that is, by allowing oneself to enter unknowing. More on unknowing in Chapter 6.

46 Tony Fry and Adam Nocek ed., *Design in Crisis. New Worlds, Philosophies and Practices* (London: Routledge, 2021); Adam Nocek, 'Between Abstraction and Insufficiency. Some Reflections on Necropolitics and the Ethics of Design Philosophy', *Design and Culture* 14, no. 1 (2022): 51–68; Claudia Mareis and Nina Paim, *Design Struggles. Intersecting Histories, Pedagogies, and Perspectives* (Amsterdam: Valiz, 2021).

into presence of unassimilable difference'[47] may take shape, then I would argue that the conditions are those offered by entering the inoperative space of full potential. As it should be clear by now, I frame this as a space of maybes. It is not a comfortable space, nor is it reassuring, but it is the only one that, for me, is worth working with.

The challenge I envision for design, then, is how to unhinge itself from instrumentality and anticipatory capture, to focus on cultivating a micropolitics of practices. The challenge is also affirming the 'roundness of whatever' by striving to multiply the range of 'possible possibles', pushing toward worlds that have not been thought of yet. This work demands the design of stratagems to enter uncertainty.

This no longer has to do with the constitution or the centrality of the human (as user, consumer, target, stakeholder, product), but with its de-creation; not with the making of the human, but with its profound, uncompromising, difficult unmaking. In other words, this is an argument for design to rethink the human as a designed artefact and subjectivity as a product of intersecting heterogenous systems of governance at scale, from the macro (the infrastructural all the way to the planetary) to the micro (the microbial, the molecular, the viral). It also means continuing the work of provincializing the normative constructs of the Western/Northern paradigm, and refusing the violent aberration of its universalizing claims, especially when practices of inclusive, socially responsive, participatory, and collaborative design are used to repurpose and 'wash' top-down, universalizing and defuturing stances.[48] Finally, it also means to think about how to deploy design to disassemble the very same systems it contributes to creating, and to dismantle, bit by bit, the equipments where control, capture and the 'disposition' of things keep on feeding on potential. In short, it is an argument for resisting reduction by design. Resistance happens in the present where it finds contingent elements to press against. The practice of speculating pragmatically against these constraints is what turns resistance into a design brief.

This is where the opportunity is given for a design that decentres the human, that supersedes the user by staying beneath those indexes and differentiations, a design that operates in and with the roundness of a life, thus a design that can shift, a little bit by a little bit, through tiny actions, through an entire range of micro-acting (micro-interventions, micro-injections, micro-infiltrations), imperceptible movements, one spatial intimacy at a time, into a non-anthropocentric mode. A mode of designing resisting reduction by expressing the roundness of whatever. A micropolitics of designing that is also a pan-sensibility to the irrevocable, irreducible uncertainty of the world.

[47] Adam Nocek, 'Human Design. A Lure for the Future', Desis Network: Philosophy Talk, Politecnico di Milano, 15 June 2022 (unpublished).

[48] Tony Fry, *Defuturing. A New Design Philosophy* (London: Bloomsbury, 2020) articulates how those operations (epistemic, ontological, political) effectively cancel the future in the presumption of knowing that what 'might be' is only a reproduction of 'what is'.

PART TWO

4 Metic Wayfinding

This is what I call 'micropolitics,' and 'molecular revolution.'
It begins with very immediate, daily, individual preoccupations,
yet remains connected to what happens at the social level,
and even, why not, at the cosmic level.
FÉLIX GUATTARI[1]

SWITCHING TO THE COSMIC

With Part Two the book switches gear. In my quest for ideas that can help in turning uncertainty into an ally, I search for those philosophies that can guide me in apprehending the full plenitude of being and the roundness of life in all their amphibolic power, as I have discussed in Part One. Thus, with this chapter I reach out to the cosmological. What I mean by cosmological is this: When I experience the totality of potential and impotential together. Recall how in the Introduction I framed uncertainty as *cosmic* to highlight the inescapable becoming of all things we all are part of. Now, with the *cosmological*, I wish to draw attention to how the cosmic can be apprehended, and to the modes of knowing, sensing and experiencing it.

To do this I draw on curated ideas from Spinoza's philosophy and from pantheism, with the aim of outlining a cosmological orientation with the following characteristics: It should be non-anthropocentric, so to rehabilitate all things, regardless of how their difference is described (living, non-living, organic, inorganic); it should repudiate hierarchies that justify extractive violence on human, non-human, species, ecosystems, environments; it should reject both the overcoding and the resacralization of nature. My cosmological orientation, in short, must assert that potential belongs not to human intention or subjective

[1] Guattari, *Soft Subversions. Texts and interviews 1977–1985*, 138.

authorship but to the incandescence and tremor of matter, prior to the enclosures that constrain beings into form and parse potential into packets. It must show that all things, from the micro to the macro, are modifications of the same (cosmic) substance, whose changes are constant but often imperceptible to human eyes. It must support the conditions of possibility for a round, *whatever* life. Moreover, aiming to steer the *thinkering* reader towards ways of crafting their existence with uncertainty on their side, the cosmological orientation I propose should be read as a 'philosophy for non-philosophers'.[2]

I begin to sketch my proposition drawing on Italian philosopher Emanuele Dattilo's recent reappraisal of pantheism,[3] followed by Spinoza's radical notion of nature. I will conclude with an overview of the mode of thinking the Greeks called *mētis*, which I invoke as the most appropriate disposition to cultivate in order to work with cosmic uncertainty. *Mētis* is the kind of intelligence 'sufficiently quick and supple, wiley and deceitful, to confront the unexpected on every occasion, to counter the most changeable of circumstances and to triumph, in unequal combat, over adversaries who are better equipped for a trial of strength'.[4] This is the meaning of the 'metic wayfinding' of the chapter's title, which takes *mētis* as the mode that ought to 'colour' the cosmological orientation proposed herein.

PANTHEISM: THE SENSIBLE GOD

Proposing pantheism as a component of my cosmological orientation may take some by surprise. After all, pantheism has a reputation for being a 'slippery concept';[5] a 'sexed-up atheism';[6] the 'position nearly everyone wants to avoid'.[7] Pantheism is often belittled condescendingly as a naïve and even absurd new-age belief. It is used as a 'bad word and a tool of automatic rhetorical dismissal',[8] when not as an insult tout court.[9] Such heated reactions are telling. Pantheism is awkward. It does not fit neatly in respectable doctrines or schools of thought.

2 Deleuze, *Negotiations*, 139–40; Marenko and Brassett, 'Introduction', 1–30.

3 Emanuele Dattilo, *Il Dio Sensibile. Saggio sul Panteismo* (Vicenza: Neri Pozza, 2021).

4 Marcel Detienne and Jean-Pierre Vernant, *Cunning Intelligence in Greek Culture and Society* (Hassocks: Harvester Press, 1978), 43. It should be pointed out that the original French title *Les Ruses De L'Intelligence: La Mètis des Grecs* could be translated more accurately as 'The Stratagems of the Intellect'.

5 Clare Carlisle, *Spinoza's Religion. A New Reading of the Ethics* (Princeton: Princeton University Press, 2021), 62.

6 Richard Dawkins, *The God Delusion* (London: Bantam, 2006), 18.

7 Mary-Jane Rubenstein, *Pantheologies. Gods, Worlds, Monsters* (New York: Columbia University Press, 2018), 4.

8 Rubenstein, *Pantheologies*, 4.

9 Ann Thomson, 'Pantheism and Enlightenment. The State of the Debate', in *Pan Tra i Filosofi. Saggi sul Panteismo da Spinoza alla New Age*, ed. Giancarlo Carabelli and Paola Zanardi (Padova: Il Poligrafo, 2010), 7–29. As Thomson points out (ibid., 23) the term 'pantheism' was coined in the late seventeenth century by the English mathematician Joseph Raphson and popularized by Irish writer John Toland, who in his eighteenth-

It is also, to this day, considered a dangerous philosophy (more on this later). But precisely because it claims that all that exists is divine, and that the divine is all there is, indistinguishable from the world; because it refutes the superiority of the human over nature; because it dispenses with the notion of the creator, I believe that a pantheistic cosmology can be a serious contender to the project of scaffolding a deep ecological metaphysics of renewal, reparation and regenesis.

This is why I find Dattilo's book *Il Dio Sensibile. Saggio sul Panteismo* (*The Sensible God. Essay on Pantheism*) so significant. Not only is *The Sensible God* a brilliant eulogy and re-interpretation of pantheism for the present; it is also a compelling argument for reclaiming pantheism's 'corroding power'[10] that has traversed as a subterranean wind the entire history of Western and non-Western thought.[11] Pantheism's key tenet – the coincidence of mind, matter and the divine – is as radical today as it was nine centuries ago, when medieval philosopher and scholar David of Dinant, who Dattilo draws on, lived in France between the twelfth and the thirteenth centuries.[12] Little is known about his life, only that in 1210 his writings were burned by the Church, and he had to go into exile to avoid the same fate. Secondary sources have preserved a fragment from his work titled *Mens Hyle Deus*, which is considered the fundamental text of pantheistic metaphysics.[13] In this fragment, David of Dinant maintains the total coincidence of mind (*Mens*), matter (*Hyle*) and the divine (*Deus*).

But the roots of pantheism are certainly much older. A lineage of pantheistic perspectives is found throughout the history of thought; for example, in the Indian Advaita Vedanta's radical nonduality; in Chinese Taoism (Laozi); in Japanese esoteric Zen schools; in the Greek pre-Socratics; in early modern European thinkers (Giordano Bruno, Nicholas of Cusa, Spinoza);[14] even in

century *Pantheisticon* writes: 'All Things are from the Whole, and the Whole is from all Thing'. John Toland, *Pantheisticon* (New York and London: Garland Publishing [reprint of the 1751 ed.], 1976), 15. Asked to explain his views, Toland is reported to have said, 'the sun is my father, the earth my mother, the world is my country, and all men are my family'. Paul Harrison, *The Elements of Pantheism. Understanding the Divinity in Nature and the Universe* (Shaftesbury; Boston; Melbourne: Element Books, 1999), 31.

10 Dattilo, *Il Dio Sensibile*, 130.

11 There was even a moment, between the third century BC and the fourth century AD, when pantheism seemed on the cusp of going mainstream in both the East and in the West. One can only imagine. Harrison, *The Elements of Pantheism*; Rubenstein, *Pantheologies*.

12 David of Dinant was a cleric, scientist and physician who taught in Paris; he could translate Greek and was influenced by Aristotle at a time when it was forbidden to give lectures on his works on metaphysics and natural philosophy. Dattilo, *Il Dio Sensible*.

13 Discovered in 1933 and published first in 1966, this fragment is the only evidence of David of Dinant's thought otherwise known only through Saint Thomas Aquinas and Albert the Great's confutations of his work during his trial in Paris. Dattilo has curated the recent publication of this fragment. David Di Dinant, *Mente Materia Dio. Mens Hyle Deus* (Genova: Il Melangolo, 2022).

14 Bruno's harmonization of divinity, universe, soul and matter, with its neo-pagan celebration of both pre-Socratic and Neoplatonic traditions, can be considered a predecessor of modern pantheism. Bruno was burned at the stake in 1600 in Rome's Campo de' Fiori. Nicholas of Cusa was suspected of pantheist heresy, although he was never condemned.

twentieth-century process philosophers (Whitehead) and physicists (Bohm). This is not the place to conduct a comparative history of pantheism. Suffice to say that among the pre-Socratic philosophers, there is the idea that all things are made by the same infinite substance with no beginning or end: for Heraclitus, this substance is fire, for Anaximander, it is the indefinite (*apeiron*), for others, the divine breath.[15] Both the Stoics and the Epicureans see the cosmos as a self-generating concatenation of matter, divinity, spirit and nature, only diverging on the quality of movement in the living universe of their respective cosmologies.[16] For others (Plotinus), the universe is made by a divine being (the One) by progressive emanation, like a balloon that inflates and creates 'a reality by its superabundance'.[17] By the mid-nineteenth century, the distinguishing feature of pantheism was the denial of a god separate and distinct from the world, which is the reason why to this day pantheism is considered 'a theological heresy by its critics precisely because it erases or understates the difference between God and creation'.[18] And this is why, as recently as 2010, His Holiness Pope Benedict XVI was at pains to single out the dangers of pantheism in his yearly address.[19] Personally, what may aggravate the supreme pontiff is for me a reason to rejoice. I will not hide the extent to which a catholic interdiction cannot but augment the affinity I feel for pantheism.

[15] Carlo Rovelli, *Anaximander, and the Birth of Science* (London: Riverhead Books, 2023).

[16] Harrison, *The Elements of Pantheism*, 20. The most well-known among the followers of Stoicism, Emperor Marcus Aurelius, writes in his *Meditations* (Book 4, 40): 'Think always of the universe as one living creature, comprising one substance and one soul: how all is absorbed into this one consciousness; how a single impulse governs all its actions; how all things collaborate in all that happens; the very web and mesh of it all'. Marcus Aurelius, *Meditations* (London: Penguin, 2006), 31.

[17] Harrison, *The Elements of Pantheism*, 22.

[18] Carlisle, *Spinoza's Religion*, 63.

[19] Benedict XVI, 'If You Want To Cultivate Peace, Protect Creation', Message of His Holiness Pope Benedict XVI for the Celebration of the World Day of Peace, 1 January 2010. In Section 13 the endorsement of anthropocentrism tilts into the condemnation of pantheism: 'Nor must we forget the very significant fact that many people experience peace and tranquillity, renewal and reinvigoration, when they come into close contact with the beauty and harmony of nature. There exists a certain reciprocity: as we care for creation, we realize that God, through creation, cares for us. On the other hand, a correct understanding of the relationship between man and the environment will not end by absolutizing nature or by considering it more important than the human person. If the Church's magisterium expresses grave misgivings about notions of the environment inspired by ecocentrism and biocentrism, it is because such notions eliminate the difference of identity and worth between the human person and other living things. In the name of a supposedly egalitarian vision of the "dignity" of all living creatures, such notions end up abolishing the distinctiveness and superior role of human beings. They also open the way to a new pantheism tinged with neo-paganism, which would see the source of man's salvation in nature alone, understood in purely naturalistic terms.'

WHY PANTHEISM MATTERS

A pantheistic universe is a universe of pure immanence with no external creator.[20] It is a universe where everything fully coincides with the divine. Put differently, the divine *is* all that exists, and all that exists *is* divine. What is meant by the 'divine' here is not a personified deity, a representation or a manifestation. Rather, it is the world as a *sensible totality* in its uncertain and incandescent unfolding. Every thing and every body participates in this divine that has no demands, no salvation mission, no prescription, no judgment, no teleology.

Pantheism offers a non-binary perspective through which I can radically rethink the relationship between mind and matter, sensible and intelligible, cause and effect. By posing the coincidence of mind and matter, pantheism tells me that the mind is not just thought, cognition, brain or language; that matter is not some sort of inert and malleable stuff waiting for an input (my input, a designer's input) to be turned into something meaningful. There is no passive, unformed matter. There is only matter with different degrees of organization and complexity. Likewise, there are no pre-existing ideas or forms waiting to be embedded. There are no blueprints. Put differently, pantheism shows that *matter thinks* and *thought materializes*. Incessantly.

On this standpoint, pantheism exposes the fallacy of elevating mind over matter; of mistaking the power of the mind for an imperative, a manoeuvre that raises the intelligible before the sensible, and essence before existence. Instead, pantheism proposes a radical nonduality where what I call 'mind' and what I call 'matter' fully coincide. Through this coincidence, pantheism breaks with instrumental causality. In reclaiming material cause against efficient cause, pantheism also poses the coincidence of creator and created, of being and acting. Gaps are recomposed. Cause coincides with the caused. Becoming *is* being. Gone is the original myth that explains how the cosmos came to be (cosmogenesis) by way of a causal relationship between ideas (first) and world (after). Instead, pantheism sees creation as an immanent process. Cosmogenesis is rewritten as morphogenesis. Matter is self-sufficient. There is no originary model. There is no blueprint.

An important implication of pantheism, and one of its strongest appeals, is that it is also a celebration of freedom from authoritarian, hierarchical thinking, exemplified by organized religion. Rather crudely put, the history of religion can be read as the history of how the divine that pervades everything is captured and split from the totality and turned into the 'sacred'. But the sacred, as it is promoted and institutionalized by organized religion, is the opposite of the divine. By separating my (divine) experience of the world, inherently 'round', into distinct segments, the divine is excised, the knowing is separated from the known. A 'Creator' or 'Maker' is invented. Thus, by reclaiming the full experi-

[20] Note the difference between 'pantheism' and 'panentheism': the former refuses any distinction between God and creation, the latter affirms it by stating that whatever exists, is *in* God, and that God is both beyond everything and present everywhere.

ence of the divine as the plenitude of my encounter with the world, pantheism refutes one of the founding ideas of Western thought: the story of creation. This is important for two reasons. First, it is a critique of the authorial position in design (and of the notion of blueprint). Second, it brings pantheism closer to Spinoza, whose key ideas concerning nature the chapter will discuss below. Before that, however, I will explain why stories of creation must be resisted.

AGAINST CREATION

Traditional creation myths tell the story of creation (including form-making) by assuming a gap between the matter of thought (*intelligible* matter, or potential) and the matter of things (*sensible* matter, or real). The image that renders well the classic story of creation is the seed placed into receiving matter, as if matter always needed an idea to be 'activated'.

Spinoza understood this and was vehemently against it. The story of creation, he says, is a superstition that humans believe in, according to which ideas are something that need execution. The belief that ideas come before execution is a powerful dogma, which constrains and hierarchizes the relationship between intelligible matter (potential) and sensible matter (real), as if the real was always situated 'downstream' in relation to a pre-existent idea. It is a double mystification: a mystification of knowledge (what 'should be' is always present as a weight and as something separate from the existent); and a mystification of potential (the potential of what exists is eroded and ultimately lost). It is according to this logic that Western thought poses something passive (*ob-ject*) in front of something active (*sub-ject*).

But my experience in, and of, the world tells me a different story. Every act is simultaneously an act of touching and being touched, of encountering and being 'encountered'. I am made in and through my encounters with the world, renewed each and every instant. Pantheism expresses precisely this formidable ethical proposition. I cannot separate the *what* from the *how*. To reiterate this point: By reclaiming the material nature of thought, pantheism breaks the causal relation between the intelligible and the sensible. It breaks the instrumental logic that sees ideas come 'before' action, as something that must be executed, obeyed or turned into normative prescription, rules and judgements. It breaks with the blueprint.

SPINOZA: THE RADICAL THE PLANET NEEDS

Spinoza's radical idea, which he re-introduced in modern thought and was the cause of his excommunication from Amsterdam's Jewish community in 1656, is that nature is a self-generating force. Not something to admire, tame or be afraid of, nature is what *everything is already*. Nature is its own cause perfectly distributed. There is nothing outside it. With his signature phrases, *Deus Sive Natura* – God or nature, expressing the idea that the divine coincides with nature, and *natura causa sui*, expressing the idea that nature is its own cause – Spinoza revolutionizes how the physical world is conceptualized. By stating that everything that exists is a modification of the same 'single substance', self-generating production with no beginning or end, Spinoza tells us that *we* are *nature* and that *nature* is *ourselves*.[21] He unlocks a new way of seeing reality, the cosmos, life itself. As architect Gökham Kodalak puts it, 'Spinoza's philosophy overlaps becoming one of the many with becoming many of the one'.[22] A single ocean, and a thousand waves. A continuum of infinite potentials and unique manifestations. Rejecting any transcendence, any idealism, any hierarchy in favour of pure immanence, Spinoza's conception is pan-sensible. Each modality has an equal capacity of being alive and being capable of modification, that is, to affect and be affected according to different degrees of speed and slowness.

His famous assertion that 'all things, although in diverse grades, are animate'[23] tells me in no ambiguous terms that the animation of *all* things exists and occurs by degrees.[24] In other words, while equal does not mean the same, a certain awareness is present everywhere and in everything.[25] From this standpoint, whatever it is that animates things, it is not agency, intentionality or innate property. It is rather a self-generating stream of intensities traversing matter and producing a multiplicity of encounters, collisions and combinations. It is this flow of matter-energy that keeps on engendering the world. Based on this 'single substance', Spinoza proposes a radical nonduality that contests the separation of matter and thought, of body and mind. Because all that exists is a modification and expression of the same substance, with no beginning or end, the eternal nature of things is to have no aim, no intention, no teleology. There is no acting distinct from being.

Was Spinoza a pantheist? Deleuze seems to have thought so when in his luminous book *Spinoza. Practical Philosophy* he wrote: 'the ethics demonstrates a substantial identity [between God and Nature] based on the oneness of substance (pantheism)'.[26] Regardless of whether he may be called a pantheist or not, Spinoza's thought offers such an uncompromising and provocative way of seeing reality, understanding life and perceiving the cosmos that it remains revolutionary to this day.[27] Spinoza is not just the first ethico-onto-epistemologist. He is the radical thinker the planet needs.

21 Warren Montag and Ted Stolze eds, *The New Spinoza* (Minneapolis and London: University of Minnesota Press, 1997).

22 Gökham Kodalak, 'Spinoza and Architecture: The Air of the Future', *Log* 49 (2020): 125.

23 Spinoza, *Ethics* II (London: Everyman, 1993), 13.

24 Alfred N. Whitehead, *Science and the Modern World* (Cambridge: Cambridge University Press, 2011), 69.

25 See 'quantum potential' (also called 'quantum choice') in neurons. Arianne Conty, 'Panpsychism. A Response to the Anthropocene Age', *The Journal of Speculative Philosophy* 35, no. 1 (2021): 27–49, 31.

26 Deleuze, *Spinoza*, 110.

27 In fact, Spinoza's *herem* (excommunication) was never rescinded. In 2021 Yitzhak Melamed, Johns Hopkins University professor and Spinoza expert, was banned from Amsterdam's historic Portuguese Synagogue, which he requested to visit during the making of the documentary '6 Reasons for the Excommunication of the Philosopher', directed by David Ofek, 2022. I am grateful to Roy Bendor for bringing this to my attention. https://go2films.com/films/spinoza-6-reasons-for-the-excommunication-of-the-philosopher/.

But Spinoza was also a maker. Deleuze calls him 'the philosopher craftsman'[28] because he supported himself by grinding lenses.[29] I imagine the assemblage of his body, bent on polishing very small glasses; his tools, a plain lathe with a spinning grinding cup; his materials, glass and light and patience. I speculate on how this assemblage informed his thinking: slowly grinding lenses while slowly grinding concepts. At risk of romanticizing him, I am drawn to speculate on the parallel between his craft and his metaphysical inquiry. It is through this parallel that Spinoza teaches me that the relation between *how* I am, *how* I know and *how* I live is the true basis of an ethical knowledge. That there is no acting distinct from being.

Spinoza's lesson (one of many) is found in how ethics can be understood, not as a set of universal rules to obey but as a practical way of inhabiting the world.[30] Like a compass offering information and steering on the routes I can choose from, ethical wisdom concerns how I navigate the complexity of the encounters I enter into and how I select those encounters that will increase my capacities and augment my power to exist.[31] With Spinoza, ethics goes beyond 'agency', 'responsibility' or 'accountability', beyond outcomes or abstract principles, to become my capacity to understand *what moves* me – which forces, which intensities, which affects. Am I moved by plenitude? By depletion? Can I sense which affects are traversing me? Where do my gestures come from? Do they originate from lack, from abundance, from fear, from hope? What is it that moves me, really?[32]

Movement traverses each and every body that exists – not just living things, but everything that has a sensible reality, including thought and mind. Spinoza calls *conatus* this cosmic tremor, this 'moving to' that traverses everything. Often explained as 'the striving to persevere in one's existence', *conatus* is perhaps more correctly described as a 'tension toward'.[33] It is because of this 'tension

[28] Deleuze, *Spinoza*, 7. For an important, if under-analysed, appraisal of Spinoza from the perspective of design practice, in particular architecture, see Peg Rawes, 'Spinoza's Geometric Ecologies', *Interstices: Journal of Architecture and Related Arts* 13, no. 13 (2012): 60–70; Kodalak, 'Spinoza and Architecture'.

[29] Especially lenses for microscopes and telescopes, such as those used by his contemporaries Hudde, Van Leeuwenhoek, Swammerdam, and Huyghens. Spinoza was highly renowned for his craft. Leibniz describes him as 'an outstanding optician, a maker of rather famous peep-tubes'. Steven Nadler, *Spinoza. A Life* (Cambridge: Cambridge University Press, 1999), 184.

[30] On the etymology of the word ethics, from the Greek *ethos*, meaning 'habitual character and disposition; habit, custom; dwelling' and how this connects to bodily disposition, habitat in the sense of my place in the world and my habitual way of life, see Rosalyn Diprose, *The Bodies of Women. Ethics, Embodiment and Sexual Difference* (London and New York: Routledge, 1994).

[31] Moira Gatens and Genevieve Lloyd, *Collective Imaginings. Spinoza, Past and Present* (London and New York: Routledge, 1999).

[32] Emanuele Dattilo, *La Vita Che Vive* (Vicenza: Neri Pozza, 2022).

[33] *Conatus* is commonly translated as effort, striving or endeavour, but these are slightly imprecise. *Conatus* is not strenuous effort, has nothing to do with lack, and is definitely not resilience. Likewise, it is not the fatigue of having to do something by necessity, yet it is not absolute freedom either. Both notions, the slavery of need, and the freedom of sovereignty, are for Spinoza superstitions.

toward' that at the cosmic level, everything vibrates.[34] This tremor, whether I perceive it or not, is the profound, irrepressible and expansive *desire to continue* that manifests itself. It is what sustains life – organic and inorganic – in all its indifferent exuberance and exuberant indifference.

A COSMOLOGICAL ORIENTATION

To test some of the ideas discussed so far in this chapter and to begin to put into practice the cosmological orientation I propose, I now ask: Can I imagine that my mind is not separate from the world, nor my experience given in discrete packets? That the object of my senses is the same as the object of my mind? That 'my' faculty of thinking, what I consider my most personal capacity, is not an individual faculty I own, but an atmosphere I am in? Can I imagine that all I perceive, sense, think is already divine?

To answer these questions, I enlist architecture critic Sanford Kwinter, who writes:

> We typically imagine that we 'think' and 'feel' and 'perceive,' as if we were both subject and origin of the experiential events that make up our lives, but in fact what thinks, feels, and perceives is a substance that is at once 'us' and is fully embedded in the world, a 'sensitive matter' (to quote Denis Diderot) that sends and receives to and from the ambient realm beyond our strict physical boundaries.[35]

On this basis, the thought experiment is this: Let us imagine that mind and matter are not separate, but that they coincide. That the matter of thought (*intelligible* matter, or potential) and the matter of things (*sensible* matter, or the real) are the same substance. Following Dattilo, another way of saying this is to say that the 'sensitive matter' (matter that 'senses') of the quotation above is *noetic* matter (matter that 'thinks').[36]

[34] Daniel Odier, *Yoga Spandakarika. The Sacred Texts at the Origins of Tantra* (Rochester, Vt.: Inner Traditions, 2004); Daniel Odier, *Desire. The Tantric Path to Awakening* (Rochester, Vt.: Inner Traditions, 2001).

[35] Sanford Kwinter, 'A Sensitive Matter. An Interview with Sanford Kwinter', *Scapegoat* 11 (2019): 67. Famously, Diderot introduces sensibility as a general property of matter that 'communicates itself just as motion does' (Denis Diderot, *Rameau's Nephew and Other Works* [Indianapolis and New York: Bobbs-Merrill, 1964], 111) in his 1769 speculative dialogue *Le Rêve de D'Alembert*, where the character D'Alembert (a partisan of substance dualism) challenges the character Diderot (a materialist, of course) to explain consciousness and thought. Diderot's originality is in collapsing any distinction (popular at the time) between different degrees of material sensitivity, for example the difference between irritability and sensitivity. Diderot argues that matter itself senses, and that sensibility is a general property of matter. For a general account of eighteenth-century debates on vitalism see Charles T. Wolfe, 'Sensibility as Vital Force or as Property of Matter in Mid-Eighteenth-century Debates', in *The Discourse of Sensibility. The Knowing Body in the Enlightenment*, ed. Henry Martyn Lloyd (Cham: Springer, 2013), 147–70.

[36] From the Greek *noesis*, concerning the intellect.

To reiterate this point: Noetic matter is matter that affords all thinking; it is all that can be thought. It is the totality of the thinkable. It is, in other words, the intelligibility of all things which concerns the potential nature of thinking: thinking's infinite 'thinkability'.[37] But I must be careful here. Noetic matter is not the sum of all the forms that I anticipate matter could potentially generate. To think this would imply to pre-ordain what matter is capable of (the blueprint, again). Rather, noetic matter is all that *may be* thinkable. It is a virtual ocean of potential matter of thought, of the intelligible *prior to* differentiation.[38]

Circling back to Kwinter's quotation above, this is why to say 'I have' a mind is both inadequate and incorrect. I do not *have* a mind; I *am in* the mind.[39] The mind is not something within me as a 'privileged' human. Mind is in all things; it extends beyond brain, knowledge and cognition, beyond (or below) consciousness and the self.[40] The whole world is sensible, thus intelligible – full of potential (and impotentiality). Its material forms are the intelligible making itself sensible. Matter, in its immediate availability and presence, is potential, and potential is matter.

This is a crucial insight. Pantheism counteracts the conventional, ingrained belief that I am a thinking subject; that I have a mind inside my brain; that I possess thoughts lodged in my head as projects, propositions and intentions to accomplish. Instead, the act of thinking is no longer a way to say 'I', to express my own conscience and to fixate on self-consciousness. It becomes an ecstatic exercise, an exhortation to become world (and sky, and ocean). I see this as an exit stratagem to access my own divinity through the roundness and the plenitude of it all. As such it requires a specific disposition, which I locate in the kind of intelligence the Greeks called *mētis*.

METIC INTELLIGENCE

In their seminal study *Cunning Intelligence in Greek Culture and Society*, Marcel Detienne and Jean-Pierre Vernant write that *mētis* implies

37 Dattilo warns us that between the notion of noetic matter and its comprehension, there is the same gap that there is between the word 'darkness' and our experience of darkness.

38 Potential is not something I can avail myself of; it is not something that I can simply choose to actuate. I am not asked to choose from a deck of cards spread in front of me, Dattilo cautions. The cards are self-selecting; there is no hand-picking them, no volition, nor intention. Potential remains beyond the ponderable.

39 Likewise, I do not 'have' ideas, I 'am' ideas. In his work on the ecological approach to perception, Kwinter mentions perceptual psychologist James Jerome Gibson who advised us to 'ask not what's inside our head, but rather what our head is inside of'. Sanford Kwinter, 'Headspace', *Frida Escobedo. Serpentine Pavillion 2018*, Catalogue (London Serpentine Galleries: Koenig Books, 2018), 75.

40 In her famous poem n. 632, American poet Emily Dickinson writes: 'The Brain – is wider than the Sky – For – put them side by side – The one the other will contain – With ease – and you – beside – The Brain is deeper than the sea – For – hold them – Blue to Blue – The one the other will absorb – As sponges – Buckets – do – The Brain is just the weight of God – For – Heft them – Pound for Pound – And they will differ – if they do – As Syllable from Sound – '. Emily Dickinson, *The Complete Poems* (London: Faber and Faber, 2016), 312.

> A complex but very coherent body of mental attitudes and intellectual behaviour which combine flair, wisdom, forethought, subtlety of mind, deception, resourcefulness, vigilance, opportunism, various skills and experience acquired over the years. It is applied to situations which are transient, shifting, disconcerting and ambiguous, situations which do not lend themselves to precise measurement, exact calculation of rigorous logic.[41]

Mētis is the mindset I need to cultivate if I want to grasp and work with uncertainty. It is the kind of astute, protean and pragmatic thinking through which I become alert to the unpredictability of events, I master the resourcefulness to respond to them, and I learn how to quickly seize opportunities. It is the practical intelligence of the craftsperson, of those who sense how things are turning and craft their deliberations accordingly, of those who know which stratagems need devising.[42] It also possesses anticipatory value as it anchors the mind while looking 'beyond the immediate present and foresee a more or less wide slice of the future'.[43]

Because *mētis* is both manipulation of what happens and flexibility to adapt to changes, it tends to be interpreted as trickery and deviousness.[44] In fact, the words used in English to translate *mētis* tend to have a pejorative connotation, such as wily, deceiving, canny, tricky.[45] That the English language has no conceptual equivalent for *mētis* is telling of how limited our cultural vocabulary is for grasping propensities and positively adapting to changing situations.

To scaffold my cosmological argument, I interpret *mētis* as an orientation to how things move, either in imperceptible instances too short to be observed – 'a space of time so brief that it is like a hair too short to be cut';[46] or so fast that the contours of things become undetectable, like the skin patterns of zebras

41 Detienne and Vernant, *Cunning Intelligence in Greek Culture and Society*, 3.

42 The Greeks applied *mētis* to a wide range of activities and practices that today would unlikely be clustered together: 'the art of the winnower, of the weaver or the carpenter, the skill of the sailor, the flair of the politician, the experienced glance of the doctor, the deceits of a character like Ulysses, the construction of enigmas and the solving of riddles, the rhetorical illusions of the Sophists'. Richard Klein, 'The Mētis of Centaurs', *Diacritics* 16, no. 2 (1986): 2.

43 Ibid., 15.

44 No wonder the epitome of *mētis* is Odysseus, an expert in tricks of all sorts, fast thinking to the point of vibrating with multicoloured iridescence. That is why Homer describes him as *pokolometis* [from *poikolos* = dappled, mottled, glittering.] This term refers 'to the sheen of a material or the glittering of a weapon, the dappled hide of a fawn, or the shining back of a snake mottled with darker patches. This many-coloured sheen or complex of appearances produces an effect of iridescence, shimmering, an interplay of reflections which the Greeks perceived as the ceaseless vibration of light' (Detienne and Vernant, *Cunning Intelligence in Greek Culture and Society*, 18). 'Shimmering sheen and shifting movement are so much a part of the nature of *mētis* that when the epithet *poikolos* is applied to an individual it is enough to indicate that he is a wiley one, a man of cunning, full of inventive ploys and tricks of every kind'. Ibid., 19.

45 Lisa Raphals, *Knowing Words. Wisdom and Cunning in the Classical Traditions of China and Greece* (Ithaca and London: Cornell University Press, 1992).

46 Detienne and Vernant, *Cunning Intelligence in Greek Culture and Society*, 309.

in a herd. It is not a coincidence that *mētis* is also about trap-making and the hunting techniques of animals, like the octopus and the fox, which most exquisitely embody *mētis* – the former via camouflaging, the latter by making itself elusive.[47] It is through these same techniques that the fisherman hunts too.[48] The octopus in particular is *mētis* personified, her shapeshifting symbolizing the un-seizability that comes from polymorphy. By enveloping her enemies in a dark cloud of ink that obscures vision she gains an escape route. She is the master of the blur as an exit stratagem.[49]

In this sense *mētis* suggests a way to gain mastery 'where there are no ready-made rules for success, no established methods, but where each new trial demands the invention of new ploys, the discovery of a way out that is hidden';[50] a way of grasping propensities where others see only a blur;[51] a way of turning the blur into an ally.

CONCLUSION

The cosmological orientation proposed by this chapter gathers inspiration from key ideas drawn on Spinoza and on Dattilo's re-interpretation of pantheism. I have enlisted the support of *mētis* to present my cosmological orientation.

The resulting 'metic wayfinding' is a way of *designing encounters* in situations that are shifting, uncertain and potentially ambiguous, situations to which rigorous logic or calculation may not be applied successfully. Metic wayfinding is a way of working in asymmetrical situations where things can change rapidly and are unknown. A metic wayfinding is a vehicle to learn how to understand the propensity of things, to act in alliance with the evolution of circumstances and

47 Trap-making takes us back to *technē* as an art of deception (Ch. 1) and design as a crafty plot. See Vilem Flusser, *The Shape of Things. A Philosophy of Design* (London: Reaktion Books, 1999).

48 'There is no difference in kind between the mētis of the fox and the cuttle-fish and that of the fisherman. The only way to triumph over an adversary endowed with mētis is to turn its own weapons against it: the fisherman's "cloud" is the unyielding answer to the "cloud" of the cuttle-fish. It is only by himself becoming, by means of his net, a bond and a circle, by himself becoming deep night, endless aporia, and elusive shape, that the man of mētis can triumph over the most cunning species in the animal world' (Detienne and Vernant, *Cunning Intelligence in Greek Culture and Society*, 42).

49 In its *Theognidea*, a collection of almost 1400 lines ascribed to him, Greek lyrical poet Theognis of Megara (mid-sixth century BC) writes [lines 213–18]: 'My heart, display toward all your friends a changeful character,
Adding into it the disposition that each one has. Adopt the disposition of the octopus, crafty in its convolutions, which takes on
The appearance of whatever rock it has dealings with.
At one moment follow along this way, but at the next change the colour of your skin:
You can be sure that cleverness proves better than inflexibility.'

50 Detienne and Vernant, *Cunning Intelligence in Greek Culture and Society*, 21.

51 Jullien, *The Propensity of Things*.

not against them without using unnecessary force, or a preordained blueprint. Referring to Spinoza's main work (*Ethics*), Deleuze points out that 'the art of the Ethics itself' is indeed the art of 'organising good encounters, composing actual relations, forming powers, experimenting'.[52] Experimentation is crucial because, as mentioned previously, I do not know in advance what my body can do – which is another key lesson from Spinoza. Chapter 6 will discuss not-knowing as an integral part of the process of cultivating a full, round life. For now, I can simply say that living with uncertainty *is* the art of living in plenitude, and a metic wayfinding is central to the project of reclaiming the uncertain and the unknown.

I conclude by recalling that in Greek mythology, Metis, the daughter of the Titan Oceanus, is Zeus' first wife. After hearing the prophecy that Metis would have a child mightier than himself, Zeus swallowed her while she was pregnant (and disguised as a fly). She reacted by building a furnace inside Zeus' body and her child (Athena) burst forth through Zeus' head. By swallowing Metis, Zeus assimilates her cunning, takes possession of the unknown and, by embodying her, gains control over unpredictability, extending his sovereignty to 'chancey ventures or surprises'.[53] Uncertainty is erased. Ever since:

> not a single cunning trick can be plotted in the universe without first passing through his mind ... nothing can surprise him, cheat his vigilance or frustrate his designs. Thanks to the metis within him Zeus is now forewarned of everything, whether good or bad, that is in store for him. For him there is no gap between a plan and its fulfilment such as enables the unexpected to intervene in the lives of other gods and mortals.[54]

Metis must be called upon to reclaim uncertainty and to resist Zeus' black overseeing glassy eye. A metic wayfinding is what I need to work with uncertainty. And it is to irrevocable, *oceanic uncertainty* that I must turn now.

[52] Deleuze, *Spinoza*, 119. Deleuze and Guattari define a body by its *longitude* (its relations of movement and rest, speed and slowness) and *latitude* (the intensive affects it is capable of). Deleuze and Guattari, *A Thousand Plateaus*, 260.

[53] Detienne and Vernant, *Cunning Intelligence in Greek Culture and Society*, 305.

[54] Ibid., 14.

5 Oceanic Uncertainty

Instead of transcending perspectives, you become skilled at never getting stuck in one. Blur becomes your *métier*.
BARRY ALLEN[1]

(UN)SETTING UNCERTAINTY

With this chapter, I go back to the beginning of the book and to the wager I raise in the Introduction: That an *allyship with uncertainty is not only possible but necessary*. This chapter addresses my wager by focusing on uncertainty in itself and by finally asking: What is uncertainty, really?

Uncertainty is, in the simplest terms, when I do not know what might or might not happen. Uncertainty signals a state, variedly described as ambiguous, indeterminate, vague, blurry, that may provoke anxiety and paralyze action but also produce bursts of creativity and disclose unexpected solutions to problems. Yes, uncertainty has a bad reputation. It is often seen as something to be wary of, to wish away or, at least, to try to manage and contain. While I do not deny that uncertainty can be debilitating, destabilizing and disempowering, I want to make a case for living with and in uncertainty as the route to achieving a fuller, rounder life.

To say that uncertainty concerns limited knowledge or inadequate understanding is only half of the story. Uncertainty is not only epistemic. Its multifaceted nature has deeper roots. Uncertainty is woven through the very fabric of the world. It is *the* very fabric of the world. Uncertainty is inescapable. It is oceanic. It is cosmic. Thus, it demands a counter-metaphysics of how it should be inhabited, seriously, radically, uncompromisingly, dangerously even.

[1] Barry Allen, 'The Cloud of Knowing. Blurring the Difference with China'. Symposium: Fuzzy Studies, part 1. *Common Knowledge* 17, no. 3 (2011): 458.

Starting from this premise, this chapter looks at images, metaphors and assumptions around uncertainty; it examines what distinguishes uncertainty from risk; it tackles the historical development of determinism, and concludes by considering Heisenberg's principle and the quantum discovery of uncertainty as foundational of the post-Newtonian world. The chapter uses this constellation to sketch a counter-metaphysics of uncertainty. My choice of describing uncertainty as *oceanic* assists me in grasping its multifaceted, vast nature and steers me to imagine an 'otherwise' of uncertainty without freezing its flow. This is where other kinds of knowledge – atmospheric, intuitive, cunning, sublunary, sideral, pan-sensible – can pool, pivot and unfold. I see this space shaped like a pause, where the unknown is a channel for the cultivation of hesitation; where ambiguity is an advantage; where not knowing is nourishment. This is the space of *maybe*s evoked by the title of the book.

THE VERTIGO OF UNCERTAINTY

But what is uncertainty, exactly? Like many other difficult-to-define notions, uncertainty is socially and culturally constructed. It is a subjective and relational affair. The same event may be interpreted as uncertain (or not) depending on the cause attributed to it. How I cope with, and react to, uncertainty is driven by a mix of personal feelings, collective beliefs, cultural expectations, affective scripts and socio-economical contexts. My expectations play a part in how I perceive and respond to uncertainty because they inform my disposition (how I prepare for uncertainty), which in turn shapes my attitude to unknown futures (how I will react to it).

Furthermore, ideas around uncertainty and how to deal with it tend to be subject-specific and to differ across disciplines, fields and sectors. For instance, the way artists may appropriate uncertainty as a source of 'chance encounters' differs from how uncertainty is viewed by statisticians and policymakers as 'risk management', or by scientists as 'ambiguity'. While these are crude generalizations, they point to a wide variety of interpretations.

So, what is uncertainty? On an immediate level, uncertainty is the by-product of imperfect information, when information is incomplete and asymmetrical, when I do not know whether something is true or false, when I know that I do not know enough. But, if I dig deeper, uncertainty is the unavoidable condition of existing in a world that is mutable, kaleidoscopic, stratified, shimmering and never 'done'. Uncertainty signals the unpredictability of tomorrow, the unknowability of the future. It is also synonymous with everything that makes life unstable and precarious – events and contingencies beyond my control.

How do I relate to uncertainty? What is my first, instinctive reaction? Do I even have one? Probably like you, I respond to uncertainty through a heady mix of anxiety and curiosity, apprehension and logic, fatalism and anger, puzzlement and powerlessness, but also, and here it is where things become interesting, with longing, desire, wonderment, courage and a readiness to yielding. My own experience of uncertainty tells me that if I try to control it not only am I likely to exacerbate it, but I may lose what uncertainty has to offer, that is, the richness of potential. Potential is what may or may not happen. It is also what I do not know in advance.

How do I describe uncertainty? Which words, images and metaphors am I drawn to? Matters of language are not secondary. The images I use to think with create worlds. They are the figurations that scaffold my constructed realities. They give tangible orientation to how the semiotic-material knots that stitch realities and worlds together come to be realized. They are also enactors of power. Thus, the metaphors I use to describe uncertainty shape how I anticipate the future. I hear uncertainty described as void, lack, or deficiency (of information, knowledge, certainties); as 'blindness', 'obstructed vision' or as a 'black hole'; as 'fog' or 'blur'. Not surprisingly, many of these expressions signal the lack of something (not enough knowledge or information), or powerlessness (inability to decide, to make a move, to choose) or apprehension (anxiety, fear, paralysis). Uncertainty is all these things, but not only. The richer aspects of uncertainty are there too, lurking. Borrowing Michael Smithson's apposite expression, uncertainty is an 'ocean' of infinite unknowability within which knowledge becomes an 'island'.[2] It is an ocean of possibilities where my capacity to choose floats. Or else said, it is the oceanic vastity of uncertainty that propels my agency. My freedom is a by-product of uncertainty. One cannot exist without the other.

Furthermore, to pose uncertainty as an oceanic space allows me to see it not only as a territory to inhabit, a zone to 'enter' and dwell in, but also in its temporal connotations as a pause, interval and recess. Put differently, my figuration wants to evoke a 'taking' space, 'making' space, 'occupying' space, which I also configure as a 'taking' time, 'making' time, 'occupying' time. In this space, hesitation, doubt, dithering, ambiguity, vagueness, opacity circulate as those modes of knowing and un-knowing whose liminality introduces stuttering temporalities.[3] I am interested in the value that uncertainty brings to the production of knowledge, and in how to capitalize on the not-knowing inherent in it. I wonder how this not-knowing can be understood not as lack, or inadequacy, but as pivotal to a specific kind of uncertainty-driven knowledge-making, with uncertainty as a counter-epistemic engine too. The questions, therefore, are: How do I positively cultivate this space of uncertainty and its unknowability?

[2] Michael Smithson, 'The Many Faces and Masks of Uncertainty', in *Uncertainty and Risk. Multidisciplinary Perspectives*, ed. Gabriele Bammer and Michael Smithson (London: Earthscan, 2008), 13–25.

[3] My list echoes cultural theorist Steven Connor's 'knowledge-feeling' list that includes 'irritation, rage, envy, lust, misery, boredom and melancholy just as much as satisfaction, assurance, excitement and triumph' (Steven Connor, *The Madness of Knowledge. On Wisdom, Ignorance and Fantasies of Knowing* [London: Reaktion, 2021], 14). He uses the term 'epistemopathy' to describe this 'production and development of complex states of feeling and imaginative projection in relation to knowledge', in other words, how I feel about what I know and what I do not know. Ibid., 10.

What are the most efficacious routes to devise to inhabit uncertainty and its unknowability without capturing and constraining its potential?

To reiterate this point: A mode of knowing driven by uncertainty 'takes' space and 'takes' time. It forces a pause. Uncertain situations ask me to ponder, reflect, assess. Sometimes the pause is experienced as inability to decide – whether for lack of, or asymmetrical access to, information. Sometimes, it is a paralysis of initiative and agency. Sometimes it is the lingering over a precipice. No matter how they manifest themselves, instances of uncertainty force me to press pause, and pressing pause can become an active stance against acceleration. This is important to reclaim uncertainty's potential as a radical gesture without falling into endorsing uncertainty as an asset for the optimization of creativity, of which more shortly.

Gestures that introduce the grain of temporality are like the *sabots* thrown by eighteenth-century weavers into the industrial looms. They reclaim time. They create time. And while the *saboteurs* were revolting against the automation that was pushing labourers to destitution, what I evoke here is a gesture whose purpose is to claw back recess from the relentless capture of potential *we* are all subjected to.[4] This stand-making against a seamless, friction-less world by means of reclaiming incertitude and hesitation as positive affects is a way of instantiating a pause within the instantaneous; of troubling immediacy and through this disturbance regain slowness; of allowing a crack to materialize between what I type in the search box and the reply. This is why I pose the vertigo of hesitation as a space to nurture. It is in this space where things may (or may not) happen.

UNCERTAINTY IS CREATIVE (AND BLEAK)

That uncertainty has the power to fuel and galvanize action by expanding the range of unthought-of connections should be familiar to anyone who has ever engaged in creative pursuits based on chance encounters – be they with ideas, images, materials, people, events. Artists have long known how to foster uncertainty in order to increase their creative chances, for example by inserting asymmetries in highly predictable situations or by shaking up routines in order to disrupt expectations and formalized behaviours. By opening up to chance, uncertainty is poised to become a collaborator in creative processes, like in the unexpected encounters among *objets trouvés*, collage-making and *cadavre exquis* the Surrealists were so fond of; or in Freudian psychoanalysis's penchant for free association and dream exploration; or in Leonardo da Vinci's counsel to stare at a peeling wall, a fire, or the clouds to 'find really marvellous ideas'. It is worth quoting at length from the entry in his diary where Leonardo notes:

[4] I am aware of the difficulty in using 'we' at any point in the text. I believe however that in this circumstance it is justified. No person, no body, no thing on the planet can be said to go untouched by planetary computation and unsubjected to processes of extraction of potential directly or indirectly, as user or abuser.

> Look at walls splashed with a number of stains, or stones of various mixed colours. If you have to invent some scene, you can see there resemblances to a number of landscapes, adorned with mountains, rivers, rocks, trees, great plains, valleys and hills, in various ways. Also, you can see various battles, and lively postures of strange figures, expressions on faces, costumes and an infinite number of things, which you can reduce to good integrated form. This happens on such walls and varicoloured stones, (which act) like the sound of bells, in whose pealing you can find every name and word that you can imagine. Do not despise my opinion, when I remind you that it should not be hard for you to stop sometimes and look into the stains of walls, or ashes of a fire, or clouds, or mud or like places, in which, if you consider them well, you may find really marvellous ideas. The mind of the painter is stimulated to new discoveries, the composition of battles of animals and men, various compositions of landscapes and monstrous things, such as devils and similar things, which may bring you honour, because *by indistinct things the mind is stimulated to new inventions.*[5]

While examples such as these illustrate the firm connection between uncertainty and creativity, they do not deflect, however, from a fundamental issue: that uncertainty is also used as a reservoir of potential to be extracted, exploited and monetized. The rhetoric of 'embracing uncertainty' to 'unlock potential' is a neoliberal mantra. So are strategies that engineer uncertainty as the Trojan horse that fire starts 'innovation' and aggressively attempts to trigger growth by choreographing controlled serendipity.[6]

This is another important wager. How do I de-link uncertainty's potential from the neoliberal capture that seizes, squeezes, swallows and spews uncertainty as an instrument for productivity and optimization? The exploitation of uncertainty's potential for 'creative' purposes is also where the bleak side of uncertainty is exposed, a festering wound cannibalizing the very thing that gives it nourishment. The planetary production of un-liveable, catastrophic precariousness – when uncertainty is artificially enforced by design – must be resisted. The swelling of the populations (human and nonhuman) and ecosystems (social, geo-political, biological) trapped in this kind of uncertainty urgently calls for it.

I have discussed resistance at length in Chapter 3, which foregrounded the necessity to switch to the impotential in conceptualizing uncertainty away from mechanisms of capture. As Chapter 6 will articulate, this calls for the design of stratagems to counteract the capture of potential that formats a life to its bare levels, erodes its richness, thins out its pulsating roundness. Here is a design brief if I ever see one.

5 Quoted in Sasha Grishin, *Uncertainty as a Creative Force in Visual Art* (London: Routledge, 2008), 115 (emphasis added).

6 Sebastian Olma, *In Defence of Serendipity. For a Radical Politics of Innovation* (London: Penguin Random House, 2016).

UNCERTAINTY IS *META*

Uncertainty is always *meta*.[7] The more I try to define it, the more slippery it becomes. Even though many similar terms can be used to describe uncertainty, significant distinctions exist: *uncertainty* suggests a lack or asymmetry of information; *vagueness* is when the exact meaning of something cannot be determined and it is not possible to distinguish between the unknowable and the unknown; *ambiguity* is when more than one meaning can be assigned to something, resulting in competing meanings; *indeterminacy* (or indeterminism) is the ontological phenomenon concerning states that are irreducibly indeterminate in themselves, independently from an external observer.[8]

Uncertainty can be further differentiated into *aleatory*, *epistemic* or *ontological*. Uncertainty around the predictability of outcomes is called *aleatory* or statistical (e.g. when I toss a coin).[9] Uncertainty that refers to situations when my knowledge is incomplete and I simply do not or cannot have all the necessary information is *epistemic*; it has to do with the limits of my knowledge, which can be measured, and is subjective.[10] Finally, *ontological* uncertainty is about states and changes of state that are assumed to be independent of an external observer, thus concerning things that are indeterminate per se; it has to do with the contingency of the world. This is radical, oceanic uncertainty.

The key distinction seems therefore to be between *epistemic* uncertainty, when I do not know something, and *ontological* uncertainty, when variability and unpredictability are said to be inherent in a given system.[11] As it will become clear in the course of this chapter, however, even this difference between epistemic

7 Michael Smithson, *Ignorance and Uncertainty. Emerging Paradigms* (New York: Springer-Verlag, 1989); Smithson, 'The Many Faces and Masks of Uncertainty'; Gabriele Bammer and Michael Smithson, eds, *Uncertainty and Risk. Multidisciplinary Perspectives* (London: Earthscan, 2008). Nikolas Rose and Filippa Lentzos, 'Governing Insecurity. Contingency Planning, Protection, Resilience', *Economy and Society* 38, no. 2 (2009): 230–54, which uses as a starting point sociologists Richard V. Ericson and Aaron Doyle's definition of uncertainty as 'the lack of secure knowledge about an unwanted outcome'. Richard Ericson and Aaron Doyle, *Uncertain Business. Risk, Insurance and the Limits of Knowledge* (Toronto: University of Toronto Press, 2004), 5.

8 Jose V. Ciprut, 'Definition, Distinctions, and Dilemmas', in *Indeterminacy: The Mapped, the Navigable, and the Uncharted*, ed. Jose V. Ciprut (Cambridge, Mass. and London: MIT Press, 2008), 1–40.

9 Probability can be distinguished between the *frequentist* (probability as the attribute of repeated events) and the *subjective* approach (or Bayesian interpretation, where probability expresses the observer's degree of belief, given the information available). This latter interpretation is subjective because knowledge varies from observer to observer. In other words, every time I say probability that means 'my' probability rather than 'the' probability.

10 All uncertainty has an irreducible element of subjectivity, and eventually any difference between aleatory and subjective uncertainty tends to dissipate.

11 Karen Barad, *Meeting the Universe Halfway. Quantum Physics and the Entanglement of Matter and Meaning* (Durham: Duke University Press, 2007); Andrew J. E. Seely, 'Embracing the Certainty of Uncertainty. Implications for Health Care and Research', *Perspectives in Biology and Medicine* 56, no. 1 (2013): 65–77; Stephen Toulmin and June Goodfield, *The Architecture of Matter* (Chicago: University of Chicago Press, 1962).

and ontological uncertainty tends to dissipate the more one delves into the incandescent matter of things (literally).

UNCERTAINTY IS RISK

One way of responding to uncertainty is by framing it as a *risk*. This is the approach found in social sciences, economics, statistics and the insurance sector.

Risk is the general term for unwanted and negatively perceived events (e.g. hazard, loss, damage, threat), and for the calculation of the probability of said unwanted events.[12] Framing something as a 'risk' implies the evaluation of a potential negative outcome. Thus, risk expresses the present calculation of a future uncertainty. It indicates in mathematical terms the statistical probability and the cost of the worst possible outcome. However, no matter how objective and scientific the assessment of a given situation is, it is always informed by socially shared beliefs, in other words, by what in this precise moment and in this current context (socio-cultural, financial, economic, legal and so on) is *perceived* as risk. There is no risk assessment (and therefore no risk per se) without contextualization.

Indeed, what is risk if not a perception? Sociologist Gerda Reith puts it bluntly when she writes: 'there is no such thing as risk in the world, only dangers we construct in our head'.[13] Far from being an intrinsic property of things, or an autonomous entity, risk is always a contextual one. It emerges from the web of connections that weaves together a potential cause *of* risk, what may be *at* risk and what I expect to be (or I perceive as) the consequences. Therefore, it is more correct to say that risk is a 'cognitive frame', rather than a real (or quasi-real) phenomenon that I experience directly.[14] In any case, what matters is the extent to which the quantification of a future contingency (my perception of risk, or a society's) becomes a guide for present anticipatory action. Thus, how I (or a society) conceptualize the relationship between uncertainty and

[12] Risk refers also to behaviours and actions that are deliberate 'risk taking' or 'edgework', and that may produce experiential benefits, such as a release from the monotony of the everyday via thrill-seeking; a way of experimenting with endurance through boundary-pushing activities; a vehicle to choose risk as the path toward self-actualization, self-growth, knowledge-growth and accomplishment. Jens O. Zinn ed., *Social Theories of Risk and Uncertainty. An Introduction* (Oxford: Blackwell, 2008); Deborah Lupton, 'Sociology and Risk', in *Beyond the Risk Society. Critical Reflections on Risk and Human Security*, ed. Gabe Mythen and Sandra Walklate (Maidenhead and New York: Open University Press, 2006), 11–24.

[13] Gerda Reith, 'Uncertain Times. The Notion of "Risk" and the Development of Modernity', *Time & Society* 13, no. 2–3 (2004): 386.

[14] In their seminal work on risk, anthropologists Mary Douglas and Aaron Wildavsky argued that the perception of risk is highly based on, and shaped by, individual opinions and collectively shared cultural beliefs; current and past social relations; memories, legacies, discourses and practices; trust in institutional expertise, distribution of knowledge and hierarchies of power. Mary Douglas and Aaron Wildavsky, *Risk and Culture. An Essay on the Selection of Technological and Environmental Dangers* (Berkeley and Los Angeles: University of California Press, 1982).

risk is instructive of where my (or that society's) priorities are. How I perceive risk reveals how I see my future. Thus, it shapes my present too.

But risk and uncertainty are not the same thing. Uncertainty cannot be measured, calculated or insured. Risk can. And while the management, governance and reduction of risk are widely researched, uncertainty – intended not as 'risk to manage', but as 'ocean to swim in' – is less so. From these considerations, it emerges that if risk is the eventuality that something bad might happen, what I experience is not risk per se but my knowledge of its (contextually constructed) calculation. Risk has to do with *knowing* (how much or how little), not with *being*. Risk is epistemic, not ontological. This leads to the familiar paradox that the more information and knowledge I have, the more uncertainty seems to grow. The more I attempt to immunize myself against accidents, failures or negative events, the more I may be inclined to see the 'future' exclusively on the basis of how risk can be assessed, locking my expectations into a mode driven by strategies of anticipatory governance such as pre-emption, prevention and precaution.

THE *PRE* MODES: PRE-EMPTION, PREVENTION, PRECAUTION

Risk can be managed through strategies of control whose goal is to neutralize real or perceived threats. This section briefly examines three of these strategies: pre-emption, prevention and precaution. Although they are all driven by the same logic, they deal with the *concept* of future risk slightly differently.

To start with, *Pre-emption* enlists the unknowability of the future into present decision-making processes; it intervenes on a specific slice of expectations curated from a wider pool of possibilities.[15] Pre-emption deals with a potential risk that has not emerged yet. Here the uncertainty is ontological. With *Prevention*, on the other hand, uncertainty is epistemic. Prevention conceptualizes the future as the replication of past occurrences and assumes that a risk (and its causes) is known and measurable.[16] Thus, prevention is based on the secular faith in scientific know-how and technical control, and on the (fiction of) objectivity in the measurement of risk. Its key concern is not the compensation for potential losses but how to reduce the chance of incurring them. Securing knowledge is fundamental, but, like in the tale of the map covering the territory narrated by Jorge Luis Borges, there is a certain utopian madness in wishing to foresee and prepare for every possible eventuality. After all, I cannot plan for what I truly do not know.[17]

[15] Louise Amoore, *The Politics of Possibility. Risk and Security Beyond Probability* (Durham: Duke University Press, 2013).

[16] Brian Massumi, 'Potential Politics and the Primacy of Preemption', *Theory & Event* 10, no. 2 (2007).

[17] François Ewald, 'The Return of Descartes' Malicious Demon. An Outline of a Philosophy of Precaution', in *Embracing Risk. The Changing Culture of Insurance and Responsibility*, ed. Tom Baker and Jonathan Simon (Chicago: University of Chicago Press, 2002), 273–301.

The asymptotic gap in knowledge leads to the third strategy: *Precaution*. Operating in the discrepancy between what empiric knowledge about future occurrences can tell me, and what I can only imagine, fear, or suspect, precaution presents itself as a promise of safety. It is precaution as a governance paradigm that impels a nation to be in a state of permanent alert, ready to respond appropriately to potential threats, disasters or crises. As a mode of governing the uncertain yet-to-come, precaution is underpinned by the discourse of prudence, and its consequences can be stifling. Think of the exhortation, highly prized by the insurance industry, to consider the worst hypothesis as the most likely to succeed. This may well result in catalysing its perverse anticipation into not *a*, but *the* possible future, inhibiting present action. By transforming the unknown into manageable packets, precaution funnels potential futures and their unpredictable trajectories into what is known to be already actualizable, which is another way of describing the process that throughout the book I call the capture of potential. By reducing the latitude of what may happen, the capture of potential also reduces the extent to which the unknowable participates in the construction of worlds and subjectivities. By stifling the emergence of other ways of existing, it contains what may diverge from, or contest, the status quo. Pre-rendering what has not been even imagined yet, makes it thinkable and erodes the creation of other possible alternatives.[18]

Furthermore, precaution acts on the social imaginary, impinges on the potential this imaginary could express (but will not), and shrinks the capacity to dream alternative futures – social, political, individual, collective.[19] Common imaginaries, especially when they manifest as forms of antagonism, resistance and insubordination, operate in the space where uncertainty is a feature of the collective, in other words, where it is social. As Rosalyn Diprose observes, common imaginaries are nourished by unscripted encounters with the world. They thrive on uncertainty. Indeed, uncertainty is essential to them. It is what makes them grow. The capture of potential weakens collective modes of dealing with uncertainty – for instance, organized systems of beliefs, be them myth-making, religions, superstitions, folk worldviews, secular faiths, revolutionary aspirations, activist world-building – with the result that coping mechanisms become increasingly individualized. This personalization of how to deal with uncertainty not only reinforces the unfair and asymmetrical distribution of resources dictating who is able to cope with what, but it also shows the fundamental fallacy of personalized responses to risk. Given that the calculation of risk can be generated only through population (not individual) analysis, it is only in the collective and the commons that strategies for coping with uncertainty can be more successfully located, not in the 'market of one'.[20]

[18] Amoore, *The Politics of Possibility*, 157.

[19] Rosalyn Diprose et al., 'Governing the Future. The Paradigm of Prudence in Political Technologies of Risk Management', *Security Dialogue* 39, no. 2–3 (2008): 267–88.

[20] Introna, 'The Algorithmic Choreography of the Impressionable Subject', 39.

THE EROSION OF DETERMINISM

In every culture and in every time people have developed ways of dealing with the uncertainty that life throws at them, in order to harness and (attempt to) explain life's radical contingency. The unknowability and unpredictability of the future have prompted individuals and societies time and time again to devise strategies of interpretation, prediction, forecast, prophecy, divination; to invent belief systems, supernatural agencies and social taboos so that causes could be attributed, adversities rebuffed and ever-present dangers exorcised; to create techniques, rituals, superstitions, apotropaic magic, rules and games in the attempt to explain (and contain) what is a fragile and precarious existence. All these strategies of management of the unknown – whether through religious, spiritual or agnostic means; through the evocation of benevolent or malevolent forces; through the suspension of belief, the recourse to delusion, even the invention of compelling and believable stories with the twofold aim of making desired outcomes more attractive and of keeping doubt at bay – are somehow not too different from what today is known as 'risk management'.[21] The difference is that, until recently, it was not called 'risk'.

If risk is the product of time and uncertainty brought together into a quantifiable relation that can be scientifically calculated, then pre-industrial times had no conception of risk. Everything happened because of the will of God. Divine providence was the conceptual framework that justified it all, chance and randomness included. It was only in seventeenth-century Europe that a cascade of social, cultural, intellectual and political transformations began to produce the notion of risk as it is understood today. This shift from providence to risk (and uncertainty) was both a conceptual transformation and a process of secularization. Uncoupled from divine providence, destiny and predestination, chance acquires an autonomous ontological dimension and becomes an object of scientific inquiry. Divine laws once set in stone become statistical probabilities. The idea that the past would determine exactly what happened next began to dissolve.

This process of 'erosion of determinism' is well-documented.[22] First, the rise of the bourgeois mercantile class with commerce as its prerogative, births the abstractions of finance and insurance. Then, the new mathematical fields of probability and statistics, developed from studies of gambling, show for the first time that seemingly random events follow recurring patterns and predictable trajectories. A new understanding of temporality as a long-term, open-ended future begins to emerge, signalling the shift from the determinism of 'what

[21] Åsa Boholm, 'The Cultural Nature of Risk. Can There Be an Anthropology of Uncertainty?' *Ethnos* 68, no. 2 (2003): 159–78; Simon Dein, 'The Anthropology of Uncertainty. Magic, Witchcraft and Risk and Forensic Implications', *Journal of Forensic Anthropology* 1, no. 1 (2016): 1–7; David Tuckett, 'Irreducible Uncertainty and its Implications. A Narrative Action Theory for Economics', *Institute for New Economic Thinking* (working paper, 2013).

[22] Ian Hacking, *The Taming of Chance* (Cambridge: Cambridge University Press, 1990).

will happen' to the probabilism of 'what might happen'.[23] God time (divine providence) becomes merchant time. The parameters of Newtonian science, which postulated the universe as an entirely predictable machine ruled by causation and linear progression, within which the concepts of space, time and matter were assumed to be fixed, absolute and immutable, begin to crumble. The new rationality triumphantly states that among the apparent chaos, laws could be discovered, patterns detected and probabilities calculated. During the European Enlightenment, any residual sense of fatalism about chance became synonymous with unreason, until the quantum discovery that the world was not deterministic in the nineteenth century tilted irreversibly the concept of causality and ushered in the era of irreducible uncertainty.[24]

UNCERTAINTY IS IRREDUCIBLE

> There is, indeed, still some dispute about the proper interpretation of Heisenberg's principle. Does the 'indeterminacy' in question mean only that we are restricted in our powers to observe and measure quantities which nevertheless have, in reality, perfectly definite and determinate values? Or does it mean that the fundamental entities of matter-theory are like clouds or claps of thunder – things which, by their very nature, have vague, indefinite boundaries, so that there are no absolutely determinate physical properties to be measured? Or is it rather a question of meaning and definition – do the equations by which our concept of 'electrons' is intellectually constructed somehow imply that the idea of an absolutely exact simultaneous measurement is devoid of physical significance? Whether one regards Heisenberg's principle as reflecting a limitation on our measurements, an essential property of material things, or a consequence of the meaning of our concepts, the practical effect of the principle is the same: though the theory explains the overall statistical patterns of events which occur in any physical situation, it obliges one to abandon all hope of predicting individual quantum events with complete accuracy.[25]

The uncertainty principle, as articulated by German physicist Werner Heisenberg in 1927, states that I cannot measure both the position and the velocity of an object. My acts of observing *and* of attempting to measure something will alter what is observed. Thus, the notions of exact position and exact velocity have no meaning together.[26]

[23] Gerd Gigerenzer et al., *The Empire of Chance. How Probability Changed Science and Everyday Life* (Cambridge: Cambridge University Press,1989); Reith, 'Uncertain Times', 386. This is exactly the opposite of what statistical predictive machines do today.

[24] Ian Hacking, *The Emergence of Probability. A Philosophical Study of Early Ideas about Probability, Induction and Statistical Inference* (Cambridge: Cambridge University Press, 1975); Hacking, *The Taming of Chance*, 181.

[25] Toulmin and Goodfield, *The Architecture of Matter*, 290.

[26] Heisenberg's concern was with attempting to measure the position of an electron. This led to the realization that, in doing so, the electron's speed would change and that, vice versa, attempting to measure the electron's speed would result in its position changing.

The debate on the specific word that Heisenberg chose to describe his principle – variously translated as inaccuracy, uncertainty, indeterminacy, un-sharpness – is ongoing and far from settled.[27] Some argue that Heisenberg's principle should be called the 'principle of indeterminacy' to signify that what came to prominence with the discoveries of quantum physics is an ontological phenomenon.[28] The vast literature discussing this point highlights the fierce diatribe between Heisenberg and fellow physicist Niels Bohr, who maintained that the real issue of quantum mechanics was indeed indeterminacy, not uncertainty.[29] For Bohr, the premise of Heisenberg's argument wrongly assumed a speed and a position impacted upon by the observer, while he (Bohr) understood the *relation* between position and momentum in semantic and ontological terms first, and only secondarily in epistemic terms. In other words, if the variables 'position' and 'momentum' cannot be determined simultaneously, then the key point is not unknowability, says Bohr, but what can be said to exist (or not) concurrently. As physicist David Peat writes, in Bohr's view:

> Every act of making a measurement is an act of interrogating the universe. The answer one receives to this interrogation depends on how the question is framed – that is, how the measurement is made. Rather than trying to unveil an underlying quantum property, the properties we observe are in a certain sense the product of the act of measurement itself. Ask a question one way and Nature has been framed into giving a certain answer. Pose the question in another way and the answer will be different. Rather than disturbing the universe, the answer to a quantum measurement is a form of co-creation between observer and observed.[30]

This is the key point: co-creation. As neither the object nor the measuring instrument exists outside or independently from their relationship, the issue is *not* epistemic.[31] Put differently, I cannot know something definite about some-

[27] Heisenberg used both *Ungenauigkeit* (imprecision, inexactness) and *Unbestimmtheit* (indefiniteness, indeterminacy, indetermination, undeterminedness or vagueness). Only in the end notes did he switch to *Unsicherheit* (uncertainty). In using this word, Heisenberg appears to have made a choice between 'inexactness' and 'indeterminacy'. In the English-language version of Heisenberg's textbook *The Physical Principles of the Quantum Theory*, published in 1930, the translation 'uncertainty' was used, hence his principle is known as the principle of uncertainty.

[28] Barad (*Meeting the Universe Halfway*) explains the difference between uncertainty and indeterminacy framing them as competing claims on how relations of reciprocity among elements should be understood.

[29] David Lindley, *Uncertainty. Einstein, Heisenberg, Bohr and the Struggle for the Soul of Science* (New York and London: Doubleday, 2007); David F. Peat, *From Certainty to Uncertainty. The Story of Science and Ideas in the Twentieth Century* (Washington DC: Joseph Henry Press, 2002); Carlo Rovelli, *Helgoland. The Strange and Beautiful Story of Quantum Physics* (London: Allen Lane, 2021).

[30] Peat, *From Certainty to Uncertainty*, 16.

[31] This is, in a nutshell, Bohr's complementarity principle, which explains the mutual exclusivity of characteristics of quantum phenomena (e.g. wave/particle, position/momentum) and is the ground for Barad's notions of intra-action and agential realism. Barad, *Meeting the Universe Halfway*, 118.

thing for which there is nothing definite to know. It may even be argued that it is indeterminacy (lack of determination) that causes uncertainty (lack of certainty).

One thing is certain (!), however. With his principle, Heisenberg did not 'discover' uncertainty. What he did was to change its meaning forever.[32] The collapse of the Newtonian categories of space, time, matter and causality had seismic repercussions beyond the realm of physics or mechanics. The fundamental indeterminacy of the post-Newtonian world, where causal laws are replaced by stochastic probability,[33] has reconfigured not only the natural world but social and subjective worlds too. The most profound impact of the principle of uncertainty remains in the challenge it brings to determinism. As physicist Stephen Buckman explains:

> In our indeterminant quantum world, particles behave in a probabilistic manner and there are many possible paths that a particle may follow. Indeed, in this quantum mechanical world the fundamental microscopic particles (electrons, protons, atoms and so on) can be in more than one quantum state (for instance, a different energy level or state of an atom) at the same time. That these so-called superpositions of states exist in the microscopic world is well known because they produce observable interference effects in measurements. However, if we perform a discrete measurement of the system, to determine its state, we always find particular value or state for the particle, rather than a mix of two or more. This seemingly bizarre consequence of quantum theory led to Schrodinger's famous 'cat paradox'.[34]

With indeterminate activity present at all levels of the visible and the invisible world, relativity undermines causality. All kinds of events resist patterning and sequencing. The universe is revealed as made not of stable or quasi-stable autonomous elements interacting with each other but of relations whose dynamic outcomes can acquire only a partial, situated, temporary and ever-mutable 'identity'. If no object exists independently from an apparatus capable of measuring it then there are no pre-existing properties in a given system. Properties do not exist per se but emerge and will be 'defined' only by acts of observation and intervention.

This is where the physicist and the philosopher concur in saying that 'reality is made up of relations rather than objects'[35] and 'relata do not precede

[32] The notion of uncertainty was, of course, already familiar. Described as slack, latitude, elbow room or ambiguity, all terms broadly denoting a general systemic unknowability, uncertainty is what spurs inquiry. It is what galvanizes the relationship between scientific theory and laboratory experiment. No research, no discovery, no inquisitiveness can occur without an uncertain starting point, a not-knowing that galvanizes curiosity into action.

[33] Stochastic distribution: a pattern that may be analysed statistically but may not be predicted precisely. Reith, 'Uncertain Times', 391.

[34] Stephen J. Buckman, 'Uncertainty in the Physical Sciences. How Big? How Small? Is It Actually There at All?', in *Uncertainty and Risk*, ed. Gabriele Bammer and Michael Smithson (London: Earthscan, 2008), 74.

[35] Rovelli, *Helgoland*, 3.

relations'.[36] The discovery of the quantum world reveals the 'incandescence' of reality at its utmost granular scale. That thing called 'reality' is a continually woven (and unwoven) universe of infinite alterity and tremor. Thus, the question of whether uncertainty is *epistemic* or *ontological*, whether it is more about what I do not know, or about something that is inherently unknowable, eventually loses traction. The indeterminate and the indeterminable are not mutually exclusive. What matters is not how they differ, but how they connect. Uncertainty is onto-epistemological because it braids the epistemic and ontological dimensions together with the tremor of invisible, incandescent matter.

In his poetic explanation of quantum theory, Rovelli writes: 'The world is a network of relative facts: relations realized when physical entities interact. A stone collides with another stone. The light from the Sun reaches my skin. You read these lines'.[37] And he continues:

> The quantum world is more tenuous than the one imagined by the old physics; it is made up of happenings, discontinuous events, without permanence. It is a world with a fine texture, intricate and fragile as Venetian lace. Every interaction is an event, and it is these light and ephemeral events that weave reality, not the heavy objects charged with absolute properties that our philosophy posited in support of those events.[38]

Far from remaining confined to the realms of physics, the radical uncertainty posed by quantum theory almost a century ago alters not only how I conceptualize my experience of the world but the most profound essence of this experience. This can be compared to what happens when I take a photo with my back to the sun. No matter how much I try to move or twist my body, my shadow will always be in the photo. There is no 'real-world' without me already in it.[39] This impossibility to measure and observe at the same time is the collapse of Newtonian determinism. It is also the collapse of the fiction of the objective, neutral and impartial observer. Besides, radical uncertainty also suggests that the absolute relationality of the universe works in tandem with the universe's utmost indifference. On one hand, this tells me that nothing can be untouched by my human intervention; on the other, that everything is perfectly immune to it.[40] The universe I partake of is indeterminate. It is undecidable. There is nothing outside it, nothing before it, absolutely nothing that grounds it.[41] Viewed as a quantum phenomenon and with the same rules found in the

36 Barad, *Meeting the Universe Halfway*, 334.

37 Rovelli, *Helgoland*, 74.

38 Ibid., 75.

39 Peat, *From Certainty to Uncertainty*, 14.

40 Connor, *The Madness of Knowledge*, 20.

41 Jonathan Basile, 'Other Matters. Karen Barad's Two Materialisms and the Science of Undecidability', *Angelaki* 25, no. 5 (2020): 3–18; Elie Ayache, 'The Medium of Contingency', *Contingency. PLI the Warwick Journal of Philosophy*, University of Warwick 22 (2011): 62–87.

indeterminate behaviour of electrons and photons, consciousness itself is nothing but the entanglement of vibrating, unstable, incandescent matter that flows in and through me, you, every body and every thing else.[42]

WITHOUT UNCERTAINTY LIFE WOULD BE VERY DULL

Over one hundred years ago, in his work on risk theory, American economist Frank H. Knight celebrated uncertainty as a highly desirable state. Without uncertainty, he writes, life would be very dull. Humans would turn into bare automata.[43]

If risk concerns a future that can be acted upon in the present via calculations, uncertainty is a much cloudier territory where the probabilistic dimension needs to include the aesthetic, the affective, the experiential. There is so much more to uncertainty than the version claimed by risk managers, insurance experts, future-proofers, economists. When I frame uncertainty solely as a risk to manage, I squash into a quantifiable nomenclature all those other aspects that make uncertainty alive and brimming with possibilities, in short, its vast oceanity. I parcel the infinite horizon of potential into discrete packets, assigning value to each on the ground of cost-benefit calculations. This parsing manoeuvre reduces the incalculable. It compresses contingency.

But contingency is like an arrow, and like an arrow it cuts through the air, moving, tending toward, alive.[44] It cannot be compressed, nor stopped. Nothing that happens is necessary, but everything that happens touches me. I am enveloped in contingency, all the time, as if I was caught in a web, but not trapped like a fly. Rather, I am like the spider who comes alive the moment the web pulls her in, vibrating with the intensity and the oceanic uncertainty of what *may be* happening.

[42] Entanglement is the 'phenomenon by which two distant objects maintain a kind of weird connection, as if they continued to speak to each other from afar' (Rovelli, *Helgoland*, 81).

[43] Frank H. Knight, *Risk, Uncertainty and Profit* (Boston: Houghton Mifflin, 1921), 348.

[44] Ayache, 'The Medium of Contingency', 62.

6 Unknowing Stratagems

The non-knowing at the heart of all knowledge is an undertaking that is meticulous, grave, and always to be taken up again.
ISABELLE STENGERS[1]

INTO UNKNOWING

In my project of articulating a counter-metaphysics and a counter-epistemology of uncertainty, this chapter turns to *unknowing*, negative knowledge and nonknowledge. The chapter has two aims. First, to reclaim unknowing, negative knowledge and nonknowledge as modes of knowing in themselves. Then, to propose a curated list of practical approaches – *stratagems* – through which this can be done. As Stengers states in the epigraph above, not knowing is at the core of knowing. It is its very own condition. I take this as a reminder that the mechanisms through which knowledge is made demand that I remain alert to how it is also unmade, obfuscated, distorted, ignored, denied. In recognizing what shapes how I know what I know, I begin to gain awareness of what I do not know, including the zone of the infamous 'unknown unknowns'.[2]

This chapter, then, is about how the known and the unknown are woven together, and how their threading can be re-owned and re-imagined. It is also about unknowing as 'learning to ignore' the deafening noise of today's knowledge

[1] Isabelle Stengers, *Thinking with Whitehead. A Free and Wild Creation of Concepts* (Cambridge, Mass. and London: Harvard University Press, 2011), 3.

[2] I refer of course to the 'known knowns, known unknowns, unknown knowns, and unknown unknowns' popularized after the response given by United States Secretary of Defence Donald Rumsfeld to a question during a U.S. Department of Defence news briefing in 2002, about the lack of evidence linking the government of Iraq with the supply of weapons of mass destruction to terrorist groups. For the full brief text see https://web.archive.org/web/20160406235718/http://archive.defense.gov/Transcripts/Transcript.aspx?TranscriptID=2636.

regimes propped by the automation of decision-making, so that what has been squashed, side-lined and captured by too much clamour, brightness, speed and exposure, can be re-sensed. To rehabilitate *unknowing*, negative knowledge and nonknowledge as modes of knowing, the notion of ignorance as an empty space, as a void or a black hole, as a space that needs filling, deserves dismissal or justifies contempt, must be disputed. This chapter's constellation sketches unknowing's nebulous contours while showing the inadequacy of Western conventions that see knowledge as clarity and light, and ignorance as darkness and opacity.[3]

Unsurprisingly, to engage with the knowledge of the unknown raises a plethora of questions about knowledge's limits, boundaries and prerogatives, questions concerning the conditions under which claims of knowledge are made and what it is that makes something worthy or un-worthy to be known.[4] It also quickly becomes slightly paradoxical. What does it mean exactly to not know? If I know that I do not know, does it still count as not knowing? Is there a difference between not knowing, nonknowledge and unknowing? How do I yield insights from what I do not know? How do I use the unknown as a way of knowing, whilst retaining its full potentiality perched on something inscrutable? How can I build around it a knowledge that is both productive (but not exploitative) and transformative (but not dogmatic)?

An initial observation is that unknowing remains relatively unattended by the humanities. Together with nonknowledge, it tends to be constructed negatively as lack (of knowledge) and darkness (of ignorance). It is often rendered as 'impenetrable fog of obscurity'.[5] But there is more to unknowing than this. Unknowing is not just the opposite of knowing. It can be 'a way of being in the world that allows it to be messy, incoherent, and imperfect'; not only 'a quasi-mystical and intentionally passive relation to that which one does not know, but rather, and perhaps more importantly, a conditioning of one's self-assured knowledge'.[6] Unknowing also concerns discarding obsolete ideas, dated beliefs and dogmatic fixations. Unknowing is, for instance, when I let go of what I no longer need to make space for the new, or when I unpick an entrenched view to re-train in what my specular 'curated ignorance' had prevented me from grasping.[7]

[3] Western epistemology is shaped by the primacy of the ocular perspective, by metaphors of vision and by a logic of visuality. According to this *view*, opacity needs to be eradicated if knowledge is to be gained. Its vagueness is wrong, destabilizing; it is what prevents knowledge from consolidating and taking its rightful semblances. For a critical discussion of ocularcentrism see Martin Jay, *Downcast Eyes. The Denigration of Vision in Twentieth-Century French Thought* (Berkeley and Los Angeles: University of California Press, 1993).

[4] It also means to reframe how I become 'expert', 'learned', 'knowledgeable', 'proficient', 'academic', 'authority' – and in the present context 'academic authority' and 'scholar'.

[5] Nicholas Rescher, *Unknowability. An Inquiry into the Limits of Knowledge* (Lanham, Md.: Lexington Books, 2009), 13.

[6] Emile Bojesen, 'Positive Ignorance. Unknowing as a Tool for Education and Educational Research', *Journal of Philosophy of Education* 53, no. 2 (2019): 397.

[7] On 'curated ignorance' see Paul Gilroy, 'Never Again. Refusing Race and Salvaging the Human', Lecture, Holberg Prize, Bergen, 4 June 2019.

Many (perhaps too many) questions surface at this point: How do I re-imagine, reclaim, re-purpose unknowing (and nonknowledge)? If ignorance can be manufactured as a vehicle of corruption, coercion and control, could it be also used in a generative and creative way? But also: What counts as knowledge? What is the status under which claims of knowledge are made? Who gets to decide? Whose knowledge gets excluded? When is a topic of study judged (un)worthy of attention? How are modes of knowing and therefore of not knowing, connected to lobbying interests and political agendas?

While this chapter will not address all of these questions, I raise them simply to point out the formidable richness of treating unknowing as a topic of inquiry. Moreover, what all these questions have in common is that they help identify a significant blind spot: that there is no knowing without unknowing.[8]

On this ground, the chapter examines the shifting boundaries between knowing and unknowing to propose modes of knowledge, my 'unknowing stratagems', that are uncertain, tentative, hesitant, un-assured, ambiguous, not fully knowledgeable yet content to inhabit their un-knowledgeability. The stratagems this chapter proposes are *learned ignorance*, when not knowing is the key to knowledge; *conjecture*, a mode of knowing that is incomplete, qualitative and contingent; *divination*, a chance-led mode of inquiry into the unknown. It also draws on selected aspects of Chinese thought that emphasize the *blur* as a figure of knowing, together with *wu wei* (active not doing), the practice of inactive efficacy. These are my *unknowing stratagems*, which I enlist as modes of entering the oceanic flow of uncertainty. As Part One foregrounded, these stratagems are necessary to reclaim uncertainty and counteract the desertification of life. I cannot but echo here Bataille's words: 'life restrained to its intelligible operations is clearly the most impoverished'.[9]

The chapter borrows from two eminent scholars of Chinese philosophy, Barry Allen and François Jullien, the argument that a shift is needed from the founding interrogation of Western ontology (What is this? What is not this?) to the *taoique*, where dyadic thinking (being-not being) dissolves in the continuity of the *Dao*.[10]

Finally, as customary, a note on the chapter's title, 'Unknowing Stratagems', a meta-statement that alludes to two distinct aspects: that the stratagems herein discussed concern unknowing; and also, that these stratagems cannot be fully known in themselves. I use the word 'stratagems' to deliberately sidestep the use of 'strategy'. Both are military terms designating a plan for action aiming

8 The blind spot is the small circular area at the back of the retina where the optic nerve enters the eyeball, devoid of rods and cones and not sensitive to light. As an example see the notion of 'white ignorance': Charles Mills, 'White Ignorance', in *Race and Epistemologies of Ignorance*, ed. Shannon Sullivan and Nancy Tuana (New York: SUNY Press, 2007), 11–39.

9 George Bataille, *The Unfinished System of Nonknowledge* (Minneapolis: Minnesota University Press, 2001), 158–9.

10 François Jullien, *The Silent Transformations* (London: Seagull, 2011), 34.

to achieve a certain objective, which is the received definition of 'strategy'.[11] A stratagem, however, relies on more clever, more cunning, more unorthodox means. It is less systematic than strategy, more direct, perhaps more intuitive, and may include subterfuge, deception and sabotage. This distinction is important because it foregrounds how the modes of knowledge-making I propose, lodged in unknowing, are located within the lineage of astute inventiveness, what the previous chapter called 'metic wayfinding'.

As per 'unknowing': there is a subtle distinction between 'unknowing' and 'nonknowledge'. The first emphasizes process, the second outcome. Agamben, for instance, distinguishes between 'not knowing' and 'nonknowledge', where not knowing (*non sapere*) concerns an unexplored territory to be conquered by knowledge; and nonknowledge (*non conoscenza*) is that zone that must remain unknowable, and therefore demands continuous vigilance.[12] Cunningly, Agamben notes that this zone of nonknowledge may eventually be found to contain nothing at all. It may not even exist (I simply do not know). In the absence of a recipe, says Agamben, all I can do is strive to maintain 'the right relationship with ignorance, allowing an absence of knowledge to guide and accompany our gestures, letting a stubborn silence clearly respond for our words'.[13]

I begin to grasp the contours of what posing unknowing as a guide may mean. It means to acknowledge and to accept, with vigilance and firmness, that a 'stubborn silence' is here to teach and must be listened to. This is how I voyage into the unknown and inhabit nonknowledge, alert to the incipience of things as they move, sensitive to their propensities, all the while plotting exits that may (or may not) plunge me further into the unknown, and its oceanic uncertainty.

THIS SHOULD NOT BE KNOWN!

Every time I engage with knowledge, especially within the institutions established to classify, preserve and transmit knowledge, I am asked to learn certain things and ignore others.[14] 'This should not be known!' is the warning issued to protect

[11] They both derive from the Greek *stratēgía* = office or command of a general, and *stratēgos* = commander.

[12] A distinction between *sapere* and *conoscere* found in the closing pages of Agamben, *Nudita'*, but regrettably lost in the translation from the Italian.

[13] Giorgio Agamben, *Nudities* (Stanford: Stanford University Press, 2010, English translation), 114.

[14] Anthropologist Michael Taussig writes about the negativity of knowing as what holds power through secrecy. If knowledge is power, then it is precisely active not knowing that makes it so. Michael Taussig, *Defacement. Public Secrecy and the Labor of the Negative* (Stanford: Stanford University Press, 1999). See also China Mieville, *The City and the City* (London: Pan, 2011) set in two cities that occupy the same geographical space but whose citizens have learned to 'unsee' each other.

what is deemed worthy of epistemic status.[15] The question of why something counts as knowledge and something else does not is Foucault's territory: How power is constituted through accepted modes of knowledge, scientific understanding and 'truth'-making dispositives. These 'general politics' and 'regimes of truth' are the result of how discourses around knowledge, namely what counts as knowledge and what does not, are constructed, reinforced and monitored by adjudicating institutions and their equipments (education systems, media, scientific organizations, administrative apparatuses, law-making bodies, policy agencies and so on).

If knowledge is socially constructed, then this process also actively builds *ignorance* through asymmetries of power, epistemic violence and mechanisms of misinformation, spin, propaganda, fabrication, denial.[16] Shaped by epistemicidal forces such as the extractive rule of colonial politics, what counts as ignorance is in itself a charged political matter. Claims to knowledge are built through a manufacturing wrapped up in secrecy, covering up, manipulation, deception and repression.[17] Alongside the study of ignorance – *agnotology* – which reveals

[15] Michel Foucault and Gilles Deleuze, 'A Conversation Between Michel Foucault and Gilles Deleuze. Intellectuals and Power', in *Language, Counter-Memory, Practice. Selected Essays and Interviews*, ed. Donald F. Bouchard (Ithaca: Cornell University Press, 1977), 219.

[16] This is not a fixed and stable relationship, though. What is deemed un-worthy, un-important, un-acceptable knowledge, can in the right conditions tilt into becoming a daring minority line, with the potential to threaten and disrupt the molar majority. As Deleuze and Guattari write, this is how marginalized modes of knowledge claw back and surge to attention. With the unruly vitality of an arrow launched into the world, with their propensity for divergence, collective agency and political immediacy, minor knowledges can attract new forces, generate new thoughts, produce new affects – they are, after all, 'crystals of becoming'. Deleuze and Guattari, *A Thousand Plateaus*, 117.

[17] A well-studied example of manufacturing ignorance is the tobacco industry. See the excellent volume by Naomi Oreskes and Erik M. Conway, *Merchants of Doubt. How a Handful of Scientists Obscured the Truth on Issues from Tobacco Smoke to Global Warming* (London: Bloomsbury, 2012); also Robert Proctor, 'Agnotology. A Missing Term to Describe the Cultural Production of Ignorance (and Its Study)', in *Agnotology. The Making and Unmaking of Ignorance*, ed. Robert Proctor and Londa Schiebinger (Stanford: Stanford University Press, 2008). Scientific research had established links to respiratory diseases since the 1950s, but the industry lobbied aggressively to manufacture knowledge (and therefore ignorance) about it. It eroded the validity of empirical fact and expert knowledge by funding decoy research and via protracted attacks in mainstream media with the aim of diminishing public capacity to evaluate risk, weigh evidence, and make informed decisions. The result was a decade-long 'debate' around issues of safety and choice that saw scientists deliberating until the 1990s. Buttressing this denialist doctrine was a form of industry 'newspeak' that marshalled terms like 'medical controversy', 'benefits of smoking' and 'freedom of choice' to drown out evidence on lung cancer and heart disease. All this amounted to an elaborate exercise in the manufacturing of ignorance characterized by the industry trifecta of 'feigning its own ignorance of hazards, while simultaneously affirming the absence of definite proof in the scientific community, while also doing all it could to manufacture ignorance on the part of the smoking public' (Proctor, Agnotology, 13). This story does not end with tobacco. The 'Tobacco Strategy' of doubt-mongering and science repudiation became the template for subsequent industry attacks on the science of climate change, when scientist-for-hire allies of the US tobacco industry, pivoted to 'fight the facts and merchandise doubt' about the science of global warming.

how ignorance is socially constructed, *epistemologies of ignorance* identify what is left out of 'canons' in order to surface the discriminatory logics upholding these processes.[18] The focus shifts to the contested and unstable borders where knowing and unknowing meet, and how these are shaped by profoundly asymmetrical power relations in the making and unmaking of knowledge. Both agnotology and the study of epistemologies of ignorance expose the often-undetectable mechanisms leading to epistemicide: the suppression, discredit and marginalization of other modes of knowing; the exclusionary practices dictating how what counts as knowledge is constructed, often relying on convenient metanarratives whose claims of commensurability intend to smooth over disjuncture across systems of thoughts and render them equivalent when they are not (e.g. whitewashing).

MODES OF UNKNOWING

The shifting relationship between knowing that I do not know – 'known unknowns' – and not knowing that I do not know – 'unknown unknowns' – is not Donald Rumsfeld's invention but was already identified by Plato's dialogue *Meno* where Socrates evinces the difference between ignorance and error.[19] When I am in error, Socrates says, I believe I know what I actually do not know. When I ignore something, I know that I lack that specific knowledge. Hence the famous Socratic saying (and paradox): *I know that I know nothing.*[20]

This idea that not knowing – 'meta-ignorance' or 'conscious ignorance' – has a value, sports a long and eclectic legacy. This is what American poet and naturalist thinker Henry David Thoreau, French philosopher George Bataille, German epistemologist Karen Knorr Cetina, English poet John Keats, and the medieval scholar and mystic Nicholas of Cusa have in common. Their views are concisely outlined below.

For Thoreau, knowledge is often positive ignorance, and ignorance is specular negative knowledge: 'My desire for knowledge is intermittent, but my desire to bathe my head in atmospheres unknown to my feet is perennial and constant. The highest that we can attain to is not knowledge but sympathy with intelligence'.[21]

[18] Stuart Firestein, *Ignorance. How It Drives Science* (Oxford: Oxford University Press, 2012); Janet Kourany and Martin Carrier eds., *Science and the Production of Ignorance. When the Quest for Knowledge is Thwarted* (Cambridge, Mass. and London: MIT Press, 2020); Erik Malewski and Nathalia Jaramillo eds., *Epistemologies of Ignorance in Education* (London: Information Age Eurospan, 2011); Proctor and Schiebinger, *Agnotology. The Making and Unmaking of Ignorance*; Jennifer Croissant, 'Agnotology. Ignorance and Absence or Toward a Sociology of Things That Aren't There', *Social Epistemology. A Journal of Knowledge, Culture, and Policy* 28, no. 1 (2014): 4–25.

[19] Plato's *Meno*.

[20] Plato's *Apology*.

[21] Henry David Thoreau, *The Writings of Henry David Thoreau* (Boston and New York: Houghton Mifflin, 1865), 240.

For Bataille, 'the secret of the richest knowledge, of a bond before knowledge, is to honestly recognize that we know nothing and to talk about the unknown'.[22] He exhorts to focus on the experience of not knowing rather than on seeking knowledge per se:

> I think it is impossible to talk about nonknowledge other than in the experience that we make of it. The experience is an experience that always has an effect like, for example, laughter or tears, or the poetic, or anguish, or ecstasy. And I don't think that it is possible to talk seriously about nonknowledge independent of its effects. Evidently, we can speak about these effects, in spite of the primary contradiction that the fact of talking about nonknowledge always represents.[23]

What Bataille is saying is that the unknown cannot be, by definition, the object of knowledge. What counts are the *effects* that the unknown has on me and the experience I have of it. These are often boundary experiences at the limit of knowledge, for example, Bataille writes: 'laughter, tears, sexual excitation, poetic emotion (envisioned at first in the form of sentiment of the beauty of nature), the sentiment of the sacred, ecstasy'.[24] A similar sentiment is evoked by philosopher and practitioner Joshua Ramey, who observes that nonknowledge, far from being ignorance, is 'the uncanny presence of forces, potentials, and realities that solicit responses prior to both knowledge and ignorance',[25] a pre-cognitive, or below cognition, space where a kind of intuitive and empathic consciousness can circulate.

In saying that the unknown cannot be an object of knowledge, but something that I can approach only by pushing to the limits of knowledge, Bataille seems to echo *The Cloud of Unknowing*, a text of medieval mysticism thought to have been written in the late fourteenth century. The counsel found in this book of spiritual guidance is: 'And so I urge you, go after experience rather than knowledge. On account of pride, knowledge may often deceive you, but this gentle, loving affection will not deceive you. Knowledge tends to breed conceit, but love builds. Knowledge is full of labor, but love, full of rest'.[26] The advice is that I am not to transcend, or try to fill the unknown, but to remain in it for as long as possible. This approach can also be called negative – or *apophantic* – knowledge: to know something by focusing on what that thing is not, and by acknowledging and accepting its unknowability.

Knorr Cetina uses negative knowledge to interrogate the limits of knowledge by drawing on experimental, high-energy physics, where negative knowledge

[22] Bataille, *The Unfinished System of Nonknowledge*, 158.

[23] Ibid., 137.

[24] Ibid., 159.

[25] Joshua Ramey, *Politics of Divination. Neoliberal Endgame and the Religion of Contingency* (London and New York: Rowman and Littlefield, 2016), 4.

[26] William Johnston ed., *The Cloud of Unknowing and the Book of Privy Counseling* (London: Random House, 2012), 188.

is incorporated into research through a focus on liminal phenomena. Liminal phenomena are objects on the fringe of what has been decided is the primary object of research. They represent universes of 'disturbances and distortions, imperfections, errors, uncertainties, and limits of research'.[27] To study these 'unsavoury' zones of liminality is to enlist them into the knowledge-making process.[28] On this basis, Knorr Cetina describes negative knowledge as 'knowledge of the limits of knowing, of the mistakes we make in trying to know, of the things that interfere with our knowing, of what we are not interested in and do not really want to know'.[29]

The cultivation of negative knowledge cannot but evoke Keats's notion of 'negative capability' – 'when man is capable of being in uncertainties, mysteries, doubts, without any irritable reaching after fact and reason'.[30] 'Negative' is used here not in a pejorative sense but to convey the idea that my potential (what I may be capable of) is made more of uncertainty than of trying to be clever, work everything out, and know it all. To cultivate negative capability, Keats's suggestion is to practise a certain nonparticipation, to make space for the unthought, to allow the mysterious or doubtful to remain just that and, importantly, to be willing to let intuition take over.

As this constellation of voices about unknowing shows, a creative state is likely to be propelled by various degrees of liminality, uncertainty, doubt, even confusion, which is something that countless practitioners – artists, designers, scientists, philosophers, writers, poets – are well aware of.[31] States of liminality and uncertainty generate a mode of knowing contiguous to the intuitive, a mode that 'narrows down the region of positive, phenomenological knowledge, while specifying the boundaries of knowledge and pinpointing the uncertainties that surround it'.[32]

This focus on the uncertain boundaries between knowing and unknowing returns in perhaps the most remarkable voice in this chapter's constellation: Nicholas of Cusa, the fifteenth-century German thinker known for his doctrine of 'learned ignorance'(*docta ignorantia*). Philosopher, theologian, diplomatic, cardinal, humanist scholar, papal legacy, traveller extraordinaire, promoter of interfaith tolerance, Nicholas of Cusa is one of the first thinkers of the modern era. Echoing Socrates, he states that true knowledge can only be found in igno-

[27] Karin Knorr Cetina, *Epistemic Cultures. How the Sciences Make Knowledge* (Cambridge, Mass. and London: Harvard University Press, 2003), 63.

[28] Karin Knorr Cetina, 'Objectual Practice', in *The Practice Turn in Contemporary Theory*, ed. Karin Knorr Cetina, Theodore R. Schatzki and Eike von Savigny (London: Routledge, 2001), 175–88.

[29] Knorr Cetina, *Epistemic Cultures*, 64.

[30] John Keats, *The Letters of John Keats*, ed. H. E. Rollins (Cambridge: Cambridge University Press, 1958), vol. I, 193.

[31] For an account of negative capability from the perspective of an artist working at the intersection of science and technology through the means of artistic practice and visual representation see Fiona Crisp, 'Negative Capability. Imaging and Imagining Fundamental Science Through Productive Doubt', *GeoHumanities* 1, no. 1 (2015): 188–97.

[32] Knorr Cetina, *Epistemic Cultures*, 63. On contiguity see Chapter 3.

rance; that becoming aware of my limitations is the highest form of knowledge; and that to be learned means to know that I do not know. This is what he calls 'learned ignorance'. The only thing I can do is to keep on dwelling in the zone where knowing turns into unknowing, keep on making conjectures, knowing that my knowledge will always be incomplete. While 'learned ignorance' may be dismissed as yet another paradox, it is in fact a powerful argument that turns ignorance into transformational learning. To know is above all to know the limits of my knowledge. The point of learning is not the acquisition of knowledge but being changed by it.

The relevance of this argument is lucidly illustrated by Boaventura de Sousa Santos who draws on Nicholas of Cusa to offer a counterpart to the violence of Western epistemicide by way of reclaiming those theories (indigenous to the West) and marginalized by it. De Sousa Santos calls this his 'search for a non-Occidentalist West'.[33] As infinite knowledge (which Cusano calls 'divine') cannot ever be reached, it can only be acknowledged in two ways: 'through our total ignorance of it; and through the limitations it imposes on the accuracy of the knowledge we have of infinite things'.[34] De Sousa Santos uses Nicholas of Cusa's example to argue that 'to be a learned ignorant in our time is to know that the epistemological diversity of the world is potentially infinite and that each way of knowing grasp it only in a very limited manner'.[35] Knowledge is not an object to obtain or a place to reach. It is a continuous process of learning at once *humble* (because it is aware of its own limits) and *plural* (because it is open to all other possible knowledge). Learned ignorance becomes a radical, timely and urgent argument for pluriversality.[36]

STRATAGEMS

Building on this, I now move to describe my stratagems for inhabiting unknowing. The section below looks at *conjecture, divination, blur, vanishing into things* and *wu wei* – to add to the *exodus, exit* and *opportunism* encountered in Chapter 3. Through these stratagems, I enter unknowing through a crack, a moment before it closes. They are modes attuned to how things come to be, because they accord status to the unthought and the less-than-cognitive. They are also less embroiled with authority, expertise and mastery. This is how I begin to cultivate the capacity to set possible possibles in motion, resist the epistemicidal capture of machines of prediction and experiment with designing new modes of existence.

[33] Boaventura De Sousa Santos, 'A Non-Occidentalist West? Learned Ignorance and Ecology of Knowledge', *Theory, Culture & Society* 26, no. 7–8 (2009): 103–25.

[34] Ibid., 114.

[35] Ibid., 115.

[36] Savransky, *Around the Day in Eighty Worlds*; Arturo Escobar, *Designs for the Pluriverse, Radical Interdependence, Autonomy, and the Making of Worlds* (Durham: Duke University Press, 2018).

Conjecture: A Leap from the Known to the Unknown

Italian historian Carlo Ginzburg is known for treating history like a forensic science that reveals a new kind of historical knowledge through the unearthing of traces and the examination of clues.[37] His approach, known as 'microhistory', breaks what he calls the self-evidence of the present. One of Ginzburg's arguments is that history is not fixed, but unstable and highly contingent, because it contains all the paths un-taken; the events that could have happened but did not; the moments of latency that remain un-realized and un-actualized.[38] On this basis, he develops his 'conjectural method'. To 'make conjecture' is a mode of knowledge-production that allows for elements of chance and unpredictability to enter the process. It uses traces to reconstruct past horizons of expectation by uncovering what could have been; it restores the uncertainty of the event by examining un-realized possible futures.[39] The roots of conjecture are in Mesopotamian divination, and in the tracking skills of the first hunters.[40] While tracking examines footprints and traces as clues of events that have already happened in the past, divination is the art of interpreting signs in order to foresee the future. As divination is examined in detail below, suffice to say that, for Ginzburg, conjecture and divination are quite similar in terms of method: 'both require minute examination of the real, however trivial, to uncover the traces of events which the observer cannot directly experience. Droppings, footprints, hairs, feathers, in the one case; animals' innards, drops of oil in water, stars, involuntary movements, in the other.'[41] The body of knowledge produced in this way – 'conjectural lore' – emerges from the concreteness of individual experience and resists quantification and measurement. Such concrete quality 'was both the strength of this kind of knowledge, and its limit – it could not make use of the powerful and terrible tool of abstraction'.[42] Ginzburg uses the wonderful expression 'elastic rigour' to explain the seemingly paradoxical nature of a mode of knowledge-production where unknowing fully participated in the knowing

[37] Among Ginzburg's works: *Il Formaggio e i Vermi. Il Cosmo di un Mugnaio del Cinquecento* (Torino: Einaudi, 1976); *Miti, Emblemi, Spie. Morfologia e Storia* (Torino: Einaudi, 1986); *Storia Notturna. Una Decifrazione del Sabba* (Torino: Einaudi, 1989); *Occhiacci di Legno. Nove Riflessioni sulla Distanza* (Milano: Feltrinelli, 1998); *Il Filo e le Tracce. Vero, Falso, Finto* (Milano: Feltrinelli, 2006); *La Lettera Uccide* (Milano: Adelphi, 2021).

[38] Carlo Ginzburg, *Clues, Myths, and the Historical Method* (Baltimore: The John Hopkins University Press, 1989).

[39] Ginzburg describes the conjectural model as a paradigm for the construction of knowledge where the division between 'rational' and 'irrational' is revealed as spurious. Carlo Ginzburg, 'Morelli, Freud and Sherlock Holmes. Clues and Scientific Method', *History Workshop* 9 (Oxford: Oxford University Press, 1980), 5–36.

[40] For the ancient Greeks, conjecture was the domain of the goddess Metis, already encountered in Chapter 4, who symbolizes divination by means of water. This kind of conjectural, divinatory, intuitive knowledge was over-shadowed (literally swallowed) by newly dominant theories of knowledge. See Chapter 4 (conclusion).

[41] Ginzburg, 'Morelli, Freud and Sherlock Holmes', 13.

[42] Ibid., 21.

through 'a whiff, a glance, an intuition'.[43] An example of this is the Sufi notion of 'firasa', the capacity to read situations and infer the future so 'to leap from the known to the unknown by inference',[44] – a leap that leads straight into divination.

Divination: Chance as an Opportunity for Sense-Making

Divination is the systematic inquiry into the unknown that uses chance as an opportunity for sense-making. Its purpose is not to give conclusive answers, nor to supply the inquirer with a definitive decision-making technique, even less to predict the future. Rather, divination should be seen as a technique of rewriting existent stories to carve new sense-making paths in the *present*. What world traditions of divination have in common is the assumption that a partial, imperfect, opaque knowledge of the unknown can be approached by interpreting selected signs and patterns. This process requires certain constant elements: signs to read, a divining agent, a framework of interpretation and a state of 'omen-mindedness', in other words, being on the look-out for possible signs from the supernatural.[45] While divinatory practices could be *prognostic* (to elaborate on unknowns still in the future) or *diagnostic* (to interpret current or past events), their key function is to handle uncertainty by the re-crafting of stories, a manoeuvre that could range from the ecstatic/intuitive to the techno/scientific.[46]

The knowledge created through divinatory means, expressed through intuitive evocation and transcending rational cognition, tends to be capacious enough to accommodate enigmatic, equivocal, divergent, even conflicting meanings. It is this ambiguity that must be treasured to inhabit the contingency of the world. Divination presupposes a knowledge that cannot be known but only recognized and interpreted by observing hints and by making conjectures based on these hints. This is why, as Agamben observes, divination is a knowledge *without subject*. What the diviner knows is that there is something they do not know.[47]

[43] Ibid., 28.

[44] Ibid.

[45] Kim Beerden, *World Full of Signs. Ancient Greek Divination in Context* (Leiden and Boston: Brill, 2013).

[46] Modern stochastic processes dealing with randomness probability can be framed as divinatory. Indeed, the term stochastic comes from the Greek *stokazomai* (meaning 'to aim at', 'conjecture' or 'guess') describing the art of conjecturing through signs.

[47] Agamben also points out that the consolidation of modern science as an autonomous domain was due, in part, precisely to the expulsion of divinatory arts from the pursuit of knowledge. From the seventeenth century onward, the subject of science became the only subject of knowledge, and any other knowledge marginalized, shunted out of the canon. The demise of divinatory sciences does not signal, however, the end of the knowledge of the unknown but rather its re-appropriation elsewhere (for instance, as unconscious cognition in psychoanalysis, and as potential captured by algorithmic machines). Giorgio Agamben, *L'Avventura* (Rome: Nottetempo, 2015).

These themes are lucidly dissected by Ramey in his *Politics of Divination.*[48] His analysis of divination focuses on how the neoliberal era of hyper-financialized capital has appropriated and monetized the contingency at the core of divinatory techniques to extract quantifiable value from the unknown. Uncertainty becomes 'futures' – contracts to buy or sell a specific asset at a future date – to speculate on, through the systematic exploitation of, and extraction of meaning from, the unknown. Market expertise becomes a modern-day version of divination, financial specialists become the equivalent of ancient seers, their oracular power siphoning plural futures into a single channel dictated by market forces, corporate interests and advertisers' agendas.

This appropriation of contingency binds the known to the unknowable and turns nonknowledge into a profitable asset. Chance becomes a fungible resource that acquires meaning only when tied to how profitable (i.e. calculable) it can be. Capture and financialization of uncertainty are the dominant logic of contemporary capitalism, which Ramey describes as the 'neoliberal religion of contingency', when contingency, chance and the unknown are at once deified, commodified and weaponized.[49]

Ramey's inquiry into divination exposes the extent to which contemporary financial and algorithmic governmentality exploit the unknown through pre-emption, capture and erosion of potential, and the terminal foreclosure of futures. Ramey calls for the 'decolonization of divination', that is, its de-linking from neoliberal capture by reclaiming what has been taken – the potential meanings contained within chance – beyond the hallucinatory pseudo-science of algorithmic capture and the Delphic distortions of disaster finance. This concerns how a reclaiming of other stories, and of an *otherwise of uncertainty* can push back against 'inevitabilism'. Other stories are needed, to incorporate chance in meaningful ways, other 'politics of divination' based on a radically re-imagined relationship with the unknown and with unknowing. Other stories are needed, to narrate how only an unscripted encounter with chance can scramble the fiction of temporal linearity, insert the future into the cracks of the present and deliciously swell the sense of what is possible.

Blur: Potential for Knowledge

Unknowing and nonknowledge are often depicted as the contamination of clarity. Fog, haze, clouds are the images often used to evoke the opacity that

48 Ramey, *Politics of Divination*. See also Robin Mackay, *The Medium of Contingency* (Manchester: Urbanomic, 2011).

49 Unlike previous eras, equally violent, extractive or authoritarian, the present is characterized by a 'transition from a knowledge-based to a *nonknowledge-based economy*, from an economy based on prediction and control to one based on the exploitation of uncertainty as such' (Ramey, *Politics of Divination*, 4). See also Luciana Parisi, 'Critical Computation: Digital Automata and General Artificial Thinking', *Theory, Culture & Society* 36, no. 2 (2019): 89–121, for a discussion of the primacy of contingency as constitutive of neoliberal techno-capital.

blurs the lucidity of thinking and prevents flawless vision. In Western thought, informed by Greek ontology and epistemology, 'to know' concerns precisely clarity, intelligibility and transparency. The object of knowledge is supposed to emerge as a well-delineated entity against the background; blurriness and opacity are seen as obstacles to knowledge.[50] From an ontological perspective knowledge must make evident the difference between being and non-being. It must push against any obstruction that threatens their distinction. Any ontological indeterminacy must be rejected to preserve the dualistic nature of the system.

Chinese thought offers a formidable counterpoint to this dualistic view because it assigns prime importance to the *blur*. Here, ontological indeterminacy is the very condition of knowing. Too much clarity is utterly suspicious. Far from being a problem with no definition, an impenetrable hurdle, a non-chartable territory or a paralysing difficulty, the blur is what 'makes knowledge inexhaustible'.[51] It is what makes knowledge possible in the first instance. Take the case of war strategy. What for the Western strategist is an obstacle to overcome – the impenetrable 'fog of war' – for their Chinese equivalent is a powerful resource. The uncertainty expressed by the blur is not an obstacle, nor the sign of a confused, ignorant or naïve mind. Instead, it is where the *potential for* knowledge resides.

This difference in how the blur is understood across two distinct cultural traditions is instructive. Chinese thought privileges interconnectedness, the flow of changeable events, the processual and the metamorphic rather than the dichotomy of being vs. non-being. Rather crudely put, what would appear illogical to a mind schooled in the Aristotelian principle of non-contradiction, such as the idea of two contraries weaving into and becoming each other, blurring the categorical distinction between 'self' and 'non-self', is the basis of Chinese thought's propensity to see 'the coherence of all change'.[52]

Once everything is interpreted as part of a continuum, the distinction between 'being' and 'non-being' tends to dissolve (in a blur). This hazy, vague, indeterminate, blurry space is the incipience of things, what Deleuze calls the virtual, Rovelli calls the incandescent matter of reality, and Zen and Tantric master Daniel Odier calls universal phantasmagoria. This is how knowledge comes from the blur, from not knowing, from uncertainty. Through the wisdom of seeing what is not visible, sensing without touching, knowing what is not known.

[50] Allen, 'The Cloud of Knowing'; Barry Allen, *Vanishing Into Things. Knowledge in Chinese Tradition* (Cambridge, Mass. and London: Harvard University Press, 2015); Barry Allen, 'War as a Problem of Knowledge. Theory of Knowledge in China's Military Philosophy', *Philosophy East and West* 65, no. 1 (2015): 1–17; François Jullien, *Detour and Access. Strategies of Meanings in China and Greece* (New York: Zone Books, 2000); François Jullien, *The Great Image Has No Form, or On the Nonobject Through Painting* (Chicago and London: University of Chicago Press, 2009).

[51] Allen, 'The Cloud of Knowing', 452.

[52] Jullien, *The Silent Transformations*, 36.

My succinct reflections around Chinese thought hint at its potential overlap with process philosophies' concepts of the virtual, the not-yet and becoming.[53] Indeed, to engage with the virtual is, in essence, to engage with not knowing. Likewise, to tune in on how the virtual might unfold – sensing its 'incipience' – is learning to stay with the unknown. And to acknowledge and accept the unknown, adapting organically to it, is the condition to work *with* it (and not against it). What is also important is how not knowing connects to the capacity to get 'unstuck' and be 'flexible and undogmatic, hence more spontaneously responsive, therefore more effective'.[54] This generative connection between nonknowledge and efficacy is the idea the rest of the chapter focuses on.

THE EFFICACY OF VANISHING INTO THINGS

To gain knowledge from the blur means also that true knowing is not about grasping a discrete object of knowledge, but rather apprehending the processes through which the world is becoming, ceaselessly. As many, too numerous to recount, have pointed out – philosophers (Whitehead, Bergson), quantum scientists (Rovelli), architecture theorists (Kwinter), Tantric practitioners (Odier), pre-Socratics (Lucretius), feminist thinkers (Braidotti, Barad), Daoist masters (Laozi) – what are called 'objects' are nothing but discrete packets arbitrarily sliced from ongoing processes whose temporality exceeds human scale. What to my eyes appears as a static form is always in the process of becoming else. Just because I cannot see it, it does not mean this process is not happening. When I misinterpret processes as objects I am stuck on origin and essence; fixated on statements and beliefs; pursuing explanations to universalize otherwise partial, precarious, impermanent knowledges.

The truth is that things have no essential nucleus, no recognizable self-identity, no immutable substance. What they are depends on *how* they relate to other things – their modes of *contiguity* and *adjacence*. In a non-dualistic universe 'opposites include and transform into each other, and nothing is permanently raised above transformation or experience'.[55] That is why objectivity must be unlearned, Allen counsels, and fixation with forms reined in. His exhortation is to 'overcome the limitation that makes us think in terms of *is* and *is not*, or in terms of boundaries and forms rather than relations and evolution. Instead of

[53] A side note about becoming and change. Western logic tends to equate becoming and change. But becoming is not always coincidental with transformation. The misunderstanding is to see change as something that happens *to* being, as if there were beings first – determinate and self-identical – upon which change is 'applied'. What is becoming does not necessarily change; it is rather through ceaseless differentiation that something maintains itself (e.g. the human body). On the other hand, 'to change is to stop being one thing and begin to be another: "whatever by being changed passes outside its own boundaries, at once this is the death of that which was before" (Lucretius). Hence the mortuary logic of our logos' (Allen, 'The Cloud of Knowing', 526–7).

[54] Allen, 'The Cloud of Knowing', 485.

[55] Ibid., 476.

things (knowing their names and how to talk about them), we spontaneously change with them, become a part of their economy'.[56]

Allen's argument is inspired by the Chinese *Dao*, the spontaneous flow of transformation that involves everything and everyone. *Dao* is simply the 'way',[57] but not in the sense of a road or path, more like a river or a canal. It is the way of flowing water.[58] *Dao* is the art of transforming with changes, which is also

> an art of knowing what is not known and what not to do. To remain fluid and capable of seizing opportunities when they are easy is in part knowing how to evade the need to act at all. A kind of not-knowing – knowing how not to act; what not to determine; when not to continue; when to defer, refrain, or consult.[59]

The 'art of knowing what is not known and what not to do' is also what informs the notion of 'vanishing into things', which concerns how 'to penetrate the actual and present and glimpse the future that is birthing'.[60] As another vivid image to think with, 'vanishing into things' speaks to the capacity to sense how things may develop *before* changes take place, and respond to them as they unfold. It is not about prophesizing or mechanically anticipating the future. As Allen puts it:

> The idea is not to possess the facts of the future and calculate; it is, rather, to affect the future discreetly by knowing where it is birthing and pliable. Such knowledge requires a kind of penetration, not from phenomena to essence, but from the obvious to the subtle, the actual to the virtual, the manifest to the latent.[61]

'Vanishing into things' is anchored in a nonduality, which is not given in opposition to dualism, but as what dissolves it.[62] While Western thought remains

[56] Ibid., 497.

[57] Compare the *Dao* to the Western notion of *method*, a term that also means *way* [from the Greek *meta* + *hodos*]. But this is where they diverge: method, as shown earlier in the section *A Note on Method*, takes me through well-known grooves, into familiar territories that yield predictable and tested outcomes. Conventional method works with what I already know, presuming and defining the obstacles to overcome, specifying 'how to' do just that.

[58] The way of flowing water makes me think of Deleuze and Guattari's 'line of flight' [*ligne de fuite*], which as Massumi points out in his 'Notes on the translation' to *A Thousand Plateaus* has nothing to do with flying, and all to do with liquid rivulets. 'Fuite [flight] covers not only the act of fleeing or eluding but also flowing, leaking, and disappearing into the distance (the vanishing point in a painting is a point de fuite). It has no relation to flying' (Deleuze and Guattari, *A Thousand Plateaus*, xvi).

[59] Allen, 'The Cloud of Knowing', 484.

[60] Allen, 'War as a Problem of Knowledge', 1.

[61] Allen, 'The Cloud of Knowing', 462. Also, the movement from the actual to the virtual must be read alongside Bergson's account of the possible and the real. See Chapter 1.

[62] On the matter of nonduality, Allen suggests using the word *emptiness* instead of *nonduality*. He also notes that what is usually taken as the opposite of nonduality (monism) is dualistic in itself insofar as 'it discriminates and attacks dualism' (Allen, 'The Cloud of

preoccupied with matters of objective reality beyond subjective perception, Chinese thought turns its attention to the cultivation of the capacity to work with potentialities and the efficacy of the response. Rather than theorizing how things came to be (origin), what they are (essence) or what their aim may be (teleology); rather than asking questions about the genesis of knowledge or its perceived status, what matters is learning to work efficaciously with potentialities.

Is this knowledge worth pursuing? Is this thing useful? How does it contribute to enhancing my capacity to act in the world? How does it enhance my vitality, that is, my capacity to grow, change and respond adequately? What moves me, really? Spinoza's lesson, again. This is about cultivating the ability to be firm whilst traversing change, changing so to elude gluey situations, retaining the ability to yield, avoiding being stuck, adopting a metic wayfinding.[63]

Working with uncertainty as an ally entails precisely this skill: learning to see processes and not things, learning to sense the flow below the apparent stability of the real. It calls for subtle artifice, that is, the *designing* of favourable conditions. It entails making the outcome of my actions appear as if it had happened by itself.[64] It calls not for the acquisition of more knowledge, but for its *loss*, like when 'sugar vanishes into water but is not gone, merely rendered imperceptible, while transforming the water with new potential'.[65] The sugar has not disappeared, only changed from its previous form into a new one. Once dissolved, it has turned water into something else. Water is now sweet. *Both* water and sugar have turned into something else. Both still exist, but in a new intensified mode.

Vanishing into things is the stratagem that perhaps more than the others highlights what design can do. Soft and resilient forms, whose edges are blurred, and are not fully distinguishable from their environment, are adapted for optimal interaction with (and merging in) other forms in the ecosystem, open to gentle sensing and response. They are the most favourable forms conducive to conviviality, symbiosis and sympathy.

Knowing', 507). So how do we express nondualism? Not through monism but through emptiness. He describes the 'practice of emptying out' in this way: 'First, you overcome all the distinctions, then you overcome your overcoming, overcome thinking of yourself as having overcome something, or having realized something others have not. Duality may seem inextricable from thought. What would we think if we made no distinctions? But of course, nondualistic thought would have to be nonobjective too. It is not thinking "emptiness" (as a paradoxical object); it is emptying thinking (of objects), emptying consciousness of objectivity, forgetting about distinctions, even the distinction between is and is not. It is not just that thought has no objects; one is not interested in them, does not care about objectivity or the lack of it – whether objects are the same or different, better or worse' (ibid., 507). Wisdom 'has no goal; its value is to keep a way open, to avoid accumulating obstructions, to sustain viability' (ibid., 469)… not a way to achieve a domain, a place or knowledge, but a 'way to stay on course amid transformation, never halting, never stuck, maintaining a perfect balance' (ibid.).

63 This ability leads back to Spinoza's art of arranging good encounters as a 'practical philosophy'. Deleuze, *Spinoza*, 119.

64 A strategy to use (in war and beyond) is the trick to make your opponent think there is a trick, when 'the trick is that there is no trick'. Allen, 'The Cloud of Knowing', 505.

65 Ibid., 529.

French philosopher and sinologist François Jullien has written arresting pages about what he calls the 'propensity of things' – 'the potential that originates not in human initiative but instead results from the very disposition of things'[66] – and how to intuitively grasp what is not actual yet, but might be; how potential can be apprehended when things are still indeterminate, and how to work with the uncertain to turn it into latitude for possible possibles. Learning how to effortlessly sense the propensity of things enhances my capacities to grow, to exist and to live. The subtle skill of sensing, and moving with, the propensity of things enables me to inhabit the mutability and unknowability of the present without being bogged down or stuck in the 'how-much-I-know'. It is an existence-enriching, affirmative mode of knowing through which I enter into the space of maybes. I acquire and cultivate this capacity not by the means of more knowing (a calculable, quantified approach that needs to be unlearned) but by a loss of it, the bold, risky and unscripted gesture of *dwelling* in maybes, where what rules is both the *unknown* (what I do not know) and the *knowing-not*: not acting, not knowing, not doing. *Wu wei.*

WU WEI: NON-ACTION THAT LEAVES NOTHING UNDONE

The Chinese notion of *wu wei* [*wu* = no + *wei* = action/doing] concerns my subtle understanding of the propensity of things so that I can act in alliance with how circumstances unfold and not against them, without using external energy or force. *Wu wei* is non-action that leaves nothing undone. It is 'the ability to act with minimum effort by going with the natural flow of things, in short, being in tune with *Dao*'.[67] The negative – *not* doing – far from signalling passive inaction or lack of agency indicates a highly cultivated stance requiring practice and effort. *Wu wei* is the intentional and skilful craft of responding to situations with optimal grace and invisible degrees of intensity. *Wu wei* cannot be pre-planned, nor scripted in advance. It is not a fully cognitive deliberation.[68] Rather, it is the art of knowing where possible futures are being birthed (*ars nasciendi*) by sensing the direction they are about to take, rather than fixating on their form and identity. It is the practice of changing with things as they change; observing the micro so as to catch a glimpse of the macro it is turning into (and vice versa). After all, the knower is able to discern the flower by

[66] Jullien, *The Propensity of Things*, 13.

[67] Jeaneane Fowler and Merv Fowler, *Chinese Religions. Beliefs and Practices* (Brighton and Portland: Sussex Academic Press, 2008), 108.

[68] While it is clear how indispensable *wu wei* is for flourishing, it is far from easy and requires persistence. There is also a distinction to be made between bad *wu wei* (the doing-nothing driven by vanity) and good *wu wei* where enough latitude is afforded so that things have room to go and obtain themselves, in thriving. Kuang-Ming Wu, '*Wu wei* after Zhuangzi', in *The Imperative of Understanding: Chinese Philosophy, Comparative Philosophy, and Onto-Hermeneutics. A Tribute Volume Dedicated to Professor Chung-ying Cheng*, ed. On-Cho Ng (New York: Global Scholarly Publications, 2008), 174–99.

looking at the seed.[69] It is also an art of vanishing into things, a practice that is quietly inventive and astutely opportunistic, which is also a metic wayfinding. I begin vanishing into things when I become 'softer, fuzzier, less distinct, less well defined, yet also larger, more complex, more integral, and effortlessly effective'.[70] More cosmic.

All my stratagems hint at how efficacious unknowing judiciously weaves itself around the seeds of the future. Far from being lodged in the mind as theory, abstraction or representation, they are practical responses that read the 'subtle signs of incipience, the beginning or becoming of things, discerning points where development remains pliable and can be inconspicuously diverted'.[71] My stratagems demand that I pay attention to less-than-perceptible, but nonetheless ongoing, transformation. Transitions I see the effects of, but where I cannot pinpoint distinct, separate moment of differentiation from one 'state' to the next: snow melting, ice becoming water, flowers blossoming, weeds ripening.

To reiterate: This perspective is profoundly non-dualistic not because it opposes dualism, but because it eliminates its presupposition. Disallowing dyadic opposition from encroaching on my modes of thinking and existing shows how to live well, richly, with pleasure and affirmation. This is the important insight of this chapter's 'unknowing stratagems'. They offer not an alternative method, but the capacity, which is both affirmative ethics and cosmological orientation, to engage with the truly unknown, where method cannot reach: Where only the *power of maybes* can truly be felt.

69 Allen, 'War as a Problem of Knowledge', 1.

70 Allen, 'The Cloud of Knowing', 529.

71 Allen, *Vanishing Into Things*, 24.

Conclusion: Whatever Designs

Who says design cannot be cosmic?
GÖKHAN KODALAK AND SANFORD KWINTER[1]

A COSMOLOGICAL ORIENTATION FOR DESIGN

As a way of concluding, I shall briefly reprise some of the themes that *The Power of Maybes* has woven in all its constellations so to bring them to bear on some final reflections on design.

The key argument that I have put forward is that uncertainty *can* become an ally. An ally to envision futures away from panic, overdetermination and stories of inevitability. An ally to release the grip of existent blueprints, predefined scripts and ingrained grooves. An ally to resist machines' capture of potential. For this to happen, however, uncertainty must be understood as cosmic and experienced in all its oceanic irrevocable force. This is the condition required for the amphibolic character of power – potential and impotential – to be embraced; for indeterminacy to be reclaimed as a source of wild delight and for the 'luminous spiral of the possible' to be inhabited fully.

There is another way of saying this. *The Power of Maybes* has claimed that the gap between intelligible matter and sensible matter must be recomposed. There is little doubt that this *gap* and what it truly means (to have lost the capacity to sense the coincidence of mind and matter) continues to have perverse consequences for human and more-than-human existence, for life in all its forms, for the planet. The radical nonduality *The Power of Maybes* has proposed through its cosmological orientation mends this breach by showing that matter thinks and thought materializes, incessantly. It shows how the coincidence of matter and thought is expressed in the tremor that traverses everything, from quanta to quasars. It exhorts me to acknowledge and honour

[1] Gökhan Kodalak and Sanford Kwinter, 'The Return of Nature', *Log* 49 (2020): 121.

this tremor in the choices I make and, in this way, participate in an ecological metaphysics for planetary renewal and reparation.

To acknowledge and honour the cosmological orientation in my own choices – my modes of knowing, being and acting – becomes even more important for designers who have a great deal to contribute to the health, reparation and wellbeing of the planet – and to its demise too. The cosmological orientation becomes a possible vision for design to eschew the lethal user/consumer paradigm upon which it remains anchored and to reach beyond the canon of human-centredness. Moving beyond human-centredness, however, does not simply mean a shift to the nonhuman or the more-than-human, although this manoeuvre, ontologically as well as epistemically, is certainly important.

Rather, my cosmological orientation invites design to shift its focus to what I see as the unquestionable centrality of cosmic matter – noetic matter – prior to the enclosures that constrain beings into form. It invites the view that power (in the sense of potential) belongs not to human intention, or subjective authorship, or identitarian agency, but to the incandescent tremor of matter. It indicates that a non-hierarchical, radical nonduality as the one I have outlined can only begin from the tiny gesture and the practice of the 'little bit'. In short, it is a vision for a *micropolitical project.* It is the small movement, one contiguous surface at a time, that connects the micro to the macro through the careful (and cunning) cultivation of astute dispositions for entering the unknown.

Mine is an exhortation for design to experiment with reimagining itself through a cosmic lens. Design's own and continually evolving ontological dimension – its world-building, existence-shaping, future-crafting power – can be expressed by placing at its core not just the human, the nonhuman, the more-than-human, the end-user or the stakeholder, but the plenitude of undifferentiated potential. Thus, to echo the question raised by the epigraph at the beginning of this chapter – 'Who says design cannot be cosmic?' – I shall respond: Design can be cosmic by way of inhabiting oceanic uncertainty, in other words, by placing potential at its core, in all its amphibolic nature.

DESIGNING WITH UNCERTAINTY

My call is therefore for design to experiment with uncertainty and with potential as a trigger for a non-anthropocentric mode that supersedes the 'user', operates beneath identitarian indexes and agencies, decentres the human and participates in the constitution of fuller, richer, modes of living. Before looking more closely at what this means however, I will pre-empt some of the objections that the concerned reader (designer or user) may wish to raise.

One objection may be that a design approach driven by uncertainty would inevitably fall short of the necessary requisites for safety that most design-driven industries and sectors depend on. How would designed products work if based on a paradigm of uncertainty and potential? How would safety be ensured? How could the consumer trust that a product – a tin opener, an airplane, a financial service, a lipstick – will deliver what was promised knowing that its design was mired in uncertainty? I ask these questions rhetorically not only to dispel any lingering doubt that the reader may have about my argument but also as an opportunity to address any concerns that my argument may have raised. What do I mean by designing with uncertainty?

To design with uncertainty means to pay attention to the *potential* that all that exists has already. It means to acknowledge and honour this potential that traverses all life, organic and inorganic, all life-forms, all that exists, without hierarchy. In this proposition I am not alone. I echo architecture theorist Sanford Kwinter and designer Bruce Mau, whose extensive collaboration has produced a unique body of work around the intersection of cosmology, aesthetics, design and pantheism, all facets of an inquiry into how design can express the continuous rather than the discontinuous, and do so in ways that are ecologically and ontologically enriching, rather than depleting.[2] Through a focus on 'a sentience-oriented, life-centred cosmology',[3] Kwinter and Mau advocate for a cosmological shift in design attitudes, practices and mindsets.

Relevant to my argument and to my cosmological orientation is the attention Kwinter and Mau pay to what they call 'kernels of potentials' around which the world forms, each a possible site of (design) intervention that calls for acknowledgement, honouring and care. Kernels of potential, like the crystals of the possible seen earlier, are nothing but the undifferentiated that can be accessed by working with uncertainty and by entering into it through a careful, astute disposition (my unknowing stratagems).

The invitation is for design to be alert and attentive to the fullness of potential, at each step of its endeavour. It is to disengage from the instrumental execution of an idea and a function, to unhinge from the blueprint and be instead the instigator of experiments with what *may be*.

With potential at its centre, some of design's fundamental questions – How are things born? How do they come to be? – will lead to different interpretations. A potential-centred design sees things coming to be not by the implementation of an idea, or through the execution of a blueprint, but through potential and the 'tension toward' that Spinoza called *conatus*, the tremor that traverses everything. Things come to be through the confluence of matter thinking and thought materializing that goes on to shape what is being generated and, by extension, the world. This is true for a plant, for a piece of writing, for a designed artefact. This capacity of being born of all things is the capacity of matter to continue generating forms through its endless transformation. To acknowledge, accept and honour that there is nothing outside self-generating matter opens a trajectory that is both stunning – instantly reverberating into how mine, yours, every body encounters the world – and generative – a portal through which new visions of how things *may be* can be accessed. It is an ethical proposition that can inform design as the ontological capacity to produce and refine the conditions of possibility for existence, for a fuller mode of living. For a life.

[2] Ecologically here in the sense of Guattari's three ecologies seen earlier. Sanford Kwinter and Bruce Mau, 'Design is Not for Us: A Simple Desultory Philippic', *Log* 51 (2021): 155–76.

[3] Kwinter and Mau, 'Design is Not for Us', 167.

A LIFE

Kwinter and Mau write that 'as designers we are not only obliged but are also most effective when we approach life with a reverence and respect and a concern for our position among all other life-forms'.[4] Moving away from the narcissism of user-centred or human-centred design, their proposal for *life-centred design* re-establishes life as the focus, the engine and the condition for any design intervention (and for design's crucial tool: the design brief).

It is important at this point to clarify how this notion of life should be interpreted. It is not 'my' life. Not 'this' life. Not the life of some (human?) to the detriment of the life of others. Not a deified 'Life' as the pinnacle of humanity. Not an imagined ideal 'Life'. Rather, life as an ongoing experiment with form, with humans only a (tiny) part of this experiment. Life, to use Kwinter's expression, is 'matter that knows reliably, stably, and continuously over time'; it is 'what makes a world *a world*'.[5] This is also an invitation to treat life and non-life not as opposed, but as part of the same continuum, only with different degrees of organization and indeterminacy. In short, life is intended as a life in its fullness, its uncertain plenitude, what I have called a 'whatever' life, what Erin Manning describes as 'the force of life-living that exceeds the shape of *this* life'.[6] Or, to borrow one last time Deleuze's words, *a* life that coincides with 'pure immanence', with the impersonal and undifferentiated flow of potential.

DESIGN AND… AND

Kwinter and Mau go on to propose a kind of life-centred design they call 'pantheistic', which they describe as based on 'the idea that designed objects might be construed as uniformly alive, uniformly freighted with energy and potential'.[7] Their call to design to attend to the energy that circulates in all things and to tilt its focus on the potential it expresses is very much aligned to mine and *The Power of Maybes*' proposition. Perhaps I care slightly less of naming this approach 'pantheistic design'. This has nothing to do with pantheism which as I have shown is a philosophy and a mode of knowing that I fully endorse. It has rather to do with pushing back against the habit, widespread in design studies, of over-denominating, which often has the effect of fabricating distortions. For this reason, I would rather not add yet another qualifier to the already long list of qualifiers that have been attached to design. Here is a inventory the reader may be familiar with: activist, agile, agonistic, affective, animistic, collaborative, conceptual, critical, decolonial, dialogic, emotional, empathic, environmental,

4 Kwinter and Mau, 'Design is Not for Us', 157.

5 Kwinter, 'A Sensitive Matter', 69. Kwinter and Mau quote biologist E.O. Wilson, who said 'rock is slow life, and life is fast rock' to underline that our body is matter animated with electricity (Kwinter and Mau, 'Design is Not for Us').

6 Erin Manning, 'Angular Perspective. Or, How Concern Shapes the Field', *Log* 49 (2020): 185.

7 Kwinter and Mau, 'Design is Not for Us', 158.

fourth-order, humanitarian, human-centred, hypervernacular, integrative, legal, meta, more-than-human, narrative, necropolitical, non-intentional, ontological, open, participatory, performative, pluriversal, problematizing, relational, social, speculative, sustainable, transdisciplinary, transitional, unemotional, universal, user-centred.[8]

While this proliferation seems to underscore the multiple and fecund directions in which design is expanding, the effect is one of inflated segmentation. The project of expanding design should be the opposite of this parcelling nomenclature that does little to advance a serious reflection around design and its impact in the world. For me, expanding design concerns in primis what design can and cannot do. What it may or not be. It concerns potential. To propose yet another design typology, or framework, or paradigm would not only defeat the point but is an approach that has become exhausted, un-generative (and a little disingenuous). I would rather not. Instead, through the approach I have developed in *The Power of Maybes*, I propose to continue mapping the unexpected encounters of design with concepts, philosophies and cosmologies, building new constellations, igniting further thoughts and delighting in the visceral intellectual pleasure of transversality.[9]

AN OTHERWISE LIFE

Uncertainty, by definition, is predicated on not-knowing. An uncertain situation is a situation whose outcome is not known in advance, one that cannot be fully assessed and resolved beforehand. This is the problem with uncertainty. As a space of un-knowing it can be (and it is) variously populated by forecasts, expectations, hopes, projections, dread, fear. To be uncertain is to know that I do not know what is coming next. Uncertainty has to do with the not-yet. It means to be certain of one thing only: That I do not know what may happen.

I take this not-knowing as a formidable resource, one that I can learn to hold as my ally through carefully curated stratagems and an astute disposition. Not-knowing harbours the wondrous and the indistinct, as well as surprise, apprehension, foreboding, open-ended expectation – expectation for something, for anything, for nothing. It is not simply curiosity for what may or may not happen, nor is it fatalism I am advocating for. Not-knowing is about the willingness to participate in the possible *maybes* that are brewing, ready to unfold into something, anything or nothing. This is what I have called the *power of maybes*.

[8] From a cursory scan of the tables of contents of the journals *Design Issues* and *Design and Culture*, issues published between 2014 and 2023.

[9] How to bring design into dialogue with non-design domains, especially philosophical, is a recurrent theme in my work. Alas, it is not about 'applying' theory to practice or prescribing normative protocols, rather a gentle push towards transdisciplinary intensification (Marenko and Brassett ed., *Deleuze and Design*). For instance, Kwinter refers to the 'growing embrace of the Hindu-Buddhist theory of nature as a continuum of articulated vibration from which all form is drawn' (Kwinter, 'A Sensitive Matter', 72) and uses references that span Buddhism, animism, Saint Francis and Heraclitus to name just a few.

To dwell in uncertainty signals the intention to inhabit this indeterminate space, as if drifting in an oceanic current rather than hurrying to cross over onto the other side. Nurturing the *power of maybes* is to be done against the grain of the linear, incremental trajectory of task-oriented and risk-managed performativity, the orthodoxy of self-management, the reproducibility of neoliberal futures, their instrumental and deterministic normativity. This has never been as important as it is now, in the context of a planetary computation dominated by calculating machines of prediction.

I contend that my take on uncertainty is the antidote necessary to push back against the capture of potential and reduction – reduction of potential, of imagination, of affect – that is algorithmic governmentality's modus operandi. Manoeuvres of capture ambush 'living experts' through anticipatory design, seamless interaction and frictionless interfaces, and turn them into 'end-users' and 'social robots'. Futures are foreclosed when uncertainty is seized, when ambiguity, indecision and hesitation are eroded by user journeys driven by predictive analytics. Under the cloak of convenience, these operations disguise the deeply biased construction of algorithmic subjects and the foreclosure of futures that have become key features of planetary computation, which is the semblance taken today by Integrated World Capitalism.

For me, pushing against reduction means reclaiming a richer, fuller, more whole, 'rounder' way of being in the world, one that is fed by the amphibolic nature of potential and that goes beneath the limitations of human-centredness. Indeed, if I constrain the idea of reclaiming such a richer, rounder life as a prerogative of the human, I will have failed already. Resisting reduction is not about becoming a better human but figuring out *how* to access, and become, world; *how* to recognize the forces that traverse me, move me and connect that slice of intensity and matter that I call 'me' to the cosmic. If this, as I have argued throughout, means to enter a cosmological territory, it is also a (micro) political project. In other words, to be cosmic becomes an act of resistance.

The Power of Maybes takes (and gives you) uncertainty as the fundamental, uncontainable, irrevocable condition of existing in the world with all its unfathomable becomings. Uncertainty *is* the irrevocable condition of existence. Everything in the world, and of the world (the human, the nonhuman and whatever else in between and beyond) is immersed in oceanic uncertainty.

Throughout this book, my aim has been to trace the contours of the 'zone of maybes' where potential circulates. It has also been to build an otherwise of uncertainty out of the tensions and divergences expressed by my constellations, and show that to access the stream of pre-personal, impersonal forces prior to cognition, consciousness and capture concerns both resistance and design. My desire was to illuminate the infinite variability of the world, so that its 'maybes' could shine like a crystal catching the light. To see these maybes in all their luminosity ultimately means one thing. That not only is an uncertain existence the richest one I may get to live, but it is only by purposefully dwelling in the plenitude of the *power of maybes* that an otherwise life may be truly possible.

The end

Bibliography

Adam, Barbara and Chris Groves (2007), *Future Matters. Action, Knowledge, Ethics*, Leiden and Boston: Brill.

Agamben, Giorgio (1999), *Potentialities. Collected Essays in Philosophy*, trans. Daniel Heller-Roazen, Stanford: Stanford University Press.

Agamben, Giorgio (2001), *La Comunita' Che Viene*, Torino: Bollati Boringhieri.

Agamben, Giorgio (2009), *Nudita'*, Rome: Nottetempo.

Agamben, Giorgio (2010), *Nudities*, Stanford: Stanford University Press.

Agamben, Giorgio (2011), *The Kingdom and the Glory. For a Theological Genealogy of Economy and Government*, Stanford: Stanford University Press.

Agamben, Giorgio (2014), *L'Uso dei Corpi*, Vicenza: Neri Pozza.

Agamben, Giorgio (2014), 'The Power of Thought', *Critical Inquiry*, 40 (2): 480–91, trans. Kalpana Seshadri, Chicago and London: University of Chicago Press.

Agamben, Giorgio (2015), *L'Avventura*, Rome: Nottetempo.

Agamben, Giorgio (2017), *Creazione e Anarchia. L'Opera nell'Eta' della Religione Capitalista*, Vicenza: Neri Pozza.

Agamben, Giorgio and Gilles Deleuze (1993), *Bartleby. La Formula della Creazione*, Macerata: Quodlibet.

Allen, Barry (2008), *Artifice and Design. Art and Technology in Human Experience*, New York: Cornell University Press.

Allen, Barry (2011), 'The Cloud of Knowing. Blurring the Difference with China'. Symposium: Fuzzy Studies, part 1. *Common Knowledge*, 17 (3): 450–532.

Allen, Barry (2015), *Vanishing Into Things. Knowledge in Chinese Tradition*, Cambridge, Mass. and London: Harvard University Press.

Allen, Barry (2015), 'War as a Problem of Knowledge. Theory of Knowledge in China's Military Philosophy', *Philosophy East and West*, 65 (1): 1–17.

Alliez, Eric and Andrew Goffey, eds (2011), *The Guattari Effect*, London and New York: Continuum.

Amoore, Louise (2013), *The Politics of Possibility. Risk and Security Beyond Probability*, Durham and London: Duke University Press.

Ayache, Elie (2011), 'The Medium of Contingency', *Contingency. PLI the Warwick Journal of Philosophy*, University of Warwick, 22: 62–87.

Bammer, Gabriele and Michael Smithson, eds (2008), *Uncertainty and Risk. Multidisciplinary Perspectives*, London: Earthscan.

Barad, Karen (2007), *Meeting the Universe Halfway. Quantum Physics and the Entanglement of Matter and Meaning*, Durham and London: Duke University Press.

Barredo Arrieta, Alejandro, Natalia Díaz-Rodríguez, Javier Del Ser, Adrien Bennetot, Siham Tabik, Alberto Barbado, Salvador Garcia, Sergio Gil-Lopez, Daniel Molina, Richard Benjamins, Raja Chatila and Francisco Herrera(2019), 'Explainable Artificial Intelligence (XAI): Concepts, Taxonomies, Opportunities and Challenges Toward Responsible AI', *Information Fusion*. http://doi.org/10.1016/j.inffus.2019.12.012

Basile, Jonathan (2020), 'Other Matters. Karen Barad's Two Materialisms and the Science of Undecidability', *Angelaki*, 25 (5): 3–18.

Bataille, George (2001), *The Unfinished System of Nonknowledge*, Minneapolis: Minnesota University Press.

Beerden, Kim (2013), *World Full of Signs. Ancient Greek Divination in Context*, Leiden and Boston: Brill.

Benedict XVI (2010), 'If You Want To Cultivate Peace, Protect Creation', Message of His Holiness Pope Benedict XVI for the Celebration of the World Day of Peace, 1 January. https://www.vatican.va/content/benedict-xvi/en/messages/peace/documents/hf_ben-xvi_mes_20091208_xliii-world-day-peace.html

Bergson, Henri (2002), *Key Writings*, London: Bloomsbury.

Bergson, Henri (2007), *The Creative Mind. An Introduction to Metaphysics*, trans. M. L. Andison, Mineola, NY: Dover Publications.

Beverungen, Armin and Stephen Dunne (2007), "I'd Prefer Not To". Bartleby and the Excesses of Interpretation', *Culture and Organization*, 13 (2): 171–83.

Björneborn, Lennart (2023), 'Adjacent Possible', in Vlad P. Glaveanu (ed.), *The Palgrave Encyclopaedia of the Possible*, Switzerland: Springer, 16–28.

Boholm, Åsa (2003), 'The Cultural Nature of Risk. Can There Be an Anthropology of Uncertainty?' *Ethnos*, 68 (2): 159–78.

Bojesen, Emile (2019), 'Positive Ignorance. Unknowing as a Tool for Education and Educational Research', *Journal of Philosophy of Education*, 53 (2): 394–406.

Braidotti, Rosi (2019), *Posthuman Knowledge*, Cambridge: Polity Press.

Braidotti, Rosi (2019), 'A Theoretical Framework for the Critical Posthumanities', *Theory, Culture & Society*, 36 (6): 31–61.

Braidotti, Rosi and Matthew Fuller (2019), 'The Posthumanities in an Era of Unexpected Consequences', *Theory, Culture & Society*, 36 (6): 3–29.

Bredekamp, Horst (1995), *The Lure of Antiquity and the Cult of the Machine. The Kunstkammer and the Evolution of Nature, Art and Technology*, Princeton: Markus Wiener Publishers.

Broeckmann, Andreas (2016), *Machine Art in the Twentieth Century*, Cambridge, Mass. and London: MIT Press.

Broussard, Meredith (2018), *Artificial Unintelligence. How Computers Misunderstand the World*, Cambridge, Mass. and London: MIT Press.

Buckman, Stephen J. (2008), 'Uncertainty in the Physical Sciences. How Big? How Small? Is It Actually There at All?', in Gabriele Bammer and Michael Smithson (eds), *Uncertainty and Risk: Multidisciplinary Perspectives*, London: Earthscan, 71–80.

Burrell, Jenna (2016), 'How the Machine "Thinks". Understanding Opacity in Machine Learning Algorithms', *Big Data and Society*, 3 (1). http://journals.sagepub.com/doi/abs/10.1177/2053951715622512 (accessed 24 October 2024).

Caló, Susana and Godofredo Pereira, eds (2022), *CERFI: Militant Analysis, Institutional Programming and Collective Equipment*, Rotterdam: Het Nieuwe Instituut.

Carlisle, Clare (2021), *Spinoza's Religion. A New Reading of the Ethics*, Princeton and Oxford: Princeton University Press.

Cheney-Lippold, John (2017), *We Are Data. Algorithms and the Making of Our Digital Selves*, New York: New York University Press.

Chia Robert, C.H. and Robin Holt (2009), *Strategy Without Design. The Silent Efficacy of Indirect Action*, Cambridge: Cambridge University Press.

Christiaens, Tim (2018), 'Neoliberalism and the Right to be Lazy. Inactivity as Resistance in Lazzarato and Agamben', *Rethinking Marxism*, 30 (2): 256–74.

Chun, Wendy (2011), *Programmed Visions. Software and Memory*. Cambridge, Mass. and London: MIT Press.

Ciprut, Jose V., ed. (2008), *Indeterminacy. The Mapped, the Navigable, and the Uncharted*, Cambridge, Mass. and London: MIT Press.

Ciprut, Jose V. (2008), 'Definition, Distinctions, and Dilemmas', in Jose V. Ciprut (ed.), *Indeterminacy. The Mapped, the Navigable, and the Uncharted*, Cambridge, Mass. and London: MIT Press, 1–40.

Cleary, Thomas (2003), *The Book of Balance and Harmony. A Taoist Handbook*, Boulder, CO: Shambhala.

Coleman, Rebecca and Jessica Ringrose (2013), 'Introduction', in *Deleuze and Research Methodologies*, Edinburgh: Edinburgh University Press, 1–22.

Colomina, Beatrice and Mark Wigley (2016), *Are We Human? Notes on an Archaeology of Design*, Baden, Switzerland: Lars Muller Publishers.

Connor, Steven (2021), *The Madness of Knowledge. On Wisdom, Ignorance and Fantasies of Knowing*, London: Reaktion.

Conty, Arianne (2021), 'Panpsychism: A Response to the Anthropocene Age', *The Journal of Speculative Philosophy*, 35 (1): 27–49.

Cooper, Barry S. (2010), 'Incomputability, Emergence and the Turing Universe', in Arturo Carsetti (ed.), *Causality, Meaningful Complexity and Embodied Cognition*, Dordrecht: Springer, 135–53.

Cooper, Barry S. (2015), 'The Machine as Data. A Computational View of Emergence and Definability', *Synthese*, 192: 1955–88.

Crawford, T. Hugo (2015), 'Thinking Hot. Risk, Prehension and Sympathy in Design', in Betti Marenko and Jamie Brassett (eds), *Deleuze and Design*, Edinburgh: Edinburgh University Press, 84–106.

Crawford, Kate (2021), *Atlas of AI. Power, Politics, and the Planetary Costs of Artificial Intelligence*, New Haven and London: Yale University Press.

Crawford, Kate and Alexander Campolo (2020), 'Enchanted Determinism. Power Without Responsibility in Artificial Intelligence', *Engaging Science, Technology, and Society*, 6: 1–19.

Crawford, Kate and Vladan Joler (2018), 'Anatomy of an AI System. The Amazon Echo as an Anatomical Map of Human Labor, Data and Planetary Resources', AI Now Institute and Share Lab. https://anatomyof.ai/ (accessed 28 October 2024).

Crisp, Fiona (2015), 'Negative Capability. Imaging and Imagining Fundamental Science Through Productive Doubt', *GeoHumanities*, 1 (1): 188–97.

Critical Computation Bureau (2021), 'Editorial. Dialogues on Recursive Colonialisms, Speculative Computation, and the Techno-Social', *e-flux*, 123. https://www.e-flux.com/journal/123/438467/editorial-dialogues-on-recursive-colonialisms-speculative-computation-and-the-techno-social/

Croissant, Jennifer (2014), 'Agnotology. Ignorance and Absence or Toward a Sociology of Things That Aren't There', *Social Epistemology. A Journal of Knowledge, Culture, and Policy*, 28 (1): 4–25.

Dattilo, Emanuele (2021), *Il Dio Sensibile. Saggio sul Panteismo*, Vicenza: Neri Pozza.

Dattilo, Emanuele (2022), *La Vita Che Vive*, Vicenza: Neri Pozza.

Dawkins, Richard (2006), *The God Delusion*, London: Bantam.

De Carolis, Massimo (1996), 'Toward a Phenomenology of Opportunism', in Paolo Virno and Michael Hardt (eds), *Radical Thought in Italy. A Potential Politics*, Minneapolis and London: University of Minnesota Press, 37–51.

Dein, Simon (2016), 'The Anthropology of Uncertainty. Magic, Witchcraft and Risk and Forensic Implications', *Journal of Forensic Anthropology*, 1 (1): 1–7.

DeLanda, Manuel (2004), 'Material Complexity', in Neil Leach, David Turnbull and Chris Williams (eds), *Digital Tectonics*, Chichester: Wiley, 14–21.

Del Campo, Manuel and Neil Leach (2022), 'Can Machines Hallucinate Architecture? AI as Design Method', *Architecture Design*, 92: 6–13. https://doi.org/10.1002/ad.2807 (accessed 28 October 2024).

Deleuze, Gilles (1988), *Spinoza. Practical Philosophy*, San Francisco: City Lights Books.

Deleuze, Gilles (1988), *Foucault*, Minneapolis and London: University of Minnesota Press.

Deleuze, Gilles (1990), *The Logic of Sense*, New York: Columbia University Press.

Deleuze, Gilles (1991), *Bergsonism*, New York: Zone Books.

Deleuze, Gilles (1994), *Difference and Repetition*, London: The Athlone Press.

Deleuze, Gilles (1995), *Negotiations*, New York: Columbia University Press.

Deleuze, Gilles (1998), *Essays Critical and Clinical*, London and New York: Verso.

Deleuze, Gilles (2005), *Pure Immanence. Essays on a Life*, New York: Zone Books.

Deleuze, Gilles (2006), *Two Regimes of Madness. Texts and Interviews 1975–1995*, New York: Semiotext(e).

Deleuze, Gilles and Félix Guattari (1988), *A Thousand Plateaus. Capitalism and Schizophrenia*, London: The Athlone Press.

Deleuze, Gilles and Claire Parnet (1987), *Dialogues*, London: The Athlone Press.

De Sousa Santos, Boaventura (2009), 'A Non-Occidentalist West? Learned Ignorance and Ecology of Knowledge', *Theory, Culture & Society*, 26 (7–8): 103–25.

De Sousa Santos, Boaventura (2018), *The End of the Cognitive Empire. The Coming of Age of Epistemologies of the South*, Durham and London: Duke University Press.

Detienne, Marcel and Jean-Pierre Vernant (1978), *Cunning Intelligence in Greek Culture and Society*, Hassocks: Harvester Press.

Dickinson, Emily (2016), *The Complete Poems*, London: Faber and Faber.

Diderot, Denis (1964), *Rameau's Nephew and Other Works*, Indianapolis and New York: The Bobbs-Merrill Company.

Dilnot, Clive (1998), 'The Science of Uncertainty: The Potential Contribution of Design to Knowledge', Proceedings of the Ohio Doctoral Education in Design Conference, 1:41.

Dilnot, Clive (2015), 'The Matter of Design', *Design Philosophy Papers*, 13 (2): 115–23.

Dinant, David di (2022), *Mente Materia Dio. Mens Hyle Deus*, Genova: Il Melangolo.

Diprose, Rosalyn (1994), *The Bodies of Women. Ethics, Embodiment and Sexual Difference*, London and New York: Routledge.

Diprose, Rosalyn, Niamh Stephenson, Catherine Mills, Kane Race and Gay Hawkins (2008), 'Governing the Future. The Paradigm of Prudence in Political Technologies of Risk Management', *Security Dialogue*, 39 (2–3): 267–88.

Domingos, Pedro (2015), *The Master Algorithm*, London: Penguin.

Dosse, François (2010), *Gilles Deleuze and Félix Guattari. Intersecting Lives*, New York: Columbia University Press.

Douglas, Mary and Aaron Wildavsky (1982), *Risk and Culture. An Essay on the Selection of Technological and Environmental Dangers*, Berkeley, CA and Los Angeles: University of California Press.

Dourish, Paul (2016), 'Algorithms and their Others. Algorithmic Culture in Context', *Big Data & Society*, 3 (2): 1–11. https://doi.org/10.1177/2053951716665128 (accessed 28 October 2024).

Elish, M. C. and danah boyd (2018), 'Situating Methods in the Magic of Big Data and AI', *Communication Monographs*, 85 (1): 57–80.

Ericson, Richard and Aaron Doyle (2004), *Uncertain Business. Risk, Insurance and the Limits of Knowledge*, Toronto: University of Toronto Press.

Escobar, Arturo (2018), *Designs for the Pluriverse, Radical Interdependence, Autonomy, and the Making of Worlds*, Durham and London: Duke University Press.

Esmark, Anders (2020), *The New Technocracy*, Bristol: Bristol University Press.

Ewald, François (2002), 'The Return of Descartes' Malicious Demon. An Outline of a Philosophy of Precaution', in Tom Baker and Jonathan Simon (eds), *Embracing Risk. The Changing Culture of Insurance and Responsibility*, Chicago and London: University of Chicago Press, 273–301.

Facer, Keri (2011), *Learning Futures. Education, Technology, and Social Change*, London and New York: Routledge.

Facer, Keri (2019), 'Storytelling in Troubled Times. What is the Role for Educators in the Deep Crises of the 21st Century?', *Literacy* 53 (1): 3–13.

Facer, Keri and Arathi Sriprakash (2021), 'Provincializing Futures Literacy. A Caution Against Codification', *Futures*, 133.

Fazi, Beatrice M. (2021), 'Beyond Human: Deep Learning, Explainability and Representation', *Theory, Culture & Society*, 38 (7–8): 55–77.

Feenberg, Andrew (2018), *Technology, Modernity, and Democracy*, London: Rowman and Littlefield.

Finn, Ed (2017), *What Algorithms Want. Imagination in the Age of Computing*, Cambridge, Mass. and London: MIT Press.

Firestein, Stuart (2012), *Ignorance. How It Drives Science*, Oxford and New York: Oxford University Press.

Floridi, Luciano (2014), *The 4th Revolution. How the Infosphere is Reshaping Human Reality*, Oxford: Oxford University Press.

Flusser, Vilem (1999), *The Shape of Things. A Philosophy of Design*, London: Reaktion Books.

Foucault, Michel (1981), 'Is It Really Important To Think? An Interview with Michel Foucault', *Liberation*, 30–31 May.

Foucault, Michel (1988), Lawrence D. Kritzman (ed.) *Politics, Philosophy, Culture. Interviews and Other Writings, 1977–1984*, London: Routledge.

Foucault, Michel (1991), 'Governmentality', in Graham Burchell, Colin Gordon and Peter Miller (eds), *The Foucault Effect. Studies in Governmentality*, Chicago and London: University of Chicago Press, 87–104.

Foucault, Michel (2002), James D. Faubion and Robert Hurley (eds), *The Essential Works of Michel Foucault, 1954–1984. Vol.* 3, London: Penguin Books.

Foucault, Michel and Gilles Deleuze (1977), 'A Conversation Between Michel Foucault and Gilles Deleuze. Intellectuals and Power', in Donald F. Bouchard (ed.), *Language, Counter-Memory, Practice. Selected Essays and Interviews*, Ithaca: Cornell University Press, 205–17.

Foucault, Michel, Félix Guattari, Gilles Deleuze and François Fourquet (1996), 'Equipments of Power. Towns, Territories and Collective Equipments', in Sylvère Lotringer (ed.), *Foucault Live. Michel Foucault Collected Interviews, 1961–1984*, New York: Semiotext(e), 105–12.

Fowler, Jeaneane and Merv Fowler (2008), *Chinese Religions. Beliefs and Practices*, Brighton and Portland: Sussex Academic Press.

Friedberg, Anna (2009), *The Virtual Window. From Alberti to Microsoft*, Cambridge, Mass. and London: MIT Press.

Fry, Tony (2020), *Defuturing. A New Design Philosophy*, London: Bloomsbury.

Fry, Tony and Adam Nocek, eds (2021), *Design in Crisis. New Worlds, Philosophies and Practices*, London: Routledge.

Galison, Peter (2010), 'Trading with the Enemy', in Michael E. Gorman (ed.), *Trading Zones and Interactional Expertise. Creating New Kinds of Collaboration*, Cambridge, Mass. and London: MIT Press, 25–52.

Galloway, Alexander (2021), *Uncomputable. Play and Politics in the Long Digital Age*, London and New York: Verso.

Gatens, Moira and Genevieve Lloyd (1999), *Collective Imaginings. Spinoza, Past and Present*, London and New York: Routledge.

Gigerenzer, Gerd, Zeno Swijtink, Theodore Porter, Lorraine Daston, John Beatty and Lorenz Kruger (1989), *The Empire of Chance. How Probability Changed Science and Everyday Life*, Cambridge: Cambridge University Press.

Gillespie, Tarleton (2014), 'The Relevance of Algorithms', in *Media Technologies. Essays on Communication, Materiality, and Society*, Tarleton Gillespie, Pablo J. Boczkowski and Kirsten A. Foot (eds), Cambridge, Mass. and London: MIT Press, 167–93.

Gillespie, Tarleton (2016), '#Trendingistrending. When Algorithms Become Culture', in Robert Seyfert and Jonathan Roberge (eds), *Algorithmic Cultures. Essays on Meaning, Performance and New Technologies*, London: Routledge, 52–74.

Gillespie, Tarleton (2016), 'Algorithm', in Benjamin Peters (ed.), *Digital Keywords. A Vocabulary of Information Society and Culture*, Princeton and Oxford: Princeton University Press, 18–30.

Gilroy, Paul (2019), 'Never Again. Refusing Race and Salvaging the Human', Lecture, Holberg Prize, Bergen, 4 June.

Ginzburg, Carlo (1976), *Il Formaggio e i Vermi. Il Cosmo di un Mugnaio del Cinquecento*, Torino: Einaudi.

Ginzburg, Carlo (1980), 'Morelli, Freud and Sherlock Holmes. Clues and Scientific Method', *History Workshop*, trans. Anna Davin, Oxford University Press, 9: 5–36.

Ginzburg, Carlo (1986), *Miti, Emblemi, Spie. Morfologia e Storia*, Torino: Einaudi.

Ginzburg, Carlo (1989), *Clues, Myths, and the Historical Method*, Baltimore: The John Hopkins University Press.

Ginzburg, Carlo (1998), *Occhiacci di Legno. Nove Riflessioni sulla Distanza*, Milano: Feltrinelli.

Ginzburg, Carlo (2006), *Il Filo e le Tracce. Vero, Falso, Finto*, Milano: Feltrinelli.

Ginzburg, Carlo (2021), *La Lettera Uccide*, Milano: Adelphi.

Golumbia, David (2009), *The Cultural Logic of Computation*, Cambridge, Mass.: Harvard University Press.

Grishin, Sasha (2008), *Uncertainty as a Creative Force in Visual Art*, London: Routledge.

Grosz, Elizabeth (1999), 'Thinking the New. Of Futures Yet Unthoughts', in Elizabeth Grosz (ed.), *Becomings. Explorations in Time, Memory, and Futures*, Ithaca: Cornell University Press, 15–28.

Grosz, Elizabeth (2005), *Time Travels. Feminism, Nature, Power*, Durham and London: Duke University Press.

Guattari, Félix (1982), *Il Capitale Mondiale Integrato. Piano Sul Pianeta*, Bologna: Cappelli.

Guattari, Félix (1995), *Chaosmosis. An Ethico-Aesthetic Paradigm*, Bloomington and Indianapolis: Indiana University Press.

Guattari, Félix (2000), *The Three Ecologies*, London and New Brunswick: The Athlone Press.

Guattari, Félix (2001), 'Singolarità e Complessità', in *Millepiani. Pensiero Globale, Cervello Sociale*, trans. Ilaria Dal Canton, Milano: Mimesis, 20: 7–26.

Guattari, Félix (2009), *Soft Subversions. Texts and Interviews 1977–1985*, New York: Semiotext(e).

Guattari, Félix (2011), *The Machinic Unconscious. Essays in Schizoanalysis*, New York: Semiotext(e).

Guattari, Félix (2011), 'The Vertigo of Immanence', in Eric Alliez and Andrew Goffey (eds), *The Guattari Effect*, London and New York: Continuum, 25–39 (interview with John Johnston).

Guattari, Félix (2015), 'Transdisciplinarity Must Become Transversality', *Theory, Culture, & Society*, 32 (5–6): 131–7.

Guattari, Félix (2016), *Lines of Flight. For Another World of Possibilities*, London: Bloomsbury.

Gunning, David, Mark Stefik, Jaesik Choi, Timothy Miller, Simone Stumpf and Guang-Zhong Yang (2019), 'XAI—Explainable Artificial Intelligence', *Science Robotics*, 4 (37).

Hacking, Ian (1975), *The Emergence of Probability. A Philosophical Study of Early Ideas about Probability, Induction and Statistical Inference*. Cambridge: Cambridge University Press.

Hacking, Ian (1990), *The Taming of Chance*, Cambridge: Cambridge University Press.

Hansen, Mark B.N. (2014), 'The Operational Present of Sensibility', *The Nordic Journal of Aesthetics*, 24 (47): 38–53.

Hansen, Mark B.N. (2015), 'Feed-Forward', in Robin Mackay (ed.), *Simulation, Exercise, Operations*, Manchester: Urbanomic, 57–61.

Harding, Susan and Daniel Rosenberg, eds (2005), *Histories of the Future*, Durham and London: Duke University Press.

Harrison, Paul (1999), *The Elements of Pantheism. Understanding the Divinity in Nature and the Universe*, Shaftesbury; Boston; Melbourne: Element Books.

Hayles, Katherine N. (2017), *Unthought. The Power of the Cognitive Nonconscious*, Chicago and London: University of Chicago Press.

Horl, Erich, Nelly Y. Pinkrah and Lotte Warnsholdt, eds (2021), *Critique and the Digital*, Zurich: Diaphanes.

Introna, Lucas, D. (2016), 'The Algorithmic Choreography of the Impressionable Subject', in Robert Seyfert and Jonathan Roberge (eds), *Algorithmic Cultures. Essays on Meaning, Performance and New Technologies*, London: Routledge, 26–50.

Ito, Joichi, ed. (2019), *Resisting Reduction. Designing Our Complex Future with Machines*, Cambridge, Mass. and London: MIT Press.

James, William (1907), 'Pragmatism. A New Name for Some Old Ways of Thinking', Lectures delivered at the Lowell Institute in Boston (November and December, 1906), and at Columbia University, New York (January, 1907). http://pdf-objects.com/files/William-James-Pragmatism.pdf (accessed 28 October 2024).

Jay, Martin (1993), *Downcast Eyes. The Denigration of Vision in Twentieth-Century French Thought*, Berkeley and Los Angeles: University of California Press.

Johansen, K. Thomas, ed. (2021), *Productive Knowledge in Ancient Philosophy. The Concept of Technê*, Cambridge and New York: Cambridge University Press.

Johnson, Steven (2010), *Where Good Ideas Come From: The Natural History of Innovation*, London and New York: Allen Lane.

Johnston, William, ed. (2012), *The Cloud of Unknowing and the Book of Privy Counseling*, London: Random House.

Jullien, François (1995), *The Propensity of Things. Toward a History of Efficacy in China*, New York: Zone Books.

Jullien, François (2000), *Detour and Access. Strategies of Meanings in China and Greece*, New York: Zone Books.

Jullien, François (2009), *The Great Image Has No Form, or On the Nonobject Through Painting*, Chicago and London: University of Chicago Press.

Jullien, François (2011), *The Silent Transformations*, London: Seagull.

Kauffman, Stuart A. (2000), *Investigations*, Oxford: Oxford University Press.

Kauffman, Stuart A. (2017), 'Beyond Physics: The Emergence and Evolution of Life', keynote speech, *Kreyon* Conference, The Complexity of the Future, Rome.

Keats, John (1958), *The Letters of John Keats*, ed. H. E. Rollins, 2 vols (Cambridge: Cambridge University Press, 1958), I.

Klein, Richard (1986), 'The Mētis of Centaurs', *Diacritics*, 16 (2): 2–13.

Knight, Frank H. (1921), *Risk, Uncertainty and Profit*, Boston: Houghton Mifflin.

Knight, Will (2017), 'The Dark Secret at the Heart of AI', *MIT Technology Review*, 120 (3): 54–63.

Knighton, Andrew (2007), 'The Bartleby Industry and Bartleby's Idleness', *ESQ: A Journal of the American Renaissance*, 1 (2): 184–215.

Knorr Cetina, Karin (2001), 'Objectual Practice', in Karin Knorr Cetina, Theodore R. Schatzki and Eike von Savigny (eds), *The Practice Turn in Contemporary Theory*, London: Routledge, 175–88.

Knorr Cetina, Karin (2003), *Epistemic Cultures. How the Sciences Make Knowledge*, Cambridge, Mass.: Harvard University Press.

Kodalak, Gökhan (2020), 'Spinoza and Architecture. The Air of the Future', *Log*, 49: 123–45.

Kodalak, Gökhan (2021), 'Cosmodality. Prolegomena to a New Architectural Metaphysics', *Log*, 52: 131–37.

Kodalak, Gökhan and Sanford Kwinter (2020), 'The Return of Nature', *Log*, 49: 119–22; 146–8; 164; 168; 182–4.

Kourany, Janet and Martin Carrier, eds (2020), *Science and the Production of Ignorance. When the Quest for Knowledge is Thwarted*, Cambridge, Mass. and London: MIT Press.

Kwinter, Sanford (2018), 'Headspace', *Frida Escobedo. Serpentine Pavillion 2018*, Catalogue, Koenig Books, 74–8.

Kwinter, Sanford (2019), 'A Sensitive Matter. An Interview with Sanford Kwinter', *Scapegoat*, 11: 66–73.

Kwinter, Sanford and Bruce Mau (2021), 'Design is Not for Us: A Simple Desultory Philippic', *Log*, 51: 155–76.

Lafargue, Paul (2023), *The Right To Be Lazy and Other Writings*, New York: New York Review of Books.

Lange, Oskar (2000), 'The Computer and the Market', in Peter Boettke (ed.), *Socialism and the Market. The Socialist Calculation Debate Revisited*, London: Routledge, 158–61.

Latour, Bruno, Martin Guinard and Eva Lin (2020), 'Coping with Planetary Wars', *e-flux*, 114, https://www.e-flux.com/journal/114/366104/coping-with-planetary-wars/

Law, John (2004), *After Method. Mess in Social Science Research*, London: Routledge.

Law, John and John Urry (2004), 'Enacting the Social', *Economy and Society*, 33 (3): 390–410.

Lemonnier, Pierre (1992), *Elements for an Anthropology of Technology*, Ann Arbor: University of Michigan.

Lindley, David (2007), *Uncertainty. Einstein, Heisenberg, Bohr and the Struggle for the Soul of Science*, New York and London: Doubleday.

Lloyd, Genevieve (1996), *Spinoza and the Ethics*, London and New York: Routledge.

Lupton, Deborah (2006), 'Sociology and Risk', in Gabe Mythen and Sandra Walklate (eds), *Beyond the Risk Society. Critical Reflections on Risk and Human Security*, Maidenhead and New York: Open University Press, 11–24.

Lury, Celia, (2020), *Problem Spaces. How and Why Methodology Matters*, Cambridge: Polity Press.

Lury, Celia and Nina Wakeford, eds (2012), *Inventive Methods. The Happening of the Social*, Abingdon and New York: Routledge.

Lyotard, Jean-François (1984), *The Postmodern Condition. A Report on Knowledge*, trans. Geoff Bennington and Brian Massumi,Minneapolis: University of Minnesota Press.

Mackay, Robin (2011), *The Medium of Contingency*, Manchester: Urbanomic.

Mackenzie, Adrian (2015), 'The Production of Prediction. What Does Machine Learning Want?', *European Journal of Cultural Studies*, 18 (4–5): 429–45.

Mackenzie, Adrian (2017), *Machine Learners. Archaeology of a Data Practice*, Cambridge, Mass. and London: MIT Press.

MacLure, Maggie (2013), 'The Wonder of Data', *Cultural Studies<>Critical Methodologies*, 13 (4): 228–32.

MacLure, Maggie (2021), 'Inquiry as Divination', *Qualitative Inquiry* 27 (5): 502–11.

Malabou, Catherine (2019), *Morphing Intelligence. From IQ Measurement to Artificial Brains*, New York: Columbia University Press.

Malevic, Kazimir (2022), *L'Inazione Come Verita Effettiva dell'Umanita*, Napoli: Cronopio.

Malewski, Erik and Nathalia Jaramillo, eds (2011), *Epistemologies of Ignorance in Education*, London: Information Age Eurospan.

Manning, Erin (2015), 'Against Method', in Phillip Vannini (ed.), *Non-Representational Methodologies. Re-Envisioning Research*, New York and London: Routledge, 52–72.

Manning, Erin (2020), 'Angular Perspective. Or, How Concern Shapes the Field', *Log*, 49: 183–95.

Marcus, Aurelius (2006), *Meditations*, London: Penguin.

Mareis, Claudia and Nina Paim, eds (2021), *Design Struggles. Intersecting Histories, Pedagogies, and Perspectives*, Amsterdam: Valiz.

Marenko, Betti (1997), *Ibridazioni. Corpi In Transito e Alchimie della Nuova Carne*, Rome: Castelvecchi.

Marenko, Betti (2014), 'Neo-Animism and Design. A New Paradigm in Object Theory', Special issue: *Design, Thing Theory and the Lives of Objects*, Leslie Atzmon ed., *Design and Culture* 6 (2): 219–42.

Marenko, Betti (2015), 'Digital Materiality, Morphogenesis and the Intelligence of the Technodigital Object', in Betti Marenko and Jamie Brassett (eds), *Deleuze and Design*, Edinburgh: Edinburgh University Press, 107–38.

Marenko, Betti (2019), 'Algorithm Magic. Gilbert Simondon and Techno-Animism', in Simone Natale and Diana Pasulka (eds), *Believing in Bits. Digital Media and the Supernatural*, New York: Oxford University Press, 213–28.

Marenko, Betti (2021), 'Stacking Complexities. Reframing Uncertainty Through Hybrid Literacies', *Design and Culture*, 13 (2): 165–84.

Marenko, Betti (2021), 'Stay Alert to the Toolification of Experience. The Technocratic Shift is Here', *Social Design Institute Position Paper*. University of the Arts London.

Marenko, Betti and Jamie Brassett, eds (2015), 'Introduction', in *Deleuze and Design*, Edinburgh: Edinburgh University Press, 1–30.

Marenko, Betti and Pim Haselager (2021), 'Marx in the Smart Living Room. What Would a Marx Oriented Approach to Smart Objects Be Like?' in Marco Rozendaal, Betti Marenko and Will Odom (eds), *Designing Smart Objects in Everyday Life. Intelligences, Agencies, Ecologies*, London: Bloomsbury, 169–84.

Marmont, Giovanni and German E. Primera (2020), 'Propositions for Inoperative Life', in Giovanni Marmont and German E. Primera (eds), *The Politics, Ethics, and Aesthetics of Inoperativity*. Special Issue. *Journal of Italian Philosophy*, 3: 9–21.

Massumi, Brian (1992), *A User's Guide to Capitalism and Schizophrenia. Deviations from Deleuze and Guattari*, Cambridge, Mass. and London: MIT Press.

Massumi, Brian (2007), 'Potential Politics and the Primacy of Preemption', *Theory & Event*, 10 (2).

Massumi, Brian (2011), *Semblance and Event. Activist Philosophy and the Occurrent Arts*, Cambridge, Mass. and London: MIT Press.

Massumi, Brian (2017), *The Principle of Unrest. Activist Philosophy in the Expanded Field*, London: Open Humanities Press.

Massumi, Brian (2018), *99 Theses of the Revaluation of Value. A Postcapitalist Manifesto*, Minneapolis and London: University of Minnesota Press.

Massumi, Brian, Jacob Ferrington, Alina Hechler and Jannell Parsons (2019), 'Affect and Immediation. An Interview with Brian Massumi', *disClosure: A Journal of Social Theory*, 28, Article 13. https://uknowledge.uky.edu/disclosure/vol28/iss1/13 (accessed 28 October 2024).

Matthias, Andreas (2004), 'The Responsibility Gap. Ascribing Responsibility for the Actions of Learning Automata', *Ethics and Information Technology*, 6: 175–83.

Maturana, Humberto R. and Francisco J. Varela (1992), *The Tree of Knowledge. The Biological Roots of Human Understanding*, Boston and London: Shambhala.

Melville, Herman (1856), 'Bartleby, the Scrivener: A Story of Wall Street', in *The Piazza Tales* (New York: Dix & Edwards; London: Sampson Low).

Mieville, China (2011), *The City and the City*, London: Pan.

Mignolo, Walter D. (2018), 'The Decolonial Option', in Walter D. Mignolo and Catherine E. Walsh (eds), *On Decoloniality. Concepts, Analytics, Praxis*, Durham and London: Duke University Press, 103–244.

Miller, Riel, ed. (2018), *Transforming the Future. Anticipation in the 21st Century*, Abingdon: Routledge, 15–50.

Miller, Tim, Piers Howe and Liz Sonenberg (2017), 'Explainable AI: Beware of Inmates Running the Asylum. Or: How I Learnt to Stop Worrying and Love the Social and Behavioural Sciences'. http://arxiv.org/abs/1712.00547

Mills, Charles (2007), 'White Ignorance', in Shannon Sullivan and Nancy Tuana (eds), *Race and Epistemologies of Ignorance*, New York: SUNY Press, 11–39.

Mittelstadt, Brent, Chris Russell and Sandra Wachter (2019), 'Explaining Explanations in AI', FAT* '19: Conference on Fairness, Accountability, and Transparency, FAT* ACM, New York.

Montag Warren and Ted Stolze, eds (1997), *The New Spinoza*, Minneapolis and London: University of Minnesota Press.

Montezemolo, Fiamma (2009), 'Tijuana, Hybridity and Beyond: A Conversation with Néstor García Canclini', *Third Text*, 23 (6): 733–50.

Munster, Anna (2013), *An Aesthesia of Networks. Conjunctive Experience in Art and Technology*, Cambridge, Mass. and London: MIT Press.

Nadler, Steven (1999), *Spinoza. A Life*, Cambridge: Cambridge University Press.

Nocek, Adam (2022), 'Between Abstraction and Insufficiency: Some Reflections on Necropolitics and the Ethics of Design Philosophy', *Design and Culture*, 14 (1): 51–68.

Nocek, Adam (2022), 'Human Design: A Lure for the Future', Desis Network: Philosophy Talk, Politecnico di Milano, 15 June (unpublished).

Odier, Daniel (2001), *Desire. The Tantric Path to Awakening*, Rochester, Vt.: Inner Traditions.

Odier, Daniel (2004), *Yoga Spandakarika. The Sacred Texts at the Origins of Tantra*, Rochester, Vt.: Inner Traditions.

Olma, Sebastian (2016), *In Defence of Serendipity. For a Radical Politics of Innovation*, London: Penguin Random House.

O'Neil, Cathy (2016), *Weapons of Math Destruction*, London: Penguin.

Oreskes, Naomi and Erik M. Conway (2012), *Merchants of Doubt. How a Handful of Scientists Obscured the Truth on Issues from Tobacco Smoke to Global Warming*, London: Bloomsbury.

Parisi, Luciana (2012), 'Speculation. A Method for the Unattainable', in Celia Lury and Nina Wakeford (eds), *Inventive Methods. The Happening of the Social*, Abingdon and New York: Routledge, 232–44.

Parisi, Luciana (2015), 'Instrumental Reason, Algorithmic Capitalism, and the Incomputable', in Matteo Pasquinelli (ed.), *Alleys of Your Mind. Augmented Intelligence and its Traumas*, Luneburg: Meson Press, 125–37.

Parisi, Luciana (2019), 'The Alien Subject of AI', *Subjectivity*, 12 (1): 27–48.

Parisi, Luciana (2019), 'Critical Computation: Digital Automata and General Artificial Thinking', *Theory, Culture & Society*, 36 (2): 89–121.

Parisi, Luciana and Antonia Majaca (2016), 'The Incomputable and Instrumental Possibility', *e-flux*, 77. https://www.e-flux.com/journal/77/76322/the-incomputable-and-instrumental-possibility/

Parisi, Luciana and William Morgan (2021), 'What is (Machine) Philosophy?', *Qui Parle*, 30 (1): 185–207.

Pasquinelli, Matteo and Vladan Joler (2021), 'The Nooscope Manifested. Artificial Intelligence as Instrument of Knowledge Extractivism', *AI and Society*, 36: 1263–80.

Peat, David F. (2002), *From Certainty to Uncertainty. The Story of Science and Ideas in the Twentieth Century*, Washington DC: Joseph Henry Press.

Petzold, Charles (2008), *The Annotated Turing. A Guided Tour through Alan Turing's Historic Paper on Computability and the Turing Machine*, Indianapolis: Wiley.

Piatti, Giulio (2016), 'The Life and the Crystal. Paths into the Virtual in Bergson, Simondon and Deleuze', *La Deleuziana*, 3: 51–8.

Pickering, Andrew (2015), 'Science, Contingency and Ontology', in Léna Soler, Emiliano Trizio and Andrew Pickering (eds), *Science As It Could Have Been. Discussing the Contingency/Inevitability Problem*, Pittsburgh: University of Pittsburgh Press, 117–28.

Proctor, Robert (2008), 'Agnotology. A Missing Term to Describe the Cultural Production of Ignorance (and Its Study)', in Robert Proctor and Londa Schiebinger (eds), *Agnotology. The Making and Unmaking of Ignorance*, Stanford: Stanford University Press, 1–33.

Proctor, Robert and Londa Schiebinger, eds (2008), *Agnotology. The Making and Unmaking of Ignorance*, Stanford: Stanford University Press.

Prozorov, Sergei (2014), *Agamben and Politics. A Critical Introduction*, Edinburgh: Edinburgh University Press.

Pye, David (1968), *The Nature and Art of Workmanship*, Cambridge: Cambridge University Press.

Querrien, Anne (2022), 'The Critique of the School in Post-'68 French Thought (2): Interview with Anne Querrien' by Jun Fujita Hirose and Yoshiyuki Sato. London: Verso. https://www.versobooks.com/en-gb/blogs/news/5492-the-critique-of-the-school-in-post-68-french-thought-2-interview-with-anne-querrienuntitled

Ramey, Joshua (2016), *Politics of Divination. Neoliberal Endgame and the Religion of Contingency*, London and New York: Rowman and Littlefield.

Raphals, Lisa (1992), *Knowing Words. Wisdom and Cunning in the Classical Traditions of China and Greece*, Ithaca and London: Cornell University Press.

Rawes, Peg (2012), 'Spinoza's Geometric Ecologies'. *Interstices: Journal of Architecture and Related Arts*, 13 (13): 60–70. https://doi.org/10.24135/ijara.v0i0.438

Reith, Gerda (2004), 'Uncertain Times. The Notion of "Risk" and the Development of Modernity', *Time & Society*, 13 (2–3): 383–402.

Rescher, Nicholas (2009), *Unknowability. An Inquiry into the Limits of Knowledge*, Lanham, Md.: Lexington Books.

Rose, Nikolas and Filippa Lentzos (2009), 'Governing Insecurity. Contingency Planning, Protection, Resilience', *Economy and Society*, 38 (2): 230–54.

Rouvroy, Antoinette (2011), 'Technology, Virtuality and Utopia. Governmentality in an Age of Autonomic Computing', in Antoinette Rouvroy and Mireille Hildebrandt (eds), *Law, Human Agency and Autonomic Computing. The Philosophy of Law Meets the Philosophy of Technology*, Abingdon and New York: Routledge, 119–40.

Rouvroy, Antoinette (2013), 'The End(s) of Critique. Data Behaviourism versus Due Process', in Mireille Hildebrandt and Katja de Vries (eds), *Privacy, Due Process and the Computational Turn. The Philosophy of Law Meets the Philosophy of Technology*, Abingdon and New York: Routledge, 143–67.

Rouvroy, Antoinette (2016), 'The Digital Regime of Truth. From the Algorithmic Governmentality to a New Rule of Law', *La Deleuziana*, 3. Conversation with Bernard Stiegler.

Rovelli, Carlo (2021), *Helgoland. The Strange and Beautiful Story of Quantum Physics*, London: Allen Lane.

Rovelli, Carlo (2023), *Anaximander, and the Birth of Science*, London: Allen Lane.

Rubenstein, Mary-Jane (2018), *Pantheologies. Gods, Worlds, Monsters*, New York: Columbia University Press.

Russell, Stuart (2019), *Human Compatible. AI and the Problem of Control*, London: Allen Lane.

St. Pierre, Elizabeth A. (2014), 'Post Qualitative Inquiry', keynote lecture, Australian Association of Research in Education, New Zealand Association of Research in Education, Brisbane, 2 December. https://www.aare.edu.au/assets/documents/Elizabeth-Adams-St.-Pierre-ppt-presentation.pdf

St. Pierre, Elizabeth A. (2019), 'Post Qualitative Inquiry in an Ontology of Immanence', *Qualitative Inquiry* 25 (1): 3–16.

St. Pierre, Elizabeth A., Alecia Y. Jackson and Lisa A. Mazzei (2016), 'New Empiricisms and New Materialisms. Conditions for New Inquiry', *Cultural Studies<>Critical Methodologies*, 16 (2): 99–110.

Salzani, Carlo (2012), 'Quodlibet. Giorgio Agamben's Anti-Utopia', *Utopian Studies*, 23 (1): 212–37.

Savransky, Martin (2021), *Around the Day in Eighty Worlds. Politics of the Pluriverse*, Durham and London: Duke University Press.

Schüll, Natasha D. (2012), *Addiction by Design. Machine Gambling in Las Vegas*. Princeton and Oxford: Princeton University Press.

Seaver, Nick (2017), 'Algorithms as Culture. Some Tactics for the Ethnography of Algorithmic Systems', *Big Data & Society*, 4 (2).

Seely, Andrew J.E. (2013), 'Embracing the Certainty of Uncertainty. Implications for Health Care and Research', *Perspectives in Biology and Medicine*, 56 (1): 65–77.

Seyfert, Robert and Jonathan Roberge, eds (2016), *Algorithmic Cultures. Essays on Meaning, Performance and New Technologies*, London: Routledge.

Simon, Herbert A. (1996), *The Sciences of the Artificial*, Cambridge, Mass. and London: MIT Press.

Smithson, Michael (1989), *Ignorance and Uncertainty. Emerging Paradigms*, New York: Springer-Verlag.

Smithson, Michael (2008), 'The Many Faces and Masks of Uncertainty', in Gabriele Bammer and Michael Smithson (eds), *Uncertainty and Risk. Multidisciplinary Perspectives*, London: Earthscan, 13–25.

Solnit, Rebecca (2014), *Men Explain Things To Me And Other Essays*, London: Granta.

Souriau, Etienne (2015), *The Different Modes of Existence*, Minneapolis: University of Minnesota Press.

Spinoza (1993), *Ethics*, London: Everyman.

Stengers, Isabelle (2011), *Thinking with Whitehead. A Free and Wild Creation of Concepts*, Cambridge, Mass. and London: Harvard University Press.

Stengers, Isabelle (2012), 'Reclaiming Animism', *e-flux*, 36. https://www.e-flux.com/journal/36/61245/reclaiming-animism/

Stengers, Isabelle (2021), 'Putting Problematization to the Test of Our Present', *Theory, Culture & Society*, 38 (2): 71–92.

Stengers, Isabelle and Didier Debaise (2017), 'The Insistence of Possibles. Towards a Speculative Pragmatism', *Parse*, 7: 12–19.

Taussig, Michael (1999), *Defacement. Public Secrecy and the Labor of the Negative*, Stanford: Stanford University Press.

Taussig, Michael (2011), *I Swear I Saw This. Drawing in Fieldwork Notebooks, Namely My Own*, Chicago and London: University of Chicago Press.

Thomson, Ann (2010), 'Pantheism and Enlightenment. The State of the Debate', in Giancarlo Carabelli and Paola Zanardi (eds), *Pan Tra i Filosofi. Saggi sul Panteismo da Spinoza alla New Age*, Padova: Il Poligrafo, 17–29.

Thoreau, Henry David (1865), *The Writings of Henry David Thoreau*, Boston and New York: Houghton Mifflin. https://www.gutenberg.org/files/42553/42553-h/42553-h.htm

Toland, John (1976), *Pantheisticon*, New York and London: Garland Publishing (reprint of the 1751 ed.).

Toulmin, Stephen and June Goodfield (1962), *The Architecture of Matter*, Chicago and London: University of Chicago Press.

Tuckett, David (2013), 'Irreducible Uncertainty and its Implications. A Narrative Action Theory for Economics', working paper, *Institute for New Economic Thinking*. https://www.ineteconomics.org/research/research-papers/irreducible-uncertainty-and-its-implications-a-narrative-action-theory-for-economics (accessed 28 October 2024).

Urry, John (2016), *What is the Future?* Cambridge: Polity Press.

Van Breda, John and Mark Swilling (2018), 'The Guiding Logics and Principles for Designing Emergent Transdisciplinary Research Processes. Learning Experiences and Reflections from a Transdisciplinary Urban Case Study in Enkanini Informal Settlement, South Africa', *Sustainability Science*, 13 (42): 1–19.

Vannini, Phillip (2015), *Non-Representational Methodologies. Re-Envisioning Research*, New York and London: Routledge.

Virno, Paolo (1996), 'The Ambivalence of Disenchantment', in Paolo Virno and Michael Hardt (eds), *Radical Thought in Italy. A Potential Politics*, Minneapolis and London: University of Minnesota Press, 13–34.

Virno, Paolo (1996), 'Virtuosity and Revolution. The Political Theory of Exodus', in Paolo Virno and Michael Hardt (eds), *Radical Thought in Italy. A Potential Politics*, Minneapolis and London: University of Minnesota Press, 189–210.

Virno, Paolo and Michael Hardt, eds (1996), *Radical Thought in Italy. A Potential Politics*, Minneapolis and London: University of Minnesota Press.

Whitehead, Alfred North (1926), *Science and the Modern World*, Cambridge: Cambridge University Press.

Wolfe, Charles T. (2013), 'Sensibility as Vital Force or as Property of Matter in Mid-Eighteenth-Century Debates', in Henry Martyn Lloyd (ed.), *The Discourse of Sensibility. The Knowing Body in the Enlightenment*, Heidelberg, New York, London: Springer, 147–70.

Wu, Kuang-Ming (2008), '*Wu wei* after Zhuangzi', in On-Cho Ng (ed.), *The Imperative of Understanding: Chinese Philosophy, Comparative Philosophy, and Onto-Hermeneutics. A Tribute Volume Dedicated to Professor Chung-ying Cheng*, New York: Global Scholarly Publications, 174–99.

Zinn, Jens O., ed. (2008), *Social Theories of Risk and Uncertainty. An Introduction*, Oxford: Blackwell.

Index